BLACK,
WHITE,
AND *The* GREY

BLACK,
WHITE,
AND *The* GREY

THE STORY OF AN UNEXPECTED FRIENDSHIP AND A BELOVED RESTAURANT

MASHAMA BAILEY AND
JOHN O. MORISANO

PHOTOGRAPHS BY
ANDREW THOMAS LEE AND
MARCUS KENNEY

(LJ)

LORENA JONES BOOKS
An imprint of TEN SPEED PRESS
California | New York

To my friends and family who have protected me, nurtured me, and helped mold me into the person I am today.
—MB

To Carol, who has made me a less-flawed human and accepts me as a work-in-progress.
—JOM

CONTENTS

PROLOGUE: FINDING JOY

BY MASHAMA BAILEY

I was born in the Bronx, New York, and lived there until I was five years old. My memories as a young child in New York City are faint and overrun by loud car noises, music, and laughter. The comforting smells of incense and cooked food wafted through the marble-floored hallways of our tenement building. I loved how those hallways echoed with the patter of my feet. At that age, I was often carted back and forth to Georgia, where my grandparents lived, so when we moved to Savannah in 1980, being there felt natural to me. I was already familiar with the South. I remembered late-afternoon thunderstorms in the summertime, eating fresh figs off my grandparents' tree, and drinking sun tea on the neighbors' back porch.

In Savannah, we lived in the Baldwin Park Neighborhood on East 41 Street, just off Waters Avenue. I remember the neighborhood being diverse. In New York, my whole tiny world had been Black and Brown. But here, I was introduced to the mix of colors, races, classes. and religious backgrounds that filled the homes on our street. I even had a friend from Ethiopia who lived just a few doors down from us. That made Savannah feel worldly. The elderly White lady up the street baked cookies for the neighborhood kids, my best friend, Dee Dee, lived around the corner with her grandparents in a big pink house, and within only a few blocks there were palm dates to eat right from the trees, and dodgeball games to win. There were always children outside playing as the old folks watched from their porches or living room windows. It was a good place to be a kid.

I attended Charles Ellis Elementary and I mostly walked the one mile from home to school. I lived the farthest away of all my friends and as we walked along, our gang grew. We often arrived at school as a group of five or six children. It was a different time and place.

I look back during my childhood years in Savannah as full of firsts: The first time I learned to ride a bike, the first time I saw the ocean, the first time I smoked a cigarette, my first kiss, and the first time I was called "nigger." It happened just after recess while we were lining up along the outer wall of the cafeteria to head back to our classroom. We were scrambling, bumping, and shoving as children tend to do while forming a line. "STOP IT! QUIT PUSHING! MRS. TURNER!" we screeched over one another. And then, pointing at me, a boy in my class exclaimed, "Mrs. Turner, she pushed me!" But I hadn't pushed him. We had all been pushing. I didn't want to say "excuse me" or "sorry" so I explained, "That's not true. He started it." And then he countered with, "YOU did, nigger," lowering his voice for the last word so that only I would hear him. That word stung me like a bee. I knew I was a Black girl and I knew that things didn't come easily for my family, like buying ice cream whenever I wanted it, but we had nice things and I never before had thought that I should feel bad about my Blackness. That word made me feel small, ugly even. I'd only heard people use the word as a way to demean others so that they could feel bigger, more powerful. I knew he didn't deserve to skip ahead of me in line and that I would not let him think he was better than me. I didn't know what to say so I called him the worst word I could think of for a White person, blurting out, "You're a cracker!" I thought I had shown that boy the ultimate disrespect. And yet I didn't feel better.

Using elementary school reasoning, I figured if I told an adult they would side with him and I would get a spanking when I got home. I'm not sure why I thought that at the time, but I did. I never said a word—not even to my parents. Did I think he was right after all? Did I think he was better than me? I was ashamed. Ashamed that I had been made to feel bad about my Blackness.

In my home, being Black felt special and unique. We had our own music, foods, speech, traditions, and style. It was hard at times but my parents did their best. They worked and went to school to better themselves for us. For a split second, I had been made to think all that wasn't good enough. But I knew it was bullshit that my parents worked hard and yet we all endured the judgments of White people, no matter their age.

That moment on the playground changed my perspective. It robbed me of a little bit of joy. I buried those feelings and from that moment on I knew that being Black wasn't a good thing to everybody. As a child, you don't feel that type of shame about yourself until someone makes you feel you should—and there's always someone who will tell you who *they* think you are.

We moved back to New York City about a year later and, as I grew older, I repressed that moment on the playground and pushed my feelings down even deeper. My world expanded and with so many different colors and cultures in New York City, that playground experience seemed so irrelevant. In a city like New York, you get to see and experience how people turn pain into art, music, and culture and how many cultures influence the environment. But when you live among so many versions of the American experience, figuring out the relationship between Black and White can easily stay in the background.

Now that we were in the North, racism was disguised in a classy suit—all dressed up and yet smelled like wet dog. The reality is that being Black and poor is hard. It is also thankless and often held against us. Fundamental rights and privileges have consistently been denied or taken away from us. In fact, much of our current state in America has been blamed on us and we often don't know what to do or how to stop the bleeding (start by applying pressure). Black folks have been conditioned to assimilate *and* keep to themselves. Since returning to Savannah to open The Grey, I have stepped back and looked at how much Black people have influenced all things *American*, and food is no exception. Racism has been baked into the clay and cast-iron pots of the cooking across this country. It took moving back to Savannah for me to realize that I'd long suppressed those feelings of rage.

Regional cooking is one of the simplest ways to learn about the different parts of a culture. One could even argue that opening a restaurant is a celebration of culture. Restaurants allow people to feel nourished or supported. They also allow someone from outside of the culture to learn or grow through exposure to different ingredients and different preparations of the same ingredients. Restaurants play a big part in changing people's perspectives. Eating together humanizes. When you are sitting across the table from someone it's easier to see your similarities than your differences.

Restaurants are woven into the fabric of cities and help provide texture and cultural understanding. In almost any city around the world, you will find the people who have migrated there represented by the themes of local restaurants. But Black folks' migration to this country was forced. Black peoples' contributions helped build these cities and provide texture. In spite of all of this, because of slavery, Blacks have adopted American culture as their own. So for me, American cooking and African American cooking are not that different.

With so many restaurants in America and all the different people who have migrated here from around the world, and all of us being exposed to each other's cultures through food, why is our society so divided? When I decided to move back to Savannah and agreed to start a restaurant with my partner, Johno Morisano, little did I know that our partnership would test this theory. It would test the basic differences in American culture and how we coexist. We were both committed to the work we had ahead of us. As a prospective business partner, Johno was grounded and focused on his goals. This intrigued me, and I was also interested in *his* culture, which is Italian American, because Italian food, once considered valueless, is now served in most households and cooked by professionals at every level, from Michelin 3-star fine-dining restaurants to neighborhood pizzerias.

Before Johno and I considered whether we had potential as partners, we asked ourselves and each other, What could we add to the industry? How would our work be different from the same old, same old? I also needed to prove to myself that Black American food is more than what people expect it to be. I wanted to show its value.

The experience of finding truth and trust in writing this book has been really difficult. Originally, this was a project Johno wanted us to do together. But, because of timing, commitments, and just being too busy to focus on too many other things than the day-to-day work, I declined. I really didn't want to write a book. I wasn't even sure if I knew how to write a book or where to begin. The story of The Grey was going to be told by Johno, and I was cool with that. Almost three years ago, Johno wrote the original manuscript—which discussed the opening and running of a restaurant, our restaurant. Months passed and the book was sold, but the agent, editor, and Johno thought that having my voice in the telling of our story was important. After hearing a new approach to having my voice in the book—I was going to provide texture and comments within the story where they seemed to fit—I was beginning to think so too. Laying my voice over and alongside Johno's text didn't seem like it would be much of strain for anyone, especially me. I would write 15,000 words, tops! I thought it would be easy, and I also thought I knew what the book was about: a retelling of how we started our restaurant.

But it turned out that Johno wanted to talk about *all* of the parts of our partnership and why it's so complicated. He wanted to delve into his relationship with race. Reading some of what he wrote was hard for me. He wrote things that were just plain insensitive. He had never said those things out loud. It made me angry and defensive. After reading his first draft I began to write, admittedly from a not-so-open place. He had brought me back to those feelings I had as a child that day at recess. I wanted to scream and call him an asshole and, in some parts, I do. Why were we even talking about race? Who wants to hear about that from a White male? What did he know about the Black community and our history in this country? Did he just adhere to the White-centric culture's stereotypes of Blacks? Why? I thought that Johno knew better than that! I had never asked him about his personal relationships with anyone Black or of color. How would I know his innermost thoughts if we had never had these conversations? On the playground that day, I learned that I was going to have to get past people like that little White boy. I worried that maybe my business partner would be another one I would need to get past.

Like our partnership, this book is unconventional. When we sent the prior version of it to friends, writers, and family members for their opinions, they came back mixed. We heard that it wasn't cohesive, my writing wasn't substantial enough, and the book read as if only Johno had written most of it. Generally speaking, the White audience thought it was great, smart, and interesting. The Black and Brown audience thought my voice was dull, marginalized, and weak. I knew I still wasn't having those conversations about race with myself or anyone else. Johno and I agreed we had missed the mark and needed to fix it. Until that feedback, I never took ownership of this project or realized the lasting impact my voice could have. So, we started over, rereading and reworking the book word by word. We agonized over each phrase to really get to the heart of what this book is actually about. We needed to find equal footing in a partnership that wasn't yet equal. We needed to figure out how to truly be co-writers, and now I feel pretty good about what we've written. The experience of writing this book is helping us find the balance in our partnership.

At our restaurant in the South, we are working on celebrating the good aspects of American culture while exposing and shedding light on the bad aspects. We know that true understanding or forgiveness is going to take a lot of listening, sacrifice from those who hold power, and a passing of the torches by those who have maintained control of the narratives. We discuss the influences of slavery and other migrations throughout the South. We celebrate the heritage of African American culture through the lens of the African Diaspora. We talk about all of our influences, from growing up in New York City to traveling around the country. We try to tell that story through our food, our design, and our service. In many ways, we are still trying to figure that out as we continue to learn from our mistakes and inspire our team. All we can hope is that through our work we can heal, gain perspective, continue to grow, and work from a place of trust and respect. In the time of a global pandemic and one of the largest uprisings in decades on behalf of Black Americans, we present an example of how uncomfortable these conversations are going to need to get.

INTRODUCTION

BY JOHN O. MORISANO

The Grey, the restaurant I co-founded in Savannah, Georgia, in 2014, was never really about just building a restaurant. There was a lot more to it than that. For me, it was about finding community and my place in it. I wanted to be part of something, and I chose Savannah as the place to do it. Building The Grey was not just my way of inserting myself into my adopted city or starting a brand that would hopefully become recognizable beyond Savannah; it was also the way I surrendered myself to something much larger than me. I knew I was going to be consumed by The Grey, by Savannah, by the South, and by all of the intricacies of race, class, and culture that would come along with my decision.

It was always about those things.

How could it not be?

I mean, for the record, I am a White guy from New York City who had already had a career. It was a highly entrepreneurial and disparate career with lots of energy expended, a great many setbacks, and a small number of things that went right. My career certainly was more than a little unorthodox. In 2011, I was picking up my life and, for reasons not completely clear to me at the time, relocating it to the Deep South. Carol, my wife of twenty-plus years, and I had no connection to the South. We had no family or friends in Savannah. We had visited the city once, the year prior. There was no job for me in Savannah. "Y'all" was an expression that had never ever left my lips and likely never ever would. But there I was making the move, and Savannah became the starting point for the rest of my life when we bought our first home there. I was forty-four. I hope that the reasons for this, or at least some of them—or the results—become clear in the pages of this book.

Within a couple of years, I also bought a dilapidated, Jim Crow–era Greyhound bus terminal on the fringe of the Historic Downtown—the geographical line where the "haves" and the "have-nots" bump up against each other regularly. The building was complete with a space that had housed a segregated lunch counter, which until 1961 (when Savannah repealed its ordinance requiring that lunch counters be segregated), only made space for Black patrons if there were not enough White customers to fill all the seats. Black people were only welcome to prepare the food and wash the dishes for the White patrons. The "colored" waiting room, restrooms, and entrance in the rear were still mostly intact. Yeah, race, class, and culture—topics that had interested me throughout my adolescence and adult life—were, for sure, front of mind.

Within a couple of days of closing escrow on the bus terminal, I broke the news to my wife that I was going to turn the building into a restaurant. Even after a long career in start-ups that most rational people, including Carol, would consider a really fucking risky way to make a living, her reaction was complete and utter shock. The restaurant industry, she rightfully pointed out, was one in which I had absolutely zero experience. I would ultimately team up with Mashama Bailey, a Black woman chef from New York City, as my business partner in this venture. Mashama would become the executive chef, my best friend, and the face of our business. This building, a tangible example of the racism and segregation of the Old South, would be co-run by a woman who, according to the laws of our United States of America, would not have been allowed to enter through the front door during the entire time it operated, from 1938 to 1964. (Savannah began quietly integrating in the fall of 1963, prior to the passage of the Civil Rights Act of 1964.)

So, in partnering with Mashama, this project, which was already intrinsically about race, class, and culture, became even more so. We even managed to add the element of gender into it as well as our collective role in a modernizing and dynamic South.

Even the name of the restaurant, a shortened version of the name of the company that first occupied the space, tipped to the social complexity of our undertaking. Here's the thing, though, I had no idea just how consuming it was going to be for us nor how bright the spotlight would be.

That's because the Savannah project was also about other factors. It was about self-preservation and self-worth. It was about trying to figure out a way, as a middle-aged, potentially washed-up White guy, to remain relevant—somewhere, somehow—in a world that moves fast. It was about the rebirth that I sought, to counter the fear and self-doubt that had emerged from the twists and turns my professional career had taken, and decisions that I might take back if I could. It was about the chip that I have had on my shoulder, throughout my entire career (and maybe even since childhood).

And it was most certainly about food and wine, which have been meaningful to me since I was a kid. At my grandparents' home, we could escape the battles of a family that thrived on conflict: a father who worked too many jobs and still never had enough money, raised too many kids, and drank too many cans of Schaeffer on any given night. My mother felt trapped by the decisions of her younger self, and with no place else to go she asked us to ride out the storm for twenty years or so. But for two hours on Sunday afternoons, Sunday Italian gravy at my grandparents taught me that food is family, refuge, and love. That has been a driving force in my life ever since.

The moment I met Mashama Bailey, in November 2013, I began to talk with her about the relevance of these childhood memories of mine. It was not long after our very first meeting, during which we decided to explore the possibility of entering into a business relationship, that I stipulated that we, Mashama and I, would have to become family if we were going to go into business together. That was important to me, and I wanted her to know that.

In retrospect, it is a minor miracle that Mashama actually agreed to even have another meeting, let alone join up with me. Think about it. Who tells a person they have just met, with whom they have no shared experiences, that in order to create a partnership in this new restaurant, not only would we have to agree to all of the deal points, we'd also have to work our fucking asses off for the next ten years or so, and we'd need to take a metaphoric blood oath? I was suggesting some sort of food *omertà* between me, a mixed-up mutt from Staten Island, and this guarded and slightly more than a little suspicious Black woman from Queens.

While we may not have shared the same formative experiences, we would come to learn that so much about the people we were when we met was astonishingly similar—our sense of commitment, loyalty, honesty, generosity, and a willingness to put ourselves out there. Maybe it was all this that made Mashama comfortable taking a leap of faith with me.

A couple of years later, after The Grey had entered the national conversation about food and wine, and was often cited as an example in the unfolding conversation about race and gender, the working dynamic we were building between us took another turn. I wanted to write our story down and find a publisher and get it out there. I thought that our relationship, the way we approached our business, the history of our building, and how the research and heartfelt honesty that went into Mashama's food and connected it to her own personal history would make for an interesting read.

When I told Mashama about the idea on several occasions, she flatly rejected wanting any involvement in writing a book. She didn't have the time in her chef's schedule, didn't know what we would write about, and, sometimes, she just didn't like an idea I pitched her because I pitched too many of them. (I often get a "No" that also includes some sort of open-hand gesture.) But she was happy for me to go and write all by my lonesome. So, I did. I wrote a partial manuscript and my agent and I, after a year or so of development, went out and sold it. The editor we were working with came up with a simple enough idea that she wanted me to consider: I lay down the story of The Grey in a complete manuscript and then when I finished, Mashama would go through my manuscript, annotating, commenting, qualifying, disagreeing, and saying when I got some stuff right.

I loved the idea. It would create a book that we would co-write and do so in a way that gave Mashama a road map. Her voice would be an overlay on mine so there would be two voices offering different vantage points on the same story—our story—but I would do the heavy lifting on the writing, and Mashama would have the surgical task of making incisive, meaningful, and closing strokes on the operation. Simple, right?

Mashama agreed and we started that summer, with me taking six weeks away from work and compiling a full draft. In this new approach to writing the book, the manuscript took a decided turn toward my own self-reflections about my relationship to race; deep, inherent, and unconscious biases; and how all of that has impacted my blossoming partnership with Mashama and the experience of living in the Deep South.

In writing this book, I have tried to be as honest as possible about my viewpoints at the time I held them. I felt that it was important to accurately reflect the way things happened in the context of when conversations were taking place, specifically when fears and stereotypes were a factor. When trying to have an honest conversation about a really difficult topic, I do not see the point of recasting through the lens of hindsight. I am certain that some people will read this and find fault in my viewpoints related to race and gender, and my evolution in understanding the innumerable benefits of my having been born White and male. And, because of the fact that I am not an academic, my viewpoint reflects my personal experience, whether qualitative or anecdotal. That is going to drive some people batshit crazy, but I will tell you that when we are sitting around the dinner table at night, drinking wine and talking about how fucked up the world is and there is not an academic in sight, that's how that conversation goes. Even when people are only partially informed, and at the end of such 'round-the-table talks, views do shift—sometimes just a little, but they do.

Finally, the idea of having Mashama lay her writing over the top of mine seemed sensible. We all thought it was going to be great until we saw the first full layout of the book and realized that the Black woman, the person we are all here to see and read about, was now stuck in the margins of the book.

So Mashama and I rented a small flat in Paris (more on that later) and locked ourselves in there every single day for five and a half weeks. We revisited every word of this book together—my passages, her passages, everything. We made sure that we agreed to timing, dialogue, and every other decision as it is presented in these pages. And we did it twice. So this is the book, *our* book. We have both put an enormous amount of energy, laughter, wine, and tears into the making of this book. It has not been easy to write, but it is written by two people who are flawed and honest. And, it was written from a point in time that covers roughly the first three years of The Grey's existence and all that went into it. Thanks for taking the time to join us as we retrace our journey, and we hope to see you at The Grey one night.

ABOUT THE RECIPES

At the end of each chapter, you will find a recipe for food we like to eat and, more importantly, food we have shared with each other, our friends, and loved ones. These recipes were inspired by the places we have been and the food memories we have made. This assortment may seem random at times; that's a reflection of the lives we have led so far. And we cannot help but be influenced by the Port City, Savannah, in which we currently live. Port cities, by circumstance or maybe by design, are amalgamations of cultures and flavors, and that might be the thing we love most about living in Savannah, and running The Grey and The Grey Market, our lunch counter and to-go shop. Because most American peoples have found their way here through the harbors of port cities at some point in their family's history, it is all of them who have given us this gift and the license to cook with flavors and foodways from all over this vast and remarkably complex world. We love that. We hope you enjoy this personal collection of recipes in the spirit of communion in which they are shared.

PART I

WM SEEKING ASPIRATIONAL BF FOR BUSINESS RELATIONSHIP

CHAPTER 1

I had nowhere else to turn. Moments before, I was content, with my friends and colleagues from The Grey. Laughing. And in a split second that was taken away.

A phone was ringing in the background. I was in that in-between state that allowed the sounds from my surroundings to intertwine with my unconscious. It took a moment or two for me to discern whether I was hearing my real phone or a conjured phone in my sleepy goings-on. Another ring and then the sound of the vibrating device on a hard surface, and it became clear.

It was most certainly my cell phone, which was across the bedroom on the desk.

I looked at my watch as I threw the covers off my lanky, six-foot-one body, my pale white skin almost glowing in the dark room. It was 12:20 a.m. on July 5, 2017. My wife, Carol, and I had spent a relatively quiet Fourth of July earlier that day, recovering from a staff party we hosted the day before in the garden of our Savannah home for the team who worked at the downtown restaurant that I co-owned, The Grey.

As I navigated the tangle of sheets, two large Rhodesian Ridgebacks, and Carol, my adrenaline began to push the grogginess from my head. The Grey was closed that Tuesday for the Independence Day holiday. I could think of no reason anyone would be calling me after midnight on a Tuesday unless it was an emergency. Having grown up in a Roman Catholic Italian household in New York City with a fireman as a father, I had become conditioned to the idea that the late-night phone call was never good news. I expected the worst.

I made it to the desk and lurched into consciousness when I saw the name "Mashama Bailey"—my business partner and the executive chef of The Grey. My worry spiked. Mashama would never call me at this time of night unless something was wrong.

Three years into our partnership and I only called Johno when I had to. This man I didn't know when we started, would check in with me constantly to see if I was getting my footing, but I rarely reached out in return. The work was hard at The Grey, and especially the building of a partnership—all of which I expected, but moving to and living in Savannah alone was harder. I felt like a fraud because I was in over my head. I was making too many mistakes at work and I was still uncomfortable talking to my "business partner," who in many

ways still felt like my boss. But this night was different. Something *terrible* had just happened. I had few choices. I knew that Johno would come if I called—he had been trying to be that type of friend to me for three years. I was never so vulnerable before; I never had to ask him to come to help me. But on this night, I needed to trust that choice. I had to trust him. So, I reached out for help.

Hopefully, she just forgot her keys and locked herself out of her apartment.

"Hey," I said, the roughness of my voice indicating that I was not completely successful in shaking off the sleep, "what's up?"

Mashama, who is almost always bright and full of energy, was anything but. As she began to speak, her voice was filled with anguish.

"Johnoooooo," she wailed, using the nickname my parents had given me. "There's been a terrible accident!" she screamed, hyperventilating into the line. And then, stuttering between breaths, she said, "I don't think Scott is alive. I haven't seen him."

Wait, what? I thought.

"What? Our Scott?" I asked, hoping that she was not talking about him, adding, "What happened?"

"I don't know. It all happened so fast. There was a car. It came out of nowhere. It hit Scott. I saw him go up onto the hood, but it was going so fast and it hit him so hard that . . . I don't know." She took another shallow breath. "Then it crashed into a pole and I think he was still on it. It was bad, Johno. It was really bad."

I knew he was dead. My entire body felt the impact. I remained frozen in the middle of Bay Street, hoping he would walk out of the wreckage. I expected to see him, hear him, hug him, but that didn't happen. I stood there in the middle of the intersection with a ringing in my ears that I will never forget. Shaken, I placed one foot in front of the other and walked forward. The moment I reached the curb, I cried out before I collapsed.

My own vision began to tunnel as I tried to process what Mashama was saying to me. Scott Waldrup was our general manager at the restaurant. He had been with us from the day we opened The Grey. He started as a bartender, but over the couple of years we had been in business, he had become our general manager and ran our wine program, two functions that reported directly to me. Other than Mashama, he was the person I spent the most time with in (and some-times out of) the restaurant. If Mashama and I were the so-called brains of the operation, Scott was its heartbeat. He loved his job and The Grey, and brought a perspective to it that was so far from my own, more conventional view of life. Scott was our moral conscience for the underrepresented—he rooted for only the underdog and the downtrodden, and he was activated in doing so. Every place needs a voice like his, and Scott was that for all of us at The Grey. He was a ginger-haired ball of energy and everyone on the team loved him. I loved him.

As I listened to her sobbing on the other end of the phone, I considered that Scott was not even thirty-one and that he was much, much too alive to die. There was no way he could be dead. Mashama must be mistaken. It was just not possible.

As I tried to slow down my brain so I could process what Mashama was saying, Carol had gotten up and was standing next to me, holding on to my arm tightly and trying to listen in and figure out what was going on.

I needed to stop talking and just get down there. "Where are you?" I asked Mashama, adding, "Carol and I will be right there."

"I'm on Barnard and Bay. The police have it all taped off. They won't let me go anywhere, but nobody is talking to me. They won't tell me what happened. Please come quick, Johno. I don't know what to do. I'm scared."

I wanted to cry out again! But I couldn't. I wanted to scream! But I couldn't. I wanted to fight and swing my arms wildly, hitting everything in my path. But I couldn't move. I sat on the concrete for only a minute but it felt like hours. No one approached me. No one saw me. I was unnoticeable to all those around me. I felt invisible. I had been with my friend. He now was gone and I needed to find him. I needed to find Scott. I got up. I looked around and still no one approached me. I hugged myself, as if gathering a shield of armor or wrapping myself in a cloak until I *was* invisible. I began to walk toward the wreckage. I heard cries and people moaning. There was glass everywhere, along with mangled pieces of metal. I continued to slowly put one foot in front of the other as I took long, slow breaths in and out, trying to steady myself from my shaking. I continued on until I saw the white SUV flipped on its side, the hood dented right down the center. I was petrified as I inched closer, looking for Scott. The ringing in my ears became louder and I hugged my shoulders tighter. I grabbed for my cloak but it was no longer there. "Miss, you can't go any farther," I heard, faintly. I continued inching forward. "Miss, you'll need to step back."

A police officer was in front of me now, standing between me and the wreckage. He held his arms out in front of him and started to move slightly side to side, like he was posted up in front of the basket, defending the basket. To get to Scott I needed to back him down. I needed a power move. "Where's my friend?" I cried. "Please!" I yelled in his face. "I need to see if he is okay." "I'm sorry," was all he said as he grabbed my arms and moved me a few feet back. I had no fight in me, so I let him. And then I just stood there, knowing.

I hung up the phone and I stood still for a second, struggling to compose myself. Carol looked at me and, because her nature was to begin to ask questions, I interjected as gently as I could before she could speak, "Please, don't ask me any questions. Go and get dressed. Mashama was in an accident. Scott might be dead."

Carol nodded.

The dogs, sensing something was wrong, were agitated, so we took a moment to get them back up onto the bed and settled as we pulled the bedroom door closed behind us. I had no idea what I was about to walk into, but the fear in Mashama's voice, something I had never ever heard from her before, worried me. My overwhelming sense was that I was heading to someplace dangerous. I had come from a family in which two of my brothers were cops, and a dad and another brother were firemen, so I felt that I needed to go down there prepared. On the way out of the house I grabbed my briefcase and made sure that my pistol, which I had purchased and begun carrying when walking home from The Grey late at night, was inside my bag. I was nervous and disoriented and its presence in my briefcase gave me a sense of control. Frankly, it calmed me. We drove the less-than-one-mile distance to where Mashama was waiting for us and where I was hoping I was going to find out that she was mistaken about Scott's fate.

The police officers held back a small crowd of people as they taped off the crime scene. They didn't want anyone to see the wreckage up close. I never saw blood or anything like that. I chose not to see it. I wanted to get close but not that close. I stood within the barricade making phone calls, trying to sound normal while reaching out to a couple of people who Scott and I had just left in the bar. I watched bodies being hauled away on stretchers, underneath the flashing lights and blaring sirens. One ambulance remained quietly in the road.

We parked the car a few blocks away from the intersection that Mashama had identified as her location and we made our way down the sidewalks packed with holiday celebrants, something for which Savannah is famous but the type of event I have mostly avoided in my time living here. And this night seemed uneasy to me. I'm sure that Mashama's phone call had so rattled me that I drove there jacked up and hyperaware, projecting tension onto the people walking by me—it was just so damned loud and disorganized. There were large groups of teens and young adults, self-segregated for the most part into Black and White, moving together as individual organisms. *Everyone was dressed in reds, whites, and blues for the holiday, but a couple of those same colors,* I thought to myself, *could just as easily connote the gangs that operated in Savannah.* I was as uncomfortable as I had ever been in Savannah in that moment because I did not know what lay ahead of us. The anxiety I absorbed from my phone call with Mashama was turning to fear with each step that I took.

I normally don't find myself in the middle of parades or national holiday celebrations. Since moving to downtown Savannah, where all of these annual events are held, this is where I see the real Savannah. Before moving here, I had learned that Savannah is 53 percent Black. But if you're living downtown you would never actually know that. It is during such events that Black Savannahians come out to celebrate alongside White Savannahians. It surprises me that Black and White people here are together so infrequently that most tourists have no sense of the true makeup of Savannah, about how diverse the different communities are. The downtown community is so insular and so separate from the rest of the city, and yet it alone represents the city that people see—residents, students, media, everyone. It's days like this that we all get to see the true essence of the city, and I hate that it ended in violence.

As we got closer to the scene, it became more apparent that something truly bad or violent had taken place. Flashing lights from the police cars that were just out of eye view were bouncing off the large storefront windows of the city's retail and tourist area, giving a strobe effect to people's movements as sirens blared all around. Most people were going about their business trying to get from one place to another, but some of the groups of teens and young adults were rowdy, yelling, swearing, bumping into each other, and taking up most of the sidewalks and walkways. Some, maybe many, were intoxicated or high from a day of partying. My paranoia continued to grow, my eyes darting from group to group, seeing the scene as a powder keg, like the evening's first act of violence was merely the precursor. All that I had learned from growing up in New York City, during one of its most violent eras, instinctively controlled my movements. I kept my head on a swivel, looking for any sign of danger that might come from any direction. I wanted to keep safe, to keep Carol safe, to find Mashama, and get us the hell out of this part of town. Violence begets violence, I remember thinking to myself.

We needed to be inside the safety of our home and not out on these streets.

I hate crowds! I am just an introvert. And, being a woman, I have my guard up when I'm out. I have always felt a little insecure whenever I'm walking through a group of people, I think *Am I going to be harassed, teased, or bullied? Will I be threatened physically? Is someone out to rob me of my rights or my dignity or my self-esteem?* I pay attention to my surroundings when I'm walking on the street and living my life. I have been trained to!

I was nervous, jumpy. Carol, a petite blonde with strength and determination evident in her gait, strode down the sidewalk, holding my left hand firmly as we moved through the crowd. My other hand remained in my briefcase, gripping my compact handgun.

Johno told me when he bought his gun. It was a year or so after we opened The Grey, and during that time there had been a string of armed robberies happening near the restaurant. Some were violent, and a local gallery owner had been killed during one. I think that everyone who lived downtown, especially the White residents, just assumed the perpetrators were kids who lived in the projects that bordered the Historic District. I knew that Johno often had it with him. I never really gave it much thought because why should I? We both know the impact of guns on our society, and that's Johno's choice to carry. But, what is odd to me is, what was it about my phone call had made him want to bring a concealed weapon? If it were violent robberies that were the catalyst for him getting the gun in the first place, was it that he was beginning to think, or had he always thought that young Black men coming into White neighborhoods, like the Historic Downtown, are a threat to him? Or, was it the fear in my voice? It never would have occurred to me to bring a gun to the scene of an accident. It just seemed like asking for trouble.

As we turned right onto Barnard Street, the scene came into full view. I saw the yellow police tape. To me, it seemed like every cop in the city was there, with emergency vehicles and police cars parked randomly at the corner of Bay and Barnard. It was bright, with emergency lights bathing everything in unnatural colors, creating an effect that seemed unreal. Police officers and onlookers were all trying to figure out what was going on.

As we got closer, we could see that within the confines of the police tape there was a group of young Black girls standing on the left side of the street. They were shaken, huddling together as a group with several police officers nearby. Then I saw her. There, sitting on the curb all by herself on the east side of

Barnard, her head in her hands, was Mashama, my business partner and the person with whom I spent almost every waking moment. "Mashama!" Carol and I called out.

I was standing near those girls while on the phone with Johno. They were talking about Scott, calling him a hero.

As I talked with Johno, overhearing those girls, I wanted them, everyone, to know Scott is a son, a brother, a boyfriend, a friend, an uncle, a nephew, an amateur hiker, an activist, and the unofficial mayor of Savannah. He always comes to work with a great attitude. He supports the staff and maintains a regular following at the Gate 2 Bar in our main dining room. He loves his downtown restaurant community and shows it by visiting his friends who work within the industry and by providing them with moral support as they sling drinks and food during their shifts. He is the life of the party and keeps The Grey staff on their toes with his antics. And just the day before, during our Fourth of July party, we all were waiting anxiously for him to reveal the winners of some stupid contest. He is like that. He is fun and he wanted to hang out with me on his favorite holiday.

"He pushed us out of the way," one girl said to me, "the guy who got hit by the car." That bothered me! They didn't even know his name! He wasn't standing with us. He couldn't speak for himself. If he hadn't been a "hero" to those girls, maybe we would have walked home together. We would *both* be safe now. I needed to move away!

She looked up in our direction and it was clear that it took her a second to realize that we were there. After a moment, she rose to her feet, pausing to steady herself, before she rushed to the perimeter of the police tape and met us, the yellow plastic separating us.

Seeing Johno and Carol was a relief. I needed someone to hold me or to talk with, someone I knew to calm me and help me stop shaking so I wouldn't implode.

She began to wail again. No discernible words could escape her throat as she sobbed. I tried to hug her, but her distress made it impossible to hang on to her.

I choked on my grief as soon as I tried to speak. And still, I don't think I was sad enough. I needed to cry more, harder and longer, until I felt nothing.

When I first met Mashama, I was struck by how she was nearly as tall as I was at six feet. Her dark skin had a sepia hue and her short, loose hair seemed carefully considered—a glint of color showing up in one of her curls and another pulled in a very intentional direction across her forehead. But now, her beautiful face was contorted by fear and shock. Her eyes were swollen and red. The warmth that her appearance usually inspires in me was gone. Her electric smile, framed by her smooth, dark skin, was replaced by pursed lips. She dragged her forearm across her nose and face to wipe away the fluids that sobbing brings. Her posture, usually commanding, was slumped and unsteady. Her chest heaved as she let the rawness of the terror out so that she might be able to finally find words.

Seeing her like this unsettled me in a way I was not prepared for. This woman who had become a steady force in my own life over the past three years, was crumbling right in front of me. For a split second I had to look away, as the kind of event that could make Mashama Bailey deflate from the inside out like this was nearly unimaginable.

After another minute or two, Carol wrapped her arms around Mashama, who finally allowed herself to be held. She began catching her breath so that she could get the words out. Carol gently released her and Mashama began to tell us what happened. "We watched the fireworks," she mustered, "and then we went to have some drinks with everybody. It was fun. We were having fun. But Scott and I were tired and hungry, so we decided to leave everyone there and get something to eat on the way home."

Actually, Scott and I met at a bar just after the fireworks. As I got there, he had been looking at pictures on his phone of him and Tart, his boyfriend. When he noticed me, he gave me a huge grin and that's when I realized that he was good and happily drunk. We line danced and ate shitty tacos at the bar to sober up before we left. We chatted lightheartedly about our secret industry crushes, giggling as we walked toward the intersection of Bay and Barnard.

"We were crossing Bay Street. We did everything right. We waited for the light, you know, until the sign told us to cross. It was us and this group of girls. They were in front of us," she said, pointing to the group of young Black girls on the other side of the street. "And as we're crossing, I heard a cop yell at us to stop. He was yelling 'Stop! Stop!' and then this car came from the other direction," she said, pointing west.

As we were crossing the street, I heard voices that were loud yet unclear. I turned to my left to see four police officers running in our direction. I hesitated for one second, maybe two, to make out what they were saying. When I turned back toward Scott, he was already a step in front of me.

"It just came out of nowhere, and it hit Scott so hard. Somehow it missed me even though we were crossing the street together. I think it just missed me. But it hit Scott. Hard. He kind of lunged forward toward those girls in front of us and it missed me and missed them and it hit him," she finished.

I don't remember Scott lunging to push those girls. I just remember him getting lifted into the air and onto the hood of the car.

A police officer came over at that moment. "You can't talk to her right now," she said to me. "You need to come back over here and sit down on the curb, ma'am," she said, directing Mashama.

The officer looked back in my direction as she led Mashama away, saying, "We haven't interviewed her yet."

"That's ridiculous," I said, raising my voice. "We're all she has here right now. She was just nearly killed. Why can't she just stand with us?"

"Sorry, that's what my supervisor tells me." And while she led Mashama back to the curb, it struck me as exactly the opposite way a victim of the evening's events should be treated.

Good policing is a gift. So is good teaching and good cooking. There will always be rules and protocol to follow, but unless one does the work from a loving place and is able to adjust for what's right in front of them, they'll never be great at it. They'll never connect with the work on a human level. Not one officer took the time to look at what was right in front of them or to make adjustments to their approach that night. Not a single one provided comfort to the witnesses.

I found another cop nearby, a young White guy. "I need to see someone in charge here. That woman there is my business partner," I said, pointing to Mashama, "and she was with our general manager and I need to find out what happened to him. Can you get me a supervisor?"

He barely nodded, and walked away.

After a few minutes, a different cop approached us, another young White guy, but he had a stripe on his uniform indicating he was a bit higher in rank than the previous two officers. "How can I help you, sir?" he asked.

"You see that woman there? I need to get her out of here. She's in shock. Then I need to find out what the hell happened to our general manager, who was with her."

He responded to my second statement first: "General manager, who was that?"

"Scott Waldrup," I said.

He took out a notebook. "Can you tell me anything about him?"

"Yeah, I can tell you about him. I just told you, he worked with us." I took a breath. "He's thirty years old with red hair and a big red beard. He was crossing the street with Mashama, and she said the car hit him."

"Who's Mashama?" he asked, mangling the pronunciation of her name and making it sound more like *Mu-sham-buh.*

Those police officers didn't care who I was or that I was almost killed. Reeling in my anguish, as I watched Johno's animated conversations with various cops, hoping that whatever they were talking about would get me out of there. The driver crashed into a pole and everything stopped. The police chasing a car on a busy downtown street in the middle of a holiday celebration, stopped. It was over. There was no ongoing chase. The case was closed. Was this the result the cops had wanted? Now let me go home so I can make myself invisible again and get off this street!

"MA-SHA-MA. My business partner," I answered, enunciating her name clearly, nodding in her direction. "And Scott, the guy she was with, was probably wearing red-white-and-blue shorts and an American-flag tank top. Fourth of July is his favorite holiday, and that's his standard outfit."

"Okay," he said, "we're still trying to figure out what's going on. There was a shooting a few blocks away, probably gang related would be my guess. We think the shooters were in the car that crashed into that pole over there when they were trying to get away." Then, pointing to something out of our line of sight, he clarified his statement with, "Just around the corner there."

"She thinks that Scott was killed," I said. "Can you tell me that? I have to call his family. Can you tell me that?"

"I can't. I don't have those details. All I can say is that there were fatalities between the two incidents, and some others went to the hospital."

I considered the word and then said it out loud, "Fatalities?" "Shit. Dammit," I added, asking next, "Which hospital are they taking the nonfatalities to?"

"I don't know," he responded.

I digested the bit of information the officer had given us. I needed a plan. I had to start to act. I needed to get a number for Scott's mother in North Carolina and call her as soon as possible.

Johno couldn't just stand there—that was too much for him. I began to see things clearer for the first time since the car made its impact. Johno and Carol looked so frightened. He needed to get us out of there. I knew he needed a distraction, he needed to mobilize. All of this was too sad to see up close—the accident, the whole thing. Was Johno frightened of the implications of what just happened? That our Scott may have been caught up in gang violence. At that point, none of this seemed about race to me, it just seemed like a horrific accident. But with the information Johno was getting, he was probably starting to have the response that White people have been conditioned to have, which is to automatically connect violence with the Black community.

This was going to be a long night.

"Okay," I said, my thoughts turning back to Mashama. "I need to get my business partner out of here. She's going into shock. I need to get her home."

Why did he keep saying that? No one gave a shit about shock! Not one police officer talked to us about our mental state. They just wanted to know what we had seen.

The officer seemed confused at the mention of Mashama again. "Who?" he asked.

"That woman sitting over there," I said, pointing in Mashama's direction.

"Which woman?" he asked, looking directly at her.

"*That* woman," I barked, because Mashama was the only woman sitting on the curb, visibly shaking and bawling her eyes out.

I felt visible again as I heard my name mentioned several times. My surroundings were beginning to come into focus.

"The Black woman?" he asked, further perplexed, like it was not possible that we were business partners, like White guys and Black women were not ever business partners.

Our partnership is not impossible; it's just not normal. I was not surprised by the officer's reaction.

"YEAH, THE BLACK WOMAN. THE ONLY WOMAN," I said, speaking in a raised voice with little regard for the fact that I was talking to a policeman and that the situation was intensifying. "I mean, what the fuck is wrong with you? There's no one else over there but her. Of course, it's the Black woman. Jesus Christ!"

If Johno were a Black man, I'm sure he would have been in handcuffs. If it had been fifty years earlier, he would have been beaten or killed for talking to a cop like that.

"Calm down, sir," he said, hesitating and then looking in Mashama's direction and then back at me. "Okay, let me see if I can have someone interview her now so you can take her home."

As Mashama sat alone on the curb crying, waiting to be interviewed, I questioned every cop and rescue worker who walked by. I wanted real information from someone about what had transpired over the last twenty minutes. But no one said anything, and the pall of a very dark night continued to smother any feelings of hope. Ambulances were not leaving the scene, rushing people to the hospital. In fact, there was an almost laissez-faire attitude among the remaining emergency personnel.

As I sat on the curb waiting to be released, I wondered why that one ambulance hadn't left yet. *Was Scott in there? Where were the helicopters?* I remember thinking that Scott wouldn't be the same if he survived.

I took a deep breath, and Carol and I hugged, quietly preparing each other for what was ahead.

"You know," I said to Carol, "he wants us to allow people into the dining room in bathing suits."

"What? Who does?"

"Scott," I answered. "We were having this argument the other day. He thinks I'm a fucking hypocrite because I preach hospitality, and to him 'hospitality' means that we've got to welcome everyone no matter how they want to express themselves. That our dress code should be that there is no dress code."

"You can't do that," Carol said, offering the same knee-jerk response I had given to Scott.

"I know. Our guests would go crazy. But Speedo Sunday is coming up in a few weeks," I said referring to the LGBTQ event Scott founded a few years prior and about which he was super-passionate, "and he thinks that everyone should be allowed to come into The Grey after the event, if they want, in their Speedos and have dinner. He truly doesn't understand why we should not let a bunch of dudes into the dining room during dinner service wearing Speedos, tank tops, and flip-flops. Like I said, he even thinks I'm an asshole for not allowing it."

Carol's response was simply a smirk, knowing Scott well, knowing that that would be his exact position on Speedos in the dining room.

Suddenly I felt overwhelmingly sad. "I hope he's okay," I said quietly. "I really hope he's okay."

I looked again toward Mashama and my sadness extended to her. She had been struggling to connect with Savannah since she had arrived here. She was a Black woman who had uprooted her entire life in New York to move to the Deep South—not an easy transition. Now it was possible that one of our closest friends here had been killed right in front of her eyes. Mashama's tenuous relationship with her adopted home had been dealt a severe blow.

I love the South and I always have, but I flat out did not feel connected to the city of Savannah. I wondered if I'd made a mistake by relocating here. I felt like I was a horse in a race with blinders on. My eyes were on the prize: building a successful business while making Savannah my home. But, after that night, my vision of the prize was getting blurry and beginning to seem unattainable.

My sadness shifted to guilt for having had a hand in convincing Mashama to move here and for not somehow protecting Scott from harm; he was part of our team, our family.

I wondered about that cop, the one who couldn't believe or did not approve of our mixed-race business partnership. Was he a bellwether for other Savannahians? Did some portion of the residents of this city think that The Grey and the two of us who owned it were an oddity?

Savannah was smaller and way more segregated than I'd imagined. In Savannah, locating Black-owned businesses is like finding a needle in a haystack. I can trace the ghosted outline of the Black business community as I drive around the part of MLK near what is now the I-16 flyover. Before moving here, I really didn't have any idea of the symbolism our partnership would represent in a town that in many ways, has digressed as much as it has progressed since the civil rights movement.

Or worse, maybe people here saw us as a threat? It had taken the South a long time to set up the society it wanted, the one we were living among. All the businesses I knew downtown were White owned. I did not know of any Black-owned businesses in Savannah's Historic District. And now here we were. When I thought about it, as we were building The Grey, my views were idealistic, maybe even idyllic. That came crashing down on this night. The realities of the place we lived and where we were building our business were now starkly evident to me. I had waltzed into town a few years earlier, accessing downtown and White society by supporting the right charities and going to the right parties. I had bought a building and identified a partner; we built a restaurant and then I had wanted to be congratulated for it. It took no time to figure out what the real Savannah was about—the centuries of conflict, the inherited and institutional inequities, the forces at play that resulted in a night like the one we were now in the midst of.

I looked at my watch—it was 12:50 a.m. Thirty minutes had elapsed since the moment I received the phone call from Mashama. This night was already shitty and it was going to get worse. In fact, I had the distinct feeling that the next few months were not going to be our best.

I felt the first twinges of anger creep into my consciousness—anger at Savannah, its leadership, and its residents. After speaking with the police officers at the accident, the mention of gang-related violence stuck with me. Had we been in New York City, that could have meant any number of different groups—Crips,

Bloods, Latin Kings, Outlaw Bikers, and about three hundred others. But in Savannah, to my knowledge, the gangs were primarily African American.

With this assumption gaining traction in my brain, I regarded the groups of Black teens on the street around me with suspicion as I was starting to conclude that some contingent of them were involved in the evening's events. I began to form thoughts, negative thoughts, about everyone who may have contributed to Scott's harm and who had us standing on this street corner on a late, sticky night not knowing the true fate of our friend. The stark segregation of our city was painted so clearly for me, in the very scene I was witnessing, in which I had become an involuntary participant. In that moment, it very briefly occurred to me that my response would be fateful.

When a crime takes place and we see it on TV or read about it in the newspaper, I think Black folks say a silent, unified prayer that the perpetrator isn't Black, hoping the incident won't magnify the stereotype that the Black community is a violent one. Whites brought us to this country through violence. We have been suppressed by violence. Now, Whites love to point at the Black community and call us violent but they never take responsibility for the violence that their society has inflicted upon us. Violence is a learned behavior and yet it seems to only shock and offend Whites when it spills into their communities.

Our business was only two and half years old, and the city in which we set it up had suddenly become the biggest threat to its long-term viability. This was the dark side of Savannah, a town known for its picturesque squares and grand urban canopy of live oak trees that shade the city's visitors and residents from the relentless summer sun. But in those shadows, there is massive dysfunction. Haves and have-nots are mostly divided along racial lines in and around Savannah's Historic District. And the people who are on the short end of the societal equation, well, their choices are so fucking limited. Who were the kids in the car? How did they get in that car on this night of all nights?

I thought back to my friends and me from my high school days. We fought to stand out, to get out of the box we, as young men, thought we were in. There was nothing I wanted more when I was twenty years old than to leave what I had grown up in, to put distance between me and a tempestuous home life, teen angst, a provincial existence in a place where I felt I was missing out on a bigger world. But I had a path that was so obvious, so easily accessed. Manhattan, THE CITY, was a free ferry ride away. My friends and I had opportunities that we took for granted, that we did not think were easy for us. We thought that the lives we were living were hard because, in the moment, they felt hard. We complained about our parents, our teachers, everyone who was keeping us from being us. We did the stupid things that adolescent boys do—fight, posture, drink, swear, smoke. We, or at least I, felt penned in, disenfranchised and, at times, screwed over. I viewed my need to get away as a struggle to get away. A few of us succumbed to the risks inherent in young existences—drugs or jail or suicide or a bad decision that turned fatal—but most of us did not. Because we were never desperate, certainly not even close to desperate enough to risk it all.

What level of desperation was at play on this night? I wondered.

The boys who crashed into Scott were young, naive Black boys in a social system that is designed for them to fail. America is in denial about our system-ization of race and class. Even in working-class communities, the disparities between Whites and Blacks result in separatism. What do we expect? For years and years, Blacks have been left to figure out how to make it without much social support. And in the South, the shades are drawn and the flags fly high. There are people who stay to themselves and don't welcome change. Prosperity for all is not in their plans. They support the American dream for themselves and their own, but they don't help others achieve it. The whole infrastructure is broken!

This drama that usually plays out in the shadows of Savannah had suddenly jumped right out onto the busy streets of downtown. No longer were the harsh realities of racism, isolation, fear, and violence strictly abstract concepts. While Scott and Mashama crossed that street, those realities moved to the front and center of our lives. As I stood waiting for my Black partner to be interviewed by mostly White cops, the bubble that I had lived my life in was now losing air.

PAPER PLANE
Serves 2

When Scott Waldrup was bartending at The Grey, before he was promoted to the position of general manager, he always offered guests a Paper Plane if they didn't know what cocktail they wanted. This was his way of saying, "Welcome! You're in the South, so have the perfect bourbon-based aperitivo."—JOM

1½ ounces Nonino amaro

1½ ounces Aperol

1½ ounces Four Roses Bourbon

1½ ounces freshly squeezed lemon juice

Fill a cocktail shaker with ice. Add the amaro, Aperol, bourbon, and lemon juice. Shake vigorously for 20 seconds (which will give you the right amount of chill and dilution).

Pour through a cocktail strainer into two coupe glasses. Clink glasses and say, "Cheers to Scott" before you take your first sip.

CHAPTER 2

When I purchased the old Greyhound bus terminal at 109 Martin Luther King Jr. Boulevard in Savannah, the actual closing was uneventful, as one might expect these things to go. That is not to say that the overall process was without drama. In fact, I thought I had a deal on the building the year before I actually purchased it. The same seller and I had reached an agreed-upon price as well as a closing date and had basically come to terms on all of the points that people come to terms on in these dealings.

Ultimately, the seller got cold feet, or at least chilly toes. He started moving away from the idea of selling the building and began talking about ways that he could help *me* by renting the building to me for five years and then at the end of that term he'd finally sell it to me, at his option, of course, which would help me with tax credits or some other bullshit that I never really understood. Which is, I think, how he intended it. He didn't strike me as a bad guy, but I distinctly remember feeling like I was getting the runaround.

To say I was frustrated is an understatement.

My last meeting with that gentleman and our realtors, during that first attempt, as I recall, ended with me pushing back from his realtor's conference room table, delivering a few choice words, the harshness of which I regretted for a brief period of time afterward, and begrudgingly writing off that particular building as not for sale.

A year later, that same seller contacted me through my real estate agent, Jacqui Mason, to say that now he wanted to sell the bus terminal. At first, I didn't return his call, but my agent convinced me that she thought he was serious this time, so I called. I mean what was the harm?

We talked and he said that he was ready.

I was very direct with him. I would buy the building but only if he was prepared to sell it at the same price we had agreed to the year prior and if he would close the deal within five days. I figured that if the guy was still on the fence about selling the building, the only way I was going to smoke him out was to move as quickly as possible.

He agreed to the five days.

I remained suspicious.

Day Five came around, and . . . well, it all went according to plan (mostly—there was a last-minute escrow negotiated to fund the removal of some of the junk he was leaving behind). Just like that, I was the proud owner of a dilapidated, structurally questionable, and filthy, yet beautiful, abandoned Greyhound bus terminal.

I was excited and nervous. I mean I owned it, but now, what would I do with it?

While Johno was in the process of securing the bus terminal, I was trying to figure out my own shit. I was working as a sous-chef in a restaurant called Prune on the Lower East of Side of Manhattan. Around that time there were some changes in the kitchen, which was the beginning of me figuring out what my next career move was going to be because I had some time to plan.

I began to think of what I needed to do to have my own restaurant. I was living in my grandmother's house on the second floor in Jamaica, Queens, New York, where she had built a one-bedroom apartment that faced the backyard. In the past, she rented that space to supplement her monthly income. My grandmother lived in this huge home that was just too much for her. As a family, with the input of her sons and other close relatives, I agreed to move in and help her with the day-to-day. Living in this little apartment gave me the privacy and peace of mind I was seeking at the time and allowed me to continue to pursue my career while making my pay a secondary concern. We helped each other. That's what family does.

Margaret Bailey exuded elegance. She stood five feet tall and was a thin-framed woman who had a frail appearance but was feisty and spoke her mind. When pushed, she pushed back. She had a good sense of humor, loved to laugh, and would occasionally tell a dirty joke or two. She was also quite the entertainer. She had a formal dining room with a table that sat twelve. She had gold-plated silverware, two different china sets, crystal glasses, cloth napkins, tablecloths, gravy boats, ladles, serving spoons, serving forks, carving knives, and platters. She knew how to host a dinner party and she hosted them often. As she got older, all of the holiday parties were at her house. While I was growing up, I helped her and it grew to be one of my favorite memories we made together.

Another woman I grew to admire, I learned of while I was in cooking school. This woman also threw dinner parties at her home, and during one of them she met an investor and from that became the chef of her own restaurant.

My grandmother had everything I needed to do the same thing and build a following. It was ideal: I would start a supper club and throw parties in Queens once a month. I wouldn't need to travel into the city to do it. I would meet an investor and run my own kitchen. If a supper club was good enough for Edna Lewis, it was good enough for me.

The day after I closed, I think it was a Friday, I was walking through 109 MLK by myself. I spent a couple of hours in there just looking at it. Absorbing it. I was almost trying to listen to it, to see if it had a story to tell. Don't get me wrong, I'm not very much a believer in the impractical or intangible. I don't believe in ghosts, the supernatural, or buildings talking to you. But in this case, I just quietly walked through it, tried to look past the filth and the neglect, and see if this building knew what it wanted to be in its next incarnation.

That evening, I was sitting at home waiting for Carol to return from her job in New York City to spend the weekend with me and our dog, Flounder, in Savannah, which was increasingly becoming our habit. After she arrived, we opened a bottle of wine and started talking about our respective weeks and, of course, our brand-new investment in the bus terminal was the primary topic of conversation.

"How do you feel about it?" Carol asked.

"Yeah, I think I feel really good. It's a stunningly beautiful building once we can remove the sludge. I think when we shine that thing up and fix what's broken, it is going to be something else. Truly unique for Savannah."

"I agree, there's really nothing like it in Savannah," she answered. "But, now that we own it, we need to figure out what to do with it. We can't have that much of our money tied up in something that's just going to sit fallow."

"Totally," I agreed.

"So?"

"I've got some ideas," I offered.

"Like what?"

"Well, we could just white box it and try to rent it as an office or to SCAD. They have the photography building right next door to it."

"Those sound reasonable. Anything else a possibility?" she pressed.

"Yeah, I mean those are good. They'd be very sound uses. But I think that space has another purpose that would be over the top," I said.

"Like what?"

"I think I'm going to turn 109 MLK into a restaurant," I declared.

Carol was silent. She gulped her wine.

I just looked at her, smiling sheepishly.

"Johno," she said calmly, taking a moment to find her words, "have you lost your fucking mind?"

"No, I don't think so."

"Who's going to run it?"

"Me."

And what army, Johno, what army?

"You're going to run a restaurant? You don't know anything about restaurants. You've done some crazy shit in your life and I have always supported you, but this one sounds, well, I don't know, kind of hairbrained. You're forty-five years old. Restaurants are notoriously difficult and they fail, they always fail."

I was prepared for her reaction. It was reasonable. I didn't blame her one bit. "Listen, you and I have traveled for all of our careers and seen good stuff. We eat out almost every night. There's nothing I love more than food and wine. Think about it. Our only true form of entertainment is eating and drinking. We are good at it. I'm good at it."

"Come on, Johno," she said pleadingly, "eating in a restaurant and owning and running a restaurant are two very different things."

"I know. But I know how food makes people happy. Think about that first time you came to my parents' house for dinner. Do you remember how that made you feel? You thought all we were going to eat were a couple of trays of antipasti and then some chicken soup with escarole, so when pasta was the next course followed by a roasted leg of lamb with potatoes and peas and then finally a salad, you were kind of blown away—we were at the table for something like four hours. You loved it. My family has always been about food."

When I think of family, I think of music, laughter, a little bit of criticism, and food. My dad played records every weekend, he particularly loves jazz, loves it loud and really doesn't care who knows it. From a very young age I can remember Miles, Coltrane, Gil Scott Heron, and many others as the theme music to the productive Saturday morning house-cleaning sessions that we bonded over. It didn't feel like bonding back in the day. Back then it felt like work. Like non-paying, hypercritical, we-better-be-appreciative-of-what-we-have work. Now my siblings and I often sit back and reminisce about the days when we couldn't leave the house until we were done with our chores. As a family we laughed pretty easily, never tried to take ourselves too seriously. But I must admit, I took myself seriously. I loved to stay in my head, write poems, and dream.

I was a very sensitive child. I was the oldest, and my brother, five years younger than me, could make me upset just by teasing me. He loved to get on my nerves. My parents were young and both their mothers would say that I was spoiled, but I just think that's how I'm made. As an adult, that sensitivity helps me in other ways. I'm intuitive and sentimental, which I think enhances my cooking. Seems like all the women in my family are made similarly—and are good cooks. My mother fed her nuclear family with mostly delicious and simple, home-cooked meals. On Sundays she would often bake chicken with all of the fixins', like mashed potatoes, gravy, and cornbread. During the week she prepared quicker meals, like meatloaf in the winter, and soup and sandwiches during the summer.

Growing up, the family gatherings were potlucks; everyone would bring their specialty. My mother did the greens, my aunt brought the macaroni and cheese, Grandma Margie made deviled eggs, and my uncle's second wife, Renee, the sweet potato pie, and the list goes on down the line. It didn't matter if we were in Georgia or New York, with one side of the family or the other, that's how it went. We share the load and help each other out. My adult relatives praised and discussed each other's doings and asked questions about ingredients and techniques. For years it never occurred to me that I was actually paying attention. As I got older and became more interested in cooking, I began asking those same questions—how do you do your lima beans, or tell me what's in your greens? Our family food traditions were about unity, sharing, and pride. About bringing over the dishes that you did best to share with the people that you love most.

Carol smiled a little bit at the memory as I thought about my life through the lens of food. For me, other than Carol, my family, my dogs, and my job, life has always been about food since I was a child. It was at my Italian grandparents' dinner table that my siblings and I found our escape from a family fed by inter-mittent, alcohol-fueled rages from a father who was too often overwhelmed by the pressures of raising a family of five on a fireman's salary in 1970s New York City, and a mother who was penned in by her circumstances and youthful life choices. At that table, we ate Sunday Gravy from a giant pot filled to its rim with crushed tomatoes and various meats and animal parts traditional to the meal—pigs' feet, beef and pork meatballs, lamb shanks, hot sausage, oxtail, and anything else the butcher had available that my grandmother, a magician when it came to creating deliciousness out of dregs, could afford.

When ready to serve, the meat was placed on two or three large platters and positioned around our table so we could pick and choose our favorite pieces. The "gravy," or pasta sauce, was mixed into a giant bowl of penne or rigatoni from which we would all fill our plates with what was always called "macaroni," regardless of the shape of the noodle. We always topped our plates with a scoop of Polly-O ricotta. As the heat from the pasta broke down the cheese, it melted into the red sauce and gently softened the acidity of the tomatoes. A long, hot green pepper from my grandparents' garden, fresh or dried depending on the time of year, was minced and used to garnish the plates of the spice-loving among us—a tradition I always insisted on being party to. Salad, crusty bread, and for the kids a taste of red wine (much more for the adults), which my grand-father made in his cellar each October from the grapes he bought at markets in Lower Manhattan, were all an indispensable part of the Sunday ritual.

It was during these meals that the worst parts of our reality slipped away and I learned about the comfort gained from food, family, laughter, and humanity. For me, the family meal represented love. And decades later, that hasn't changed.

Maybe the question isn't "can you run a restaurant?" but "should you run a restaurant?"

Running a restaurant is a fantasized version of what a family meal can be. Many people, investors, cooks, restaurateurs, and servers, come into this business thinking that all they have to do is show up to work and everything is going to go according to plan. That never happens. Any given day you could walk into the restaurant and your back server no-shows because she got picked up the night before on a parole violation, your GM's kid is sick with the flu, there's a leaky pipe under the dish machine, the proteins never got delivered from the

purveyor, and your lead bartender is fucking hung over. Meanwhile you have a full dining room and a giant roach crawls across the bar. Granted, not all of these things happen in one night, but I am sure you will see them over a week or two. So, folks need to think real hard about opening a restaurant because it's not just about candelabras and the soft music playing in the background. Or the signature ingredient that makes your Dover sole magical. Restaurants are about people. People who wake up every day, and, no matter what their day was like the day before, still enjoy serving and feeding people. *Should I run a restaurant?* was the question I had been asking myself and the question Johno should have been asking himself too.

I looked at Carol as I sipped my wine. I smiled calmly at her. "I can do this," I said. "I am going to be successful at it. I have to be. And Savannah needs the kind of place that I think I can build. I just feel it."

She smiled back, not quite as confidently as me, but clinked my glass anyway, "Well, I hope you're right."

MARGIE'S DEVILED EGGS
Serves 6

12 eggs

½ cup of your favorite mayonnaise

3 tablespoons spicy mustard (Dijon or brown)

1 tablespoon apple cider vinegar

1 teaspoon garlic powder

Kosher Salt

1 tablespoon sweet paprika

We could count on my grandmother to bring the deviled eggs to every family gathering. No one else's rival hers!—MB

Fill a medium sauce pot halfway with water and bring to a boil over high heat. Once the water is boiling, using tongs, a slotted spoon, or a small mesh strainer, carefully lower the eggs into the water. Set your timer to 10 minutes. Once the water returns to a boil, decrease the heat to medium.

Meanwhile, fill a bowl with ice water and nest another bowl in it.

When the timer goes off, transfer the eggs from the pot to the water bath and leave them to cool for 3 to 5 minutes.

Peel the eggs. Slice in half lengthwise and separate the whites and yolks. Place the yolks in the bowl of a food processor. Add the mayonnaise, mustard, vinegar, and garlic powder. Process until smooth. If the mixture is too thick (pastelike), add a tablespoon of water or a dash or two of vinegar. Taste and season with salt as needed.

Transfer the yolk mixture to a pastry bag and fill the halved whites. Alternatively, spoon the filling into the halves. Arrange the eggs on a serving plate and refrigerate for 4 hours before serving. Sprinkle with the paprika and serve cold.

CHAPTER 3

I had been in the industry for over two decades. I was then a sous-chef for just under four years at a thirty-four-seat restaurant that I loved. I had already been a private chef, server, and line cook, and had washed a ton of dishes. All of this had pushed me to be a better cook. I also was firmly adopting the necessary work ethic from my bosses who held us accountable and treated us all like owners of those businesses. Even with all of that, you won't know if you are truly prepared for something bigger until you take that risk.

As a first-time restaurateur, I had no idea how complicated and interconnected the operations of a restaurant truly are. I didn't understand the various roles of the chef, general manager, and owner beyond the fact that I knew that a chef cooked, a manager managed, and owners sweated all of the finances and every last detail (at least I do). But I was about to find out pretty damn fast.

During the summer, I began work on the schematic plan for the restaurant with the design-and-build teams I'd engaged. Jeremy Levitt and Andrew Cohen, the principals of Parts and Labor Design, a firm in New York City often referred to as "PLD," had quickly become my near-constant companions during the early development and planning stages.

"How many seats do you want in the restaurant?" they asked one morning as we spoke on the telephone, me sitting in my house in Savannah and them in their office, then on Broadway and Houston, in Lower Manhattan.

Jeremy, a big guy from Michigan who, at just under six feet, has a sleepiness about him that belies an extreme intensity in his work. His voice is baritone and he often speaks in a manner that is hushed and conspiratorial. During the creative process, he's a rapid-fire talker who will suddenly pause mid-sentence, go silent for some period of time, search the file folders of his brain for the color, curve, or method he is looking for, and then resume his spiel. He's tattooed, thickly built, and just as comfortable reasoning something out or fighting for it—hard. And while he grew up the son of a lawyer in the suburbs of Detroit, it's the grit of that city that he prefers to wear on his sleeve. These complexities coalesce in a way that make him a lot of fun to be around and a very good designer.

Andrew is a smaller package at five feet eight inches. Partially balding in front, the remainder of his dark, curly hair surrounds a genial face and deep-set eyes that are his most prominent feature. Conversely, his outward intensity sometimes overshadows an immensely thoughtful guy who has a sharp sense of humor and laughs easily. He is quick to crack a joke, insightful, and, when necessary, a tough opponent on the other side of an issue. He is an excellent complement to Jeremy, bringing balance to the table when it is called for, while keeping the architecture and spatial design moving forward in their projects.

Our combined relationship quickly transcended a purely professional one. They collectively became my sounding board for almost every decision I made related to the buildout and opening of the restaurant. We shared aesthetic tastes, appreciated each other and, mostly, just had a lot of fun. It was usually very easy between us and there was as much banter as there was work.

In response to the question they posed on the phone about seat count, I answered, "How many seats can we fit?"

"It's more complicated than that,". "We have to get this right in every way. You have to worry about how much food your kitchen can get out. That depends on your menu, your chef, your service model, your team. All of it," they said, trying to shed some light on the larger picture for me.

The inner workings of a restaurant *are* complicated. These three were in over their heads, asking questions that should be answered by a chef, service manager, or, hell, even a restaurant consultant.

Kitchen, smitchen, my internal voice said. I was, as we entered this phase of the project, very much worried about getting bogged down in design hell and sweating things that did not need to be sweated. I had close to a million dollars sunk into the purchase of a building that would remain nonperforming until the restaurant opened, and a budget of another couple million to fund the buildout. Speed and efficiency were my main concerns. A yet-to-be-engaged kitchen team serving food in an actual restaurant was such an abstract concept to me at that stage that I almost could not consider it a serious concern, as it related to cramming in as many seats as we could because seats, in my accountant's brain, equaled revenue and, hopefully, profit.

"Why does it have to be this complicated?" I asked. "Sure, we have to invest in this space to make it beautiful and unique in Savannah. If we pull that off, we're off to great start. Then I've got to figure out how to put an entire experience together because most places in Savannah, I think, are chasing tourist dollars and no one is just trying to serve the community in the downtown area, at least that I can see. That's our opportunity—give Savannah a complete experience. So, yeah, we have to build out the right space; I couldn't agree more. But, also, from an economics point of view, we need to build a restaurant with as many seats as possible and the kitchen will have to service that restaurant."

Jeremy groaned, still too new to our relationship to express his true feelings about how dangerous he found my oversimplification, and quipped sarcastically, "Sure. Whatever you say." Taking a slow pause, he added with a laugh, "Let's see how your chef feels about that."

Seat count doesn't matter if the kitchen can't feed them. The dishpit needs to be the right size, the walk-ins need to be the right size, the prep cooks need room to prep, and the chefs need room to cook. In a perfect world, all of these pieces have to fit together, but most restaurants aren't set up perfectly. So, we just make it work.

"You do know you need to hire a chef soon. Right?" Andrew added immediately after Jeremy spoke, demonstrating what would become a long-term pattern of them tag-teaming me in our conversations about buildout and functionality.

I did know that. Kind of.

Well, I knew I did not know how to cook beyond doing so in my own personal kitchen. And I knew, just from witnessing the goings-on in any successful restaurant I had been in over the course of my life, that there were innumerable factors that went into its success. The truth was that I was scared shitless throughout this process about all the pieces that were ultimately going to have to be assembled, coalesced, and fine-tuned. A chef may have been the next (giant) piece of the puzzle, but it would still be a puzzle after that person arrived on the scene.

I put them off with "Let's just keep going on the design and get as many seats in as we can. I *will* start thinking about a chef."

Silence on the other end of the phone.

"I promise," I offered with my requisite amount of faux confidence.

PLD had just begun to get their footing as independent restaurant designers. From Johno's perspective, I don't think he could have teamed up with a better group. Between their bantering with one another and their ease in communicating, the design phase seemed to truly bring creativity from all sides. However, these guys were still dreaming, prioritizing the design of the space

over the function of the space. Johno probably should have stopped everything at that point and either found his chef or hired a restaurant consultant who could work from the inside out, someone who knew how restaurants and service worked. That was a missed opportunity.

A few hours later, my phone rang. It was Larry, our kitchen design consultant (and one of the few people on our team who never got used to calling me Johno). "Hey, John, I'm working on this layout for the kitchen, and I really need a seat count. How many seats does Parts and Labor have slated for the main dining room?"

"Holy fuck" now ricocheted around the inside my head. I had just come up for air after the PLD phone call and now Larry's question shined the same bright light on my extreme ignorance about the restaurant business. My throat closed up a bit and I had to actually gasp for a breath before answering him.

"We're working on that, Larry," I said softly, tamping down the fear that was beginning to dominate my reaction to everything.

"Okay," he replied, with some frustration in his own voice. "I really need to know that. I need to know what kind of food you're cooking too."

I nodded to the handset and mumbled, "Uh huh."

Larry had been designing kitchens in Atlanta and throughout the South for decades. He was a personable guy, probably ten or so years older than me, but one who didn't spend a lot of time suffering fools and novices. He was respectful of me, his client, but also took the shortest route to get to the point when it came to his time. He continued, "It's virtually impossible to design a kitchen when I don't know what you want to cook. For instance, do I need a pasta station, multiple fryers, a flat top? Are you doing Asian food? Southern? Ethiopian?"

"I don't know, Larry," I snapped, "but I am pretty sure it's not going to be Ethiopian. Beyond that, whatever the chef that I find cooks, that's what we will be serving."

Back in New York City, I was searching for my culinary voice. Port cities like Savannah are tremendously influenced by cultures and cuisines from all parts of the world. Maybe, if I had been in these early discussions, Ethiopian food wouldn't have seemed so farfetched because I would have pointed out that African influences make perfect sense in a city like Savannah. There is a

Geechee Gullah community alive and well in the area and there are African American folks who still uphold the African traditions of farming and cooking throughout the surrounding region.

"Okay, I got it. Fine," Larry said, giving in just a bit. "But I do need a seat count at this point. That's going to have a real impact on how we structure the dishpit and how much space we devote to it. We don't have a lot of space in this kitchen and it all starts with the dishpit. Then I can work backward and placeholder some of the cooking equipment."

Dishpit? I was pretty sure I had never heard that term before. *What's the big deal about a dishpit?* I wondered. A new pang of fear struck me. *Is there like a restaurant glossary or encyclopedia out there somewhere, so I could at least get the jargon down? God, I suck.*

The fact is that I had likely skipped all of that stuff when thinking about what this undertaking entailed. I focused on the aesthetics and creating a space that people were going to feel comfortable in, that was special. I guess, because all of my personal experiences in restaurants were eating in them, I was a front-of-house guy, through and through, before I even knew it. It almost confused me that Larry and PLD were asking me these questions because they were the consultants and designers and I had never even heard of a dishpit.

The end result of all of this back and forth is that the dishpit ended up being too small for the restaurant. Larry had the space spec'd for dishes only but no one considered all of the rest of it. The dishes, the glasses, the silverware, the pots, and the pans. The dishpit occupies the far-left corner of the kitchen and needs at least two people to run it. These two people are so necessary in supporting the complete dining experience. They work closely together and that setup is not ideal. The dishpit is a permanent reminder of someone needing to stop and think about how this restaurant would function realistically.

"I'm waiting on that number, Larry," was my half-hearted response. "I'll send it to you as soon as I have a final count from PLD. They promised me something shortly."

I hung up and Googled "dishpit."

Then, after taking a few seconds to read some generic descriptions, I called the PLD boys back. "Hey, guys. Back to that conversation we were having earlier today, we really need a seat count at this point for Larry. We're trying to lay out the dishpit and I'm sure you guys well know that we can't do that without a seat count. This is high priority. I'm starting to get concerned about where we're going to fit the dishpit, depending on how big it needs to be, and that, again, as you guys know, is partially a function of seat count."

Silence from the other end of the phone as I did the dishpit two-step. I could practically hear them roll their eyes. I had no doubt that Andrew was mouthing to Jeremy something along the lines of "This guy's going to spend a whole lot of fucking money and completely fail at this."

It was a genuine possibility that I was in over my head. I mean, what kind of restaurant owner has never heard of a dishpit?

"Legit," was all Jeremy said back to me, one of his standard responses, along with "dope," when he did not have an answer or an answer was not deserved.

Maybe I need to take this chef thing seriously, I thought as I hung up.

This part of the restaurant's development I find completely frustrating because every single thing they are talking about affects me, the organization of the back of the house, the kitchen team, and everything that goes on in the kitchen. I wish I had been there for this. I am not sure I would have been able to greatly improve things, but I know that I could have offered the perspective that comes with experience.

CLAMS OREGANATA
Serves 4

This is a version of a dish that we have eaten together in a lot of different cities and countries that always reminds us of New York City . . . City Island, Little Italy, Queens, and Staten Island.—MB and JOM

Fill a large bowl or pot with 1 gallon of cold water and the ¼ cup salt. Scrub the clams and soak overnight in the salted water to purge them of sand and silt.

Rinse the purged clams. Transfer to a deep skillet with a tight-fitting lid. Steam over high heat just until the clams open, about 4 minutes. Strain and reserve the liquid. Remove and discard the top shells of each clam, collecting any liquid that drains from the bottom shell. Using a small paring knife, cut under a clam to release it from its shell. Set the clam in its shell on a baking sheet large enough to hold all of the clams and then repeat for the remaining ones.

In a sauté pan over medium heat, melt the butter. Add the panko and toast until golden brown, tossing continuously to prevent overbrowning. Transfer the panko to a mixing bowl and add the parsley, oregano, garlic, cheese, red chile flakes, remaining 1 teaspoon salt, the black pepper, and reserved clam liquid and mix well. Let stand for 10 minutes.

Preheat the broiler. Using a soupspoon, fill each clamshell with the panko mixture. Broil for approximately 3 minutes, watching carefully to ensure the clams don't burn. Serve immediately.

¼ cup kosher salt, plus 1 teaspoon

24 littleneck clams

1 cup butter

2 cups plain panko

½ cup finely chopped flat-leaf parsley

1 tablespoon finely chopped oregano

6 cloves garlic, minced

¼ cup grated Parmigiano-Reggiano cheese

2 teaspoons crushed red chile flakes

Cracked black pepper

½ cup dry white wine

CHAPTER 4

Even though throughout most of my adult life I have eaten 90 percent of my meals in restaurants, the relationship among seat count, dishpit, walk-in space, storage, and product flow had never occurred to me before.

I had keenly tracked my personal experiences in restaurants. This was partly why I believed that I had a point of view worth sharing with other people—our future team and guests. I have always paid attention to the food, the service, the ambiance, and whether they all came together to create a completely satisfying experience, a completely awful experience, or, worst of all, a mediocre and incomplete experience that left me confused or wanting something more, or something else.

I did not, however, give much, if any, consideration to the fact that by the time the food had reached me, the die was already cast. All of the decisions that led to the food's procurement, preparation, plating, and delivery were made well before I ever saw it. The food on my plate was the end result of the talent (or lack thereof) of the executive chef, owner, general manager, the team, and everything else that went into the planning of getting that food to me at the appropriate temperature and its intended quality. While logically this is a very simple concept to grasp, it was just not one that I had ever considered before.

The night of the seat count–dishpit conversation, I did not sleep a single second. Jeremy, Andrew, and Larry were all right. I needed help, and the fact that I did not, as of yet, have any, when such crucial and costly decisions were being made about the kitchen and the elements necessary to prepare our food, was turning a consistent, base-level, buzzing fear into a near panic as the night sweats and insomnia accelerated this cycle, loosening my grasp on the project management.

And through this, the only thing I knew for sure was that I did not want to hire just a chef. I needed to find a partner, a true business partner. I needed someone who would be completely in it with me and not just on board for a paycheck.

Stay the hell away from this, businesspeople. Until you realize you love it and you're not just in it for a paycheck, you will not survive. There are tons of sacrifices that you endure. You miss birthdays, weekends, nightly dinners, holidays, everything. And your restaurant "family" consists of people you will have been in the trenches of service with but who in many ways are no substitute for your true family, who loves you unconditionally. Unless you can accept all of those aspects of restaurant life, don't do it.

People who are new to start-ups often worry about preserving their equity rather than sharing it with the people who are able to help them build something of value. Over my years doing this work, I learned to not be that person, because that type of thinking is often shortsighted.

Owning 100 percent of something that you cannot grow by your lonesome amounts to nothing. Owning a lesser portion of a growing, thriving entity, because your partners are properly incentivized, has a higher likelihood of adding up to something meaningful.

Finding a business partner, however, would be far more difficult and riskier than hiring a chef that I could fire if things didn't go well.

Immediately after my dishpit epiphany, I committed to the task of finding a business partner who would serve as our executive chef. Instead of passively looking and hoping, which had been my strategy till then, I decided that my search needed to become very active and intensive.

All right! Yes, let's insert some culinary inspiration and experience.

I did this knowing full well that the person I was looking for was likely not in Savannah. I had been in town for two and a half years at that point, and while there was certainly some good food to be found, most downtown restaurants were catering to visitors and travelers.

Much of the culinary focus was on what restaurant owners expected visitors to want from a town like Savannah: shrimp and grits, fried green tomatoes, and she-crab soup with a splash of sherry. For the most part, cuisine in the Historic District had very little to do with the growing seasons, the history of food in the area, or, for that matter, what chefs wanted to cook and eat. It seemed to me that it was much more driven by profit margins and preconceptions about how visiting guests would respond to a Savannah menu.

Many of the mom-and-pop places in the Historic District that were telling the story of the region over the last fifty to a hundred years are gone. So for me, I needed to look toward the traditions carried on within the homes in the Low Country. To eat from one modern restaurant to another is one kind of research, but to truly understand why, in certain regions, we only farm oysters in months with names that contain the letter "R," or when greens are best eaten, or even what makes dishes like hoppin' John to be Southern and special, I needed to ask questions and read books. I needed to be invited into

the inner circles that helped keep the regional traditions of the Golden Coast alive and well. Over the last thirty years, the closing of flagship restaurants and beloved neighborhood eateries that were no longer in vogue has left a void for aspiring chefs looking for inspiration in and around Savannah. Moving back to this region and having the advantage (or disadvantage) of viewing it from a Northern perspective is powerful. Getting information about food and traditions from local folks helps add depth and soul to a dish. By asking the questions and listening to people's oral histories, not only does that reinforce the need to keep the old, comfortable dishes alive and strong, but it gives me and other chefs the opportunity to create new dishes that are personal and invoke memory.

That is not to say that in those couple of years of exploring the culinary land-scape in downtown Savannah there were not plenty of places that I enjoyed. They were comfortable and familiar. It was as if the tourism board had helped conceptualize and build many of them. There was not, however, a place in which the chef was the clear driving force, pushing the envelope because of a compulsion or just straight-up passion. There was no place that made its guests really have to think about why they were eating this dish or that. Service, in many of the places I frequented, did not appear to be a priority. I wanted to build and be part of a place that led with its food and where everything else was in support of that food—the wine, the service, the team, the aesthetic. I am not sure that I had the vocabulary at that point to say that I was seeking to build a chef-driven restaurant, but, in hindsight, I was quite dead set on that very thing.

I love that! Same here! Savannah just seems like a city that is ready for more. Many people stayed committed to small and local places, but the real driver for Savannah is tourism, and that changes the expectations of many diners in the city. People want Southern food; it's delicious. The kind that many of us see on TV and that will put you to sleep—heavy foods laced with fat and sugar that will raise your blood pressure and cause other health problems. I can image a board room full of ad executives in the 1950s searching for ways to promote domestic travel in this country. Travel to Savannah on the Greyhound bus to come sit in the squares of the city. Live oaks, cobblestone streets, horse-drawn carriage rides, fried shrimp, and sweet tea. It worked and it still works today.

So, I set out to find someone different, someone who was not at all who Savannahians expected to find in the kitchen of a downtown Savannah restau-rant. I didn't want shrimp and grits anywhere near our menu. I didn't want soul food, barbecue, or any of the processed-food or butter- and fat-laden dishes that television chefs had convinced Americans, including me, constituted Southern food. If the restaurant we were building was going to separate itself, we needed to think differently. We needed to build something that was disruptive, something that would make Savannah diners take notice because it was new to them—something that would both comfort and surprise them. It needed to be something that locals could ultimately call their own because it was distinctly Savannahian. That abstract definition was the best I had at that moment.

Correct me if I am wrong, but I think that the history of Blacks cooking in professional kitchens in America is as long as the country is old, and exactly what some people would expect. When I see liver and onions over grits, smothered pork chops, and collard greens or fried catfish on a menu, I think a Black person is cooking. There are some popular restaurants in Savannah serving those dishes (or food that reminds me of them) and there are certainly a lot of Black folks cooking in those kitchens. I know this feeds old stereotypes and yet those are the dishes that people want to eat when they visit—the good, old-fashioned plate of "fill in the blank" way of dining. As a Black chef, I am always wondering how I am perceived and how I am constantly managing people's expectations of me. Many people assume that these foods are all I know how to cook, and I am happy to cook and serve the food I was raised on—often, that's the food that I crave—but I also wanted to explore Southern food through the lens of a girl who was raised between the North and the South and felt compelled to understand my ancestry through my cooking.

Alas, the first discovery I made when I began my search for someone different was that the chef pool in America was primarily filled with macho White guys who have an overabundance of cutlery tattoos and, often, testosterone-swelled egos from working in boy's club kitchens. Additionally, chefs, at least by reputation, are not known to be great collaborators. Finding a business partner who could run our kitchen was, I was discovering quickly, going to be far more challenging than I had initially thought. Identifying someone who could bring a completely different perspective, and do so cooperatively and immediately, seemed impossible.

Don't get me wrong. In spite of their decreasing popularity in recent years, I'm not against White men. I happen to be one. While there is much wrong with a homogenous group setting all of the rules in a theoretically diverse society, there is nothing inherently wrong with being White and male.

As a rule, I normally don't trust White men and their motives. There is nothing wrong with being who you are, but their lack of awareness of their inherent benefits confuses me, and they have done a pretty shitty job of understanding

gender and race. They view those of us who don't look like them or adhere to their "values" as threats. Even though I see the source of power shifting, glacially, it is still inherently beneficial to be White and male.

The trouble starts when the White guy looks around the room and all he sees are other White guys who look like him and think like him, whether by design, coincidence, or circumstance. That's when the risk that an idea that *is* inherently fucking stupid or subjugating or evil starts to sound, well, not so fucking stupid to them. That's when individuality turns into groupthink turns into gang mentality, and that is when their decision making, management style, and humanity erode.

And, as for tattoos, I love them. I have a bunch, and I keep getting more—they are becoming the greatest visual representation of my midlife search for connection to the people and things that are important to me. My first tattoo was a Hagar the Horrible knockoff that I got when I was eighteen (hidden on my hip so my parents wouldn't find out) as an ode to my Norwegian grandfather, Ole, whose name inspired my nickname "Johno." The next was a small skull and crossbones on my left shoulder blade, which I had done when I was living in Paris in my twenties and was in an extreme Guns N' Roses phase. From there, a Crown of Thorns banded my far-too-small bicep to bear such a tattoo, reminding me that I once firmly believed in God. Another memorialized the first and only marathon I have ever run. And lately, my wife, my dogs, my love for art, and my shortcomings are the subjects of choice for my current crop.

So when I looked at the people, the guys, who were candidates for the position of chef and business partner, they mostly looked and acted a whole lot like me. Right down to the cropped hair, pale skin, perpetual five o'clock shadow, and penchant for wearing their hearts on their sleeves in the form of ink. That was who was most visible to me, so naturally that was who I met.

In culinary school, I was asked to write about a chef who inspired me. At first, I insisted that I wanted to write about my grandmothers. They were the best cooks that I have known to date. But I wasn't allowed. The essay had to be about a professional chef who had been trained in a hotel or restaurant. None of the most visible of those people looked anything like me. I did my research and found a woman who did. She had run restaurants and written cookbooks. To find someone different, I had to look in different places. If you look behind those standing in front, you see that there is a silent army—the next generation—behind them, upholding your standards along with theirs. Those folks are usually more diverse and colorful than the ones in front of them. I love that! I am that!

My initial search yielded outreach to about ten guys from around the country, ranging from New York City to Atlanta, Charleston, New Orleans, and the West Coast. Of those ten, I began meaningful discussions with four or five of them. The first of note was a nice guy from Atlanta who I had met through a local restaurateur I had gotten to know.

When I called the young chef, we made the obligatory small talk for a bit. He was a tad awkward, but I suppose he felt the same about me, as I had no idea how to interview a chef or even what to ask him that was remotely relevant.

I wondered, *Do I say something along the lines of "Do you like to cook?" Is that a fair question? Or maybe it would be better to ask, "What do you like to cook?"*

Pro-Tip: I like asking cooks, "What station are you working on the line? What cooking magazines do you read and why? What cookbooks are you reading right now? What is your favorite knife? Where's the last place you were impressed by the chef? What was the dish that did it?"

Instead, I asked nothing of him. I just dove right in with, "I'm working on a project in Savannah. I'm looking for a chef, well, really a business partner, and I wanted to see if you might be interested in talking about it."

"Sure. Yeah. I might be. I love Savannah," he answered.

Silence on the phone.

Was it my turn already?

"Um, I'm new to this. I'm not really sure what we do next. You want to meet?" I asked.

"Sure. Yeah, that's a good idea. Why don't you drive up to Atlanta and come to the restaurant? Eat dinner here and then we can have a beer afterward and talk about your project."

Wow, this guy's brilliant, I thought. Eat the food that he is cooking as a way to get to understand him? I can see how he cooks and what his personality is like all in the same trip!

So, Carol and I drove to Atlanta, got a hotel room for the night, and went to the restaurant where he was cooking.

His food was good. Solid.

We met with him and, to my surprise, his girlfriend, after dinner for a couple of beers (or wine in our case). They were a sweet couple. She did the talking. She told us all about him, his background, his cooking style, and what they were thinking of—as a couple—in terms of his next gig. It was more like being with an actor and his manager discussing a potential role. He said very little.

The next morning, I called Jeremy and Andrew, who I had briefed about my trip to Atlanta to meet the first candidate, to tell them how dinner went.

"How was it?" one of them asked excitedly.

"It was good. Solid. Lot of seafood. He was a dead-nice guy, but the girlfriend ran the show. He reminded me of someone I could have grown up with on Staten Island. Kind of rough around the edges in a really familiar way to me. The kind of guy you could hang out and have a beer with after you got to know him a little better. His girlfriend was with him and she seemed nice but also kind of in charge. That makes me a little nervous." And then I added, "His food was a little messy too; it lacked a certain amount of precision and didn't look all that great."

"But the food, it tasted good?" Andrew asked.

"Yeah, it was good. Solid. I liked it. I think he could be in the running. Just needs a little more attention to detail. And I'm not sure why the girlfriend was there, although she seemed nice enough."

"But he can't plate is what you're saying, right?" Jeremy nearly shouted.

"Well, he can plate. It's just kind of messy, I guess. It was okay," I answered, a bit proud of myself for using the restaurant professional term "plate."

"Forget him. You can't have a chef who can't plate in the restaurant we're building. That'll ruin everything," Jeremy continued.

I hung on, about to say something in the young chef's defense. After all, everyone kept telling me that I needed a chef in very short order. How can the originators of that demand just dismiss a potential candidate before they learned anything about him?

But I was not quick enough, and Andrew immediately agreed with Jeremy. "Jeremy's right . . ." he began to say.

Jeremy was fired up and cut off his business partner, interjecting, "Yeah, that's all we need, Sloppy Plates McGee, your long-lost cousin from Staten Island, running the kitchen, putting out sloppy food. Probably should forget this guy."

"Yeah, we probably should forget this guy," Andrew added for good measure.

"But his food was good," I offered meekly, not fully willing to give up on him just yet but not at all confident in my ability to pick a chef, "it was solid." The conversation about Sloppy Plates McGee, however, was already over.

A few months later I would have my meeting with Jeremy and Andrew in their offices. I thought that these guys were going to be just assholes, kind of how they sound here. These dudes were so engaged and excited about this project that you could see them going above and beyond the design aspect. They were invested in the end results, the service, the flow, and even the chef. It was clear from my first meeting with them that they really wanted the best fit. I had been cooking for a while and still questioned whether I was ready for this next step even after I told myself that I was. I remember the confidence I left with after meeting them in their office. The three of us hit it off right away.

The next guy was in New York City. Good cook. *Really* good. Lots of tattoos. We had several meetings. His wife/business partner attended all of them and did a lot of the talking, which, again, seemed odd to me, as I was trying to get into business with a chef and not the chef's partner or significant other.

He was a fairly notable chef in New York City, and so a relationship with him would be more complicated. He would come along with an identity that people knew, at least in New York and the food-centric scene beyond that city. We hit it off, but I had some serious trepidation about this type of arrangement from the beginning. I knew so little about restaurants that I felt that I needed a person who would fully commit to our partnership. I was not looking for someone who just wanted to put his or her name on a project because they created the menu, taught someone how to cook it, and then managed it all, remotely, far from Savannah (which, in retrospect, was likely the only kind of deal that could have worked for most candidates, so my plan may have been doomed from the outset).

Sure, he could possibly be a business partner . . . of sorts. A long-distance relationship would not be an optimal solution, but we decided to continue the conversation because we liked each other and the first time I ate in his restaurant, I really, truly liked the food—a lot. It was inventive, fun, and, most importantly, delicious.

And while I was talking with him over a period of several weeks, I went back to his restaurant a couple more times in an effort to better understand him and his food. My experience each time was a little more disappointing. The execution and consistency of the food was not as it was on my first visit and I never saw him there despite the fact that it was his only operating restaurant at that time. I found this worrisome because I was of the belief, mistakenly or not, that chefs and owners of successful restaurants were pretty much chained to them, yet during my three visits, I went zero for three on catching him in his place.

When I chose to do this work, I thought I was making the decision to be there every single day, plate every single dish, and train every single person. That's hard and unrealistic. It's so hard to do this work when you are there, in it, every day. Setting up your team is really your job because you have to be able to step away to maintain perspective. I can empathize, though, because if your team loses focus or your cooks aren't tasting the food coming off their stations, so many things can fall through the cracks. This is a hard business to grow and even more grueling to nurture.

The final time I ate there, Carol and I took seats at the bar as soon as it opened early on a Sunday evening. We were two of only three people in the entire place, with a solo diner sitting to our left. As we took our seats, the staff barely acknowledged our presence or served us. Instead, they mostly congregated at the far end of the bar to trade stories about how "fucked up" they were the night before, with a specific story told by a young bartender taking a decidedly graphic and kind of gross turn. It was safe to say that it was not a super-appetizing introduction to our meal and I left that evening feeling dubious about whether this could go anywhere.

I met with the chef and his wife one more time after that Sunday to have an honest conversation about what each of us needed from a potential partnership and what our respective capacities were to take on such a project. I continued to find him very sincere in his passion for food and restaurants but, I guessed, that he was also overwhelmed by juggling his current space and another two restaurants in the making. As a guy who was, at that point in time, completely drowning in the process of trying to open my own, single restaurant, I honestly could not imagine what it would be like to be in his shoes and taking on so much simultaneously. As we talked back and forth, I shared my concerns about whether or not he had the bandwidth to really give my project the attention it would need and illustrated my concerns, perhaps insensitively, by talking about my three consecutive experiences in his existing space and the inconsistency I found in those experiences. I, regretfully, also shared the story of his team on the last night I was there and recounted his bartender's story verbatim.

Okay, wait. This is starting to get painful to hear but I guess these are the growing pains of inexperience and part of the process. Knowing Johno like I do now, I can see why he went through these conversations to figure out exactly what he was looking for. With him being new to all of this, the restaurant business and its idiosyncrasies, this clearly was a jumping-off point for him to begin to truly understand the culture of this business. The chef, the overinserted spouse/business partner, the hungover bartender, and distracted servers waiting for a bartender to drop unsolicited gossip from the night before are all real parts of this business. It's really interesting to see Johno's reaction to it for the first time. It's funny that it never occurred to him that he would soon find himself in that same role as this chef/owner while creating and protecting the culture of The Grey and supporting our team.

Our conversation was straightforward and professional and he took my feedback in stride. After all, as the saying goes, everyone's got an opinion and I was just offering mine. He was noticeably bothered by my telling of my final visit to his restaurant and I often wonder, in retrospect, if it was necessary to share that part with him.

After a while, the conversation grew more awkward with my lack of restaurant experience coming up as a counter argument to my observations, which I not only deserved but was true. We went around a bit more with me countering that restaurants are businesses and I did have some experience in those, but it all seemed kind of fruitless at that point and our meeting came to something of an abrupt end.

For the record, I did get an email from the offending bartender the day after meeting with the chef and his wife in which he apologized for his behavior and the lousy service. A very classy move on the chef's part and I really appreciated him for that.

When enough time had passed, the chef and I exchanged a final, pleasant email, agreed we were not a good fit for each other, and wrapped up the relationship as it had started—amicably.

I continued the search. I made more phone calls. I expanded my network. I reached out to more restaurateurs in Atlanta and New York. I called anyone

I knew who even liked food and asked them who they knew.

I mostly met macho White guy after macho White guy after macho White guy. I saw more chef knife tattoos than I care to count.

Each day I was in Savannah, I walked from the idyllic square where my house was located and, with dog in tow, head to the garbage dump that had been the bus terminal and hoped intensely for a miracle that would help me restore the soul of that space. Construction had not yet started, so it was still in the same condition it had been in for the past dozen years, and it was quite a juxtaposition to the physical beauty that had come to define Savannah for me.

The one-mile walk between my home and the bus terminal became almost a metaphor for all that Savannah represented to me. Exiting my front door into the steam of the day, the cloyingly sweet smell from the paper mill located several miles north on the Savannah River initially made me wish I had oxygen in tow as well as my dog, but over time this odor became as familiar and comforting to me as the live oaks that dominated the Historic District. The daily walk was my way of stitching myself into the fabric of Savannah—my dog and I becoming a constant of the morning scenery.

I passed people and places that were becoming a part of my life. I eagerly anticipated walking by the hulking, live oak tree not far from my house that had a one-foot-diameter, six-inch-deep, eye-level knot in its trunk that students from Savannah College of Art and Design (SCAD), I assumed, had turned into a miniature stage that they updated regularly with an artistic vignette. I said, "Hey!" to the homeless residents of the squares, the negotiations over territory happening when nobody, at least not me, was looking. They braved the stifling heat of the Savannah summers so they could still remain relatively warm in the winters. Each morning I nodded to the men in suits going to their banking jobs or the hotel workers or store clerks or tourists. There were the retirees out walking their dogs or on their constitutionals, as well as gaunt African American men riding bikes, looking older than what I guessed their years to be, who seemed to have no place in particular to go. They would hang out in a square by the river, socializing the day away. One gentleman with a gray beard always made a point of yelling out at me "Ridgeback" as I walked by his square, reminding me that he knew the breed of my constant companion.

At the end of my walk, I would always end up at the bus terminal, which, with its dark history and seemingly bright future, in many ways became my own personal metaphor for rebirth.

And yet, the future restaurant site remained a disaster.

I guess that was to be expected with a long-abandoned building. Inside it, there were mini mountains of disregarded and forgotten possessions that still needed to be cleaned away. Window and door openings were covered with makeshift barriers of plywood and garbage bags that barely kept the outside from coming in. Some of the piles seemed to be organized, but most of the junk was strewn around the rose-and-black terrazzo floor.

Nothing scurried around any longer, but the carcasses of things that had made this place their home littered the floor. Dead palmetto bugs, the polite Southern name for giant flying cockroaches, lay in large, exoskeletal numbers everywhere. The droppings from other vermin, something I was familiar with as a kid from New York City, were obvious and abundant. Black pellets coated everything and made it seem as if someone had seasoned the entire place with bucketsful of rat and mouse shit. The floors, shelves, piles of old tools, broken-down machinery, and wooden crates that contained God knows what were entombed in a caustic mixture of dust and mold.

But every time I entered the building, from the day I bought it, I tried to imagine what it must have been like in 1938, when the bus terminal opened for business—the heyday of "separate but equal."

Separate but equal. It was once a way for the people of Savannah and other places in this country to give comfort to Whites while instilling laws and practices that justified inequality, subjugation, and racism toward Blacks. Thank goodness those practices aren't legal anymore but traces of that way of thinking still exist.

I would stand in the middle of the main waiting room and think about what it would have been like to have been in this room when it was bustling and people were there on their way to someplace else. The travelers must have felt excited, or nervous, or sad as they walked through the doors during that bygone era. And why not? Back then, they were in route to family, friends, a wedding, a funeral, or boot camp—the first stop on their way to war. The human condition creates such an expansive range of emotions, and most every one of them would have been experienced at some point by the travelers who came through this building during its twenty-six years in operation.

And what did the Black people who needed to get somewhere feel when they were in this space? As someone who, since early adulthood, has been trying to examine my own feelings around race and racism, this thought was at the forefront of my mind and, in a way, a factor in my decision to purchase the building. Blacks were required to enter through a back door near the restrooms that were designated for them so they would not stray and impinge upon the sanctity of the White waiting room in order to relieve themselves. Their waiting area was a claustrophobia-inducing five-by-ten-foot box, yet they were still traveling for all of the same reasons as their White counterparts (love, loss, war, work)—their emotions inevitably choked off by the omnipresent oppression built into the building's very layout.

Some Black people may have felt anger. Some Black people may have felt fear. And then, some may have turned inward, trying to mask their excitement surrounding their pending travel or the arrival of a loved one in an attempt not to draw attention to themselves. Traveling in the South at that time was very dangerous, more dangerous than any of us could have imagined. I would have probably felt nervous and afraid because of all the harm and danger I would have been exposed to that would have been out of my control. A lot of Black people must have felt like that when they had to expose themselves to White people who viewed themselves as the authority—be it the bus driver, a White passenger, or the clerk at the information booth.

Each visit, I would try and take it all in—the entire picture. It would stir up a twinge of something within me. History, maybe. Something both hopeful and dark.

And one day, standing there in the middle of the junk-filled, epically dirty waiting room, it hit me like I had been punched in the gut. I was breathless with excitement.

I immediately called Jeremy and Andrew at PLD and said, "Guys, I figured it out."

"What?" they asked in unison.

"The chef," I said. "I figured out the chef."

"Not Sloppy Plates?" Jeremy asked, an alarmed tone in his voice.

"No, not Sloppy Plates," I snapped. "I don't know who the chef is, but I know who the chef should be."

They waited for me to continue.

"A Black woman."

"Okay," they answered, waiting for more.

"An African American woman is who should run this place with me. I need to find someone who is classically trained, would move to Savannah, wants to get into business with me, cooks kick-ass food, knows how to plate, can run a kitchen, and wants to do all of that now. If she can cook Italian, I feel like she would be the Holy Grail."

There was a pregnant pause, a muffled chuckle, and then, "Oh, that's all you need? Simple enough!" Andrew said, his tone doing little to mask his skepticism concerning my requirements.

"Why not? That person exists. She has to. I saw a really talented Black woman on *Chopped* last night," I said, referencing the Food Network television show I was obsessed with at the time.

Why does a Black woman have to be able to cook Italian when an Italian woman isn't expected to cook anything else? I can tell you that I didn't value my own cultural contributions to American cuisine until I began to learn and cook the foods from other countries. I can also tell you that I needed to work and train myself in other cuisines before I began to value my own. I can feel my frustration bubble up again whenever I hear conversations like this one.

"Well, then get *her,* because that is going to be one tall order to fill," Andrew said. "I don't think the statistics are in your favor."

"Think about it, guys. It was a segregated bus terminal. It's in the South. Savannah is a majority Black city," I said, pleading my case.

Savannah *is* a majority Black city, but downtown Savannah is pretty much White unless you live in the projects. So, not only would Black folks have to learn about a Black chef running this kitchen, they would also have to want to come downtown to see what I was doing. It didn't seem like a tall order to me but actually it was, to think that just because a Black chef is running the kitchen that would be enough incentive to get the Black community to come to the restaurant. I thought that when Black people found out that I was there, they would start to come out, but, in reality, that didn't happen right away. It took a few years and now I think we are beginning to share a pride in the food

that The Grey serves as a representation of this region and the larger community, especially in the African American heritage inherent in it all.

"If I don't find a Black woman to run this place with me, I'm just a carpetbagger from New York City who opened another restaurant. But," I added, finishing my point, "if I find that person, that woman . . . well, then that's a story people can wrap their arms around. That's the way we have the voice to reach all of Savannah. All of the South. That's the only way we are going to make an impact—and maybe, a real fucking impact."

Jeremy chimed in with "Legit."

I waited silently for something more than that, and he complied. "Does that all make sense? Sure, it does. But Johno, you need a great chef. This place needs a great chef. Is there a Black woman out there who is also a great head chef? Of course there is," he said, answering his own question. "But really, dude, the chances of you finding her and her moving to Savannah to be your partner are, like, nada. They're zero, dude. Let's say you find her. Let's say she can cook. She still would have to want to even do this. Andrew's right. It's a very tall order with so few Black women in professional kitchens to begin with. You can't key in on that."

This conversation strikes me as ridiculous. Three White men talking about finding a Black woman chef as though she's a unicorn of some sort, a mystical creature with talents that could only be dreamed of. Turns out, I am that Black woman that they were discussing, that business partner that Johno was seeking. So, why was I so hard to find? Why is it that it was so hard to believe that someone like me, who had been cooking in restaurants for years, and who has traveled abroad to cook and eat, wasn't making an impact on the perception of what an American chef looks like?

During the beginning of my cooking career, I decided to leave the professional restaurant kitchen, and become a personal chef. When I told my father, he immediately hated the idea, in part because his grandmother, Anna Hollis Ford, was a domestic for a White family. She worked while she raised her daughter, missing family holidays and birthdays. Those sacrifices left scars that were passed down to him and then to me. He didn't care that there was a trend in my industry toward personal cheffing because the economics were such that it was a way for chefs to save some money while honing their craft. My plan was to do that and then reenter a professional kitchen down the road at a higher level. He just thought all of it was a step backward. My parents wanted a different future for me. They struggled to see past the White-male-dominated aspect of restaurant kitchens or the servitude implied in working in someone's home and believed either of those things would make my career ascent even more difficult. This made it hard for them to have faith that I could do it and that cooking and leading a kitchen, a professional kitchen, was a step toward the future that I was becoming more interested in achieving. Working as a chef and inspiring a team to follow you is a position that holds power through its creative voice and independence. This is not how these positions have been viewed in the past in Black households but instead were and, maybe, are stigmatized because of the history of servitude connected with food service and hospitality. My father still struggles with some of these ideas and history behind my chosen career.

I guess the ridiculous part of the conversation that these three White men were having is that it was necessary to have it at all. There are people like me, *women* like me, in kitchens all over America and yet, for the most part, we are still invisible and that *is* ridiculous.

Andrew added, "And you don't have that kind of time. You need a chef right now. You can't start looking for a hen's tooth. Not this far into it."

They were right. When I was doing my search, I learned that approximately 15 percent of all chefs and head cooks in America are Black. That means that Black women make up some low single-digit percentage of the total cooks in professional kitchens in the entire United States—aka, Andrew's aforementioned hen's tooth.

I didn't have the luxury of time. The path of least resistance was definitely the quickest. But I likely had committed to my new plan that day. As far as I could see, there was no real way to disrupt food and restaurants the way that other industries were being disrupted—through technology. The service experience is too much of a personal one. Sure, you can install a reservation system that uses technology to better track your guests' personal information and behaviors, but that was an enhancement to the overall experience and not a disrupter.

No, disrupting this industry was going to require a human disruption. It was going to have to result from the whole being greater than the sum of its parts. The way I was going to do that was to find someone who was starkly different from me and the two most easily identifiable differentiators, in my overly simplified view, were race and gender.

I was a White man. I wanted to find a Black woman.

STEAK TARTARE
Serves 4

With a good glass of red wine, like Bordeaux or a Nebbiolo, this is one of those perfect snacky foods that can be lunch or dinner, depending on the portion size. It will make your party guests think you're sophisticated (and a badass), even though it's really simple to throw together. Ask the butcher to coarsely grind the steak to save you from finely chopping it by hand.—MB and JOM

In a large bowl, combine the beef, mustard, shallot, olive oil, Berbere spice, vinegar, and salt. Mix gently, making sure to incorporate well. Cover and refrigerate for at least 1 hour or up to 4 hours. Refrigerate four small serving plates.

Portion the tartare mixture among the chilled plates. If you are feeling fancy, use a 3-inch round ring form to do this. Gently crack a quail egg, separate the yolk from the white, and place the yolk in the center of one of the portions. Repeat for the remaining three servings. Serve with crostini.

1 pound prime New York strip steak, coarsely ground or chopped

1 tablespoon Dijon mustard

1 shallot, finely chopped

3 tablespoons extra-virgin olive oil

½ teaspoon Berbere spice or sumac

1 tablespoon apple cider vinegar, plus more as needed

1 teaspoon kosher salt

4 quail eggs

Crostini, crackers, or toasted bread for serving

CHAPTER 5

During the summer and fall, in addition to designing the restaurant with PLD, the preservation architects, and Larry, I was also reading every book I could find written by relevant restaurateurs, chefs, and businesspeople. I was reading books on restaurant management, hospitality, service, wine, cooking, team building, and every related memoir that sounded the least bit interesting.

I was still driving to and from New York City a lot during this period because, well, technically, Carol and I still lived there. Flounder, our 115-pound dog, was not going to fit under an airplane seat, so he and I became very familiar with the 815 miles of I-95 pavement, covering it as often as three times a month. I developed the habit of listening to some of those books I had purchased during my thirteen hours of driving solitude. It was an efficient way to pass the time and listen to different people's points of view on all things restaurant and hospitality. Danny Meyer, Charlie Trotter, Julia Child, and many others occupied my brain and distracted me from the monotony of the landscape.

I, too, am very familiar with the drive up and down I-95. I feel like it's in my blood. My father's from New York and my mother is from Georgia, and for holidays, birthdays, and special occasions, they would pile my brother, sister, and me in the car with a cooler of snacks for the trip and make that drive as often as my mother saw fit, only stopping for gas and bathroom breaks. When you're little, and they throw you in the backseat with a pillow and a blanket and leave at 4 a.m., you're there by dinner time. It wasn't until I got older that I realized what a drag that drive could be.

During one drive in early September, I listened to *Blood, Bones & Butter: The Inadvertent Education of a Reluctant Chef,* a narrative written by a woman named Gabrielle Hamilton. It was her story of growing up in a complicated family and how she ended up the owner and chef of one of New York City's most iconic restaurants in the past twenty years. Back in the day, I knew Prune, her restaurant on the Lower East Side of Manhattan, because it was a lauded destination restaurant situated between my office in Greenwich Village and my apartment in Tribeca. I had been there in the earlier days of its existence when it was triangulated between my own world of work and home.

Ms. Hamilton wrote incisively about culture, food, and kitchens, and there was a steady, underlying tenderness in her writing around her profession and the people with whom she worked. She wrote, as far as I could tell, honestly about the ups and downs of her life, pre- and post-Prune's opening, in a way that connected the reader to her experiences. It certainly connected me to her experiences. She addressed the diversity of her restaurant, a cooking line that was mostly women—gay women, straight women, Black and Brown women. She did not seem to see herself as someone who actively pursued diversity, but, rather, someone who lived it.

Around the same time that I listened to her book, I was also getting past the initial phases of a conversation with an executive chef candidate from New Orleans. I had already flown him to Savannah after our phone conversations went so well. He made food for me at my house, and that guy could cook. I mean *really* cook. It was the best food I had tasted so far in my chef search.

He had cooked all around New Orleans over a decade and then had a gap in his career for the next couple of years. A gap, I quickly learned through discussions with restaurant professionals, is usually not a good thing in the food and beverage business, as it often signaled an issue of something personal—marriage, divorce, substance dependency, or maybe the guy was just an asshole in the kitchen and wore out his welcome in a particular city. It could have been any of those or that he burned out for a period of time or entertained a career change, but whether it was for those reasons or another, a big gap is a red flag.

Sometimes you just need to step away. I'm not sure what happened to that chef, but I stepped away for an extended time because I needed a new perspective and that's hard to get when you're working in a professional kitchen day after day. I'm always looking for motivation, that thing that will keep pushing me forward. I was also so broke. Line cooks make no money so I became a personal chef for one family on Park Avenue for almost four years. Working in that part of the city was fun! Those people had money, the apartments, the fashion, the sidewalk cafes, and little reading nooks made me feel like I was getting a real inside look at how rich people lived. And believe me, I was paying attention. I would often find myself window-shopping, pretending that I could afford to go inside the little neighborhood shops. I worked close to all the museums and great markets, which I took full advantage of. For a while those distractions kept me engaged. I had been earning a decent wage and saving money, which started to establish a financial foundation that would allow me to reconsider going back into the prestigious professional kitchens around the city, where I would earn a lot less but would be honing my skills in a much more structured and controlled way. I was even thinking about traveling to enrich my culinary repertoire. I could now afford my own apartment while paying back my college loans. For me, the downside of personal cheffing was that the few culinary skills

I had were starting to regress and the family and I were becoming codependent. Leaving this and going straight back to restaurants didn't seem like the right move. Also, working in that neighborhood for rich White people reminded me of my father's fear that I would become complacent and reduce myself to being the help—his grievances were starting to ring true. I needed to take a sharp left turn on the culinary road I was heading down.

The Institute of Culinary Education (ICE) in New York City is where I'd continued my schooling after undergrad. I had kept connected through the school newsletter and often referred to it when I was in the market for a new job. That was where I learned about La Varenne, a cooking school founded in 1975 by Anne Willan, an English-born culinary instructor who was living and teaching in France. Anne was the first person to offer professional cooking courses in France taught both in English and French. This attracted many non-French-speaking American chefs, like Tanya Holland, Virginia Willis, and Jonathan Waxman, who wanted to advance their culinary careers. When I was interested in attending, Anne was no longer offering professional classes. Back then what she was offering were positions for English- and French-speaking culinary professionals to help her run the recreational cooking classes at her chateau in Burgundy. If accepted, I would work at the chateau and in the garden, cook meals for the staff, and, in general, do most of the heavy lifting for the first eight weeks. After I completed that portion of the program, I would then work for four additional weeks at a Michelin-starred restaurant in the region. In exchange for my hard work, I would receive free room and board and would gain access to Anne's network of award-winning chefs and culinary professionals from around the world. This sounded like the recharge that I needed, so I applied and, shortly after, I got accepted.

Between the personal cheffing and my time in France, I took a four-and-half-year break from working in restaurant kitchens, and during that time I gained new perspective that reenergized me and gave me the confidence to go back into professional kitchens—this time, with a whole new set of skills.

I liked this guy well enough, and I liked his food a whole lot. And, most importantly, I was getting desperate to find a chef as the architectural and design plans for the restaurant—including the kitchen—would be locked down over the next few months.

Before I knew it, I had begun negotiating with him to come on board. Because I was concerned about his recent past and the gap in his experience, I did not plan to offer him a partnership, so I was effectively defaulting to finding a placeholder chef for the time being. He was the most talented of the several people that I'd considered to that point, so he would likely be the one. Sure, he was kind of a macho White guy (sans cutlery tattoos), but his background, before his hiatus, had been promising. He had won some awards and made some "best of" lists during his career and, generally, he seemed like a decent guy and a very good cook.

I even put him on the phone with Jeremy and Andrew, and they agreed that he sounded as if he knew how to run a professional kitchen. He talked the talk of a leader who was reinvigorated about his career.

The clock was also ticking because he was simultaneously entertaining another job offer in New Orleans. He was putting a fair amount of pressure on me to decide on whether we were going to work together. I was susceptible to the pressure because I had insisted that the design of the restaurant move forward no matter what. Carol and I had so much money tied up in the building that I was not willing to let up on the gas at all. I wanted this piece of real estate to become revenue producing in the shortest amount of time possible. I was so ignorant about restaurant operations that I had convinced myself that any mistakes we might make because we did not have a chef on board as we were designing the kitchen, bars, and other functionality would just have to be corrected or overcome once we did have the right people in place. That, along with the fact the budget was already ballooning and I was far too cheap to add the expense of an actual restaurant consultant to help with the process while I continued my chef search, meant, in short, I was winging it.

I think it is interesting that Johno never wanted to stop and really assess where they were in the process. Did he need advice or help? His emotions were at ten on the dial; he was frazzled, but he just kept pushing. I am not sure I could have done that. I may have just called up Sloppy Plates.

At night, I would climb into my bed with my dog Flounder (Carol was spending most of her time in New York City) and simply stare at the ceiling, a television that I wasn't watching playing in the background, as I thought about all of the ways that this undertaking could blow up in my face. In the morning, if I fell asleep at all, I would wake up in the fetal position, covers pulled up taut to my chin and the sheets sweat soaked. Even loyal Flounder moved as far from me on the mattress as possible, not willing to give up his own peaceful night's sleep to ease my nerves.

I was nearly paralyzed with fear in those days and weeks—hire someone who I knew was not the long-term choice or do nothing and continue to design a kitchen and restaurant in a chef vacuum. Further, I knew that if I hired New Orleans–guy, even as stand-in, my hope of finding a Black woman as my business partner would become even more of a challenge than it seemed initially. Human nature, my nature, being what it is, meant that if I had a chef on board, well, I would likely use all of my energy managing that person and learning to run a restaurant rather than finding my ideal business partner down the road.

After I got to our apartment in New York City the evening of the drive during which I had listened to *Blood, Bones & Butter*, I was completely energized. I was, of course, punchy from the thirteen hours in a car, but I was buzzing with electricity. I couldn't wait to tell Carol all about Chef Hamilton and her book.

As Carol and I sat together over a late dinner at a nearby Indian restaurant, I shared my takeaways from the book. "Her fondest memories from childhood are about food—just like me. She cooks the food she wants to eat—the kind of food I want to eat. She cooks from the heart," I explained. "She's not messing around with all of the shit that's trendy—foams and molecular gastronomy. She stays away from the bullshit. We need to go to her place. I think you'll love it. I haven't been there in years, but I really enjoyed it when I went."

"Yeah, let's do it," Carol said, needing no convincing to go out to eat good food.

"And," I went on, "she had this line in her book that really hit me. She was talking about how cooks push the envelope to stand out, maybe plate something in a vessel never intended for it simply because you could or because it might surprise the diner. She just summed it up perfectly. She said that she would 'never serve anything but a martini in a martini glass. Preferably gin,' and I immediately thought *Yeah! I totally get what she means.*"

Carol laughed at the line, knowing exactly why it would resonate with me. "Yeah, that sounds like you. Forget progress, you like things the way they are supposed to be. The way they were."

"I like things that are classic," I retorted. "Levis. Chuck Taylors. The things that never go out of style . . . a martini never goes out of style, but ceviche in a martini glass, um, no thanks."

"Ha, yeah, how about those mustard-yellow sweatpants you always wear. There's no way those things ever were or ever will be in style," she said, continuing to laugh while sopping up some lamb vindaloo with a piece of naan. "You might be stretching your love for classics just a little."

"Springsteen," I snapped, "classic."

"Listen, Staten Island–boy, I'm from Jersey. Don't talk to me about Springsteen."

"Whatever," was my lame retort as we continued to eat, talk, and laugh off an exhausting day.

As I reflected further on Hamilton's book, I could not help but be taken in by the fact that she seemed to run her restaurant the way I thought I wanted to run mine—like a family but with professionalism. She treated people with respect. She worked hard and insisted on perfection, but wrote as if everyone on her team enjoyed being there and that she was there for them. She wrote about food in a way I respected—she revered it.

"Why don't you call her?" Carol asked.

"What do you mean call her? I can't do that. I don't even know her."

"Well, it sounds like this woman might be able to offer some advice and her restaurant is only a mile from here. You could just walk down there. She probably doesn't bite. Maybe she would even want to team up with you."

I laughed out loud. "Sure, why not?" I said, jokingly, cutting into a samosa, "Yeah, I am sure she's just dying to team up with me. While I am at it, I'll call Alice Waters, Joel Robuchon, and Lidia Bastianich, as I'm sure they're also dying to get into business with me in Savannah, Georgia. I could just do a rotating slate of the world's great chefs. I love that idea."

"Now, now," Carol said, looking at me stabbing a piece of chicken from a plate, "try not to be an asshole."

"I was just kidding," I said, "but I do think you're right about her giving me some advice."

"Yeah, I figured you would have learned that I usually am after twenty years together."

"Maybe I'll write her a note and see if she responds," I said, trailing off and digging into some aloo gobi.

So, I did just that. I wrote her a letter, which took me nearly a week to craft, and I hand delivered it to her restaurant one afternoon in the middle of pre-service. I had no idea what kind of person Chef Hamilton was, but from her book she seemed to me to be someone who was generous of spirit, so I dropped off the note and hoped for the best.

JOHN O. MORISANO
NEW YORK, NY

September 6, 2013
Ms. Gabrielle Hamilton
c/o Prune
54 East 1st Street
New York, NY 10003

Hey Gabrielle,

My name is John O. Morisano and you do not know me so I thought dropping off a note was better than flagging you down in your restaurant in the middle of service. Having already known Prune from my days living downtown, I read your book recently and I really loved it— the writing, the storytelling, honesty, et al. In fact, I thought so highly of it that I was emboldened enough to write this note.

Which probably has you asking the obvious question as to why I would be writing you a note at all. Well if you will bear with me for just a few moments, I am going to tell you but, in full disclosure, it meanders a bit.

Long story short is that I have been a founder/creator/operator of a number of media, technology and art-related businesses, primarily here in NYC, for the last couple of decades. Most have been small start-ups and turnarounds. A couple of years ago my wife and I bought a place in Savannah as an investment property as part of a longer-term plan but I found myself really drawn to the city. That led to me investing in some new business ventures down there which, among other things, include the purchase of two historically significant, albeit dilapidated, buildings. We are in the process of performing a restoration on the first of the two buildings— a 1938 Greyhound Bus Terminal of art deco design. The second will follow. The challenge now is what do we put in these buildings.

One of my own personal interests is food and wine, which stems from an eerily similar place to what you describe in your book. A second interest that has occupied much of my attention over the last five years is women's empowerment. This has manifested itself in the form of an online magazine for women of which I am a co-founder and a board seat I fill at UN Women—the UN's organization dedicated to women's rights in developing nations. The unlikely intersection of these two interests is why I thought you would be a great person to contact.

As I contemplate the use of the buildings for which I am now the proud owner and I consider the market conditions in Savannah, the idea of participating in elevating the overall food experience in Savannah is very interesting to me. It is a little bit of "the land that time forgot" compared to some of its contemporaries when it comes to food. As such I am on a minor fact-finding mission to discuss food, food's potential position in Savannah, opportunities, and, in particular, women chefs. I say the last thing because I also have thoughts on how, if I go the food route, leading with women can have a positive social impact in this market, particularly with at-risk girls and young women. But that is a way longer meandering.

So after all that background (don't judge my writing by your own standards please), here is the ask — I was wondering if you would be interested in sparing a little of your time to discuss some of these things with me. I am in NYC through mid next week and would be happy to meet up at a time that is convenient for you or just get on the phone for a bit if that is easier. If you would rather not, I totally get that too.

Anyway, thanks for taking the time and I look forward to hearing from you.

Regards,

John O. Morisano

Simultaneously, in terms of the timing of restaurant design, the walls were closing in and my sleepless nights were near constant. I was becoming a physical and emotional mess—losing weight and generally acting unstable, with my temper often getting the best of me and the insomnia making me unable to focus and accident-prone—which resulted in forgetting to check both ways at a stop sign and crashing my car one morning.

I obsessively assessed my options, which were also shrinking: hire the guy from New Orleans to buy some time and at least have a chef who could take the lead on helping design a kitchen and help open the restaurant, or cut bait and take my chances that I would find a person who might give the advice and direction I desperately needed.

Every time I faced this conundrum, I always came back to the same answer: We would only have one chance to win over the people of Savannah when we opened. Savannahians have a reputation, I was learning in my time living and working there, as people who do not have a lot of patience for things they do not like or that they feel did not fit their vision of what makes Savannah *Savannah*. They could embrace new businesses or could, just as quickly, turn their backs on them. There were challenges galore and working toward the best chance of early success was always my goal. Being perceived as a carpetbagger was a risk I could not mitigate. I was a New Yorker, a Yankee. Creating something new for the market, an elevated and chef-driven restaurant, was not a risk I had any interest in mitigating. I wanted to raise the bar, and I was most certainly committed to the elements that I believed would do it. But building something honest and inclusive, something that reflected as much of Savannah as possible, and doing so with the right person, was an aspect of the risk I felt I could manage—if only I could find that person. Ultimately, I accepted that meant that I could not simply hire just any chef, especially another guy who looked like me, despite how well he cooked. Reaching out to Ms. Hamilton was a long shot, sure. But stepping into the unknown was what this journey had been about from the very beginning, so why not just keep doing that?

Damn, this guy was asking for a lot. No wonder he was constantly curled up in the fetal position!

I called the guy in New Orleans to tell him it was not going to work out between us.

After a week of not hearing from Chef Hamilton, I sent an email to an address at the restaurant, noting that I had dropped off a letter for the chef. I knew I was being a nudge, but I figured at that point I didn't have anything to lose.

And what happened? Chef Hamilton responded and she agreed to meet with me. So, I wasn't dead yet.

The morning of our meeting, I showed up a little early dressed in my standard gear—blazer, jeans, button-down. She arrived and immediately brewed us a fresh pot of coffee. She was generous with her time and her attention. I enjoyed every second of being in her presence and the advice that she offered.

I showed her my plans for the bus terminal and how I was determined to try and reach the larger Savannah community—not just the downtown, White community. I told her how I wanted to partner with someone different from me and reiterated what I had written in my goofy letter to her, about being interested in working with a woman and someone who could help me reach young, at-risk people, which, in the case of Historic Savannah, is largely interchangeable with the Black community. She asked questions, direct questions. She made me laugh and she made me very, very nervous.

She mentioned a young woman who was working at Prune—Mashama Bailey. She thought that maybe we should meet and said she would consider making an introduction, but she wanted a little time to think about it and talk to Ms. Bailey. She then offered me a few more names of people she knew who were impacting their communities through food and restaurants. But, at that moment, all I heard was that one name, Mashama Bailey.

For three weeks, I didn't hear back from Chef Hamilton. I waited. Design of the restaurant and kitchen continued. I grew more nervous.

From what I knew of Savannahians, they seemed like a tough group of people to win over. Walking into this city of unknowns was going to be a real challenge. Savannah seemed like the type of city that would keep you honest, where people ask questions and force you to be introspective and have a point of view. I had looked into relocating to Charleston and thought about working in other cities in the South. I was familiar with Savannah. I had attended grade school there. I remembered oak trees on Victory Drive, the beach at Tybee, the sandbox playground on River Street next to the Waving Girl statue. Yet, when I left, I never considered going back to live there.

I started thinking about reaching out to my old friend, Sloppy Plates McGee—the only one of the chefs with whom I had met and had not yet put a hard stop on the relationship. I had just sort of let that one fizzle out. I thought briefly about checking in with the guy from New Orleans, but I knew that I couldn't go back to him.

Maybe I had blown it by not going with the short-term solution. The saying about a bird in the hand being better than two in the bush existed for a reason. Taking a flyer on someone I didn't know may not have been a perfectly thought-out plan.

And then at the end of that third week, early on a Sunday morning, I was driving with Carol and my phone dinged. At a traffic light in Habersham Village in Savannah, I noticed it was an email from Chef Hamilton. I pulled over immediately and read it. She had just made a virtual introduction to her sous-chef, Mashama Bailey.

During this time, I was starting to get restless with my day-to-day duties at the restaurant. I had been a sous-chef for only a couple of years and I had yet to fully step into that role. Sure, I was providing station support for my fellow staff members, writing prep lists, cooking some of the more important and delicate menu items, and I was ordering supplies. But I wanted more! I was feeling a little sorry for myself. I felt as if I was missing out on something, like I was not recognizing opportunities for development, like they were slipping through my fingers. I was waiting for someone to offer me an opportunity on a silver platter. And I was putting that responsibility on others rather than discovering my own untapped talents. I felt as if I wasn't receiving the recognition I deserved. I had a chip on my shoulder! I had been cooking for years and I felt that I was too old and too young to be in a rut. My engagement was shifting, I was losing focus.

In spite of being surrounded by wonderful, hardworking, creative people, I needed to explore my own interests in food and culture. In recent years, I had briefly traveled to Spain and New Orleans. I ate paella in the markets of Barcelona and churros with hot chocolate in Madrid. I savored boudin and gumbo in the Treme. The food in these places was vastly different but left the same lasting impression on me, motivating me to continue to work toward my career goals and find my own footing in the culinary world.

In my restlessness, I was picking up cooking projects in my free time, working with a neighborhood chef in Queens, doing some catering, and working on my supper club dinners as a way of figuring out my next step.

I put my car in park and remained on the side of the road while I typed out an email to Mashama. Within a day, we had a time set to meet at my office in New York City. I could not wait.

It was time for me to move on. I was planning my second supper club and this time I wanted to switch up the guest list from having local, neighborhood friends attend to hosting people who could offer me some advice and possibly funding to help me open my own small restaurant.

Walter "Sonny" Winfrey Jr. was my paternal grandmother's cousin. He and his wife, Ruth, were a bit younger than my grandmother, but they often attended any number of events that she held. Even though Sonny was younger than my grandmother, they grew up together so he knew her well and could advise my siblings and me on how not to get on her bad side. He told us stories about their upbringing, how they had to fight for everything.

Sonny was a true "Hollis," from Forsyth, Georgia. He was strong and a true gentleman. Motivated by our family history, he built a successful career and life. His mom, along with my great-grandmother, and some of their fourteen other siblings, were forced north without their father in the late 1920s. Their dad, my great-great-grandfather, Robert Hollis, had been pulled out of his house one night by a group of White men pretending they had work for him. Instead, they lynched him. Those same men returned the next day and gave the family an ultimatum that drove them off their land permanently. They stole my family's land and burned all the records that proved its ownership. Robert's family had to move immediately. A few more than half of his children went to New York City and the other half to Tennessee. His wife, my great-great-grandmother, along with her daughters, including Sonny's mother and my grandmother, who was just a baby at the time, went to New York.

My cousin Sonny was on the list of the small group of guests I had gathered around my grandmother's dining room table for this supper club. He was an accountant with a little storefront in Queens Village, New York, and I wanted to ask him for business advice. Even as a child growing up, I could see that Sonny had a steady way about him. My grandmother trusted him with everything... but her money! And, believe it or not, for her that was a compliment.

It was time for me to put my plan into action. With my grandmother's best china on display, we started with a chopped salad that had some beautiful fall greens that I had bought in the city at the Wednesday Union Square Farmers' Market. I lightly dressed them so they would stand out on their own. For the main course, I presented a whole-roasted striped bass stuffed with herbs and citrus. I roasted the citrus in the pan with the fish and mixed it with a little olive oil as a sauce. We ate that with sautéed spinach and roasted potatoes. I can't recall what I made for dessert, but I am sure it was simple because I only ever make simple desserts. Well, I could tell you that none of that other stuff mattered because all Sonny could talk about was that fish. He loved it! It invoked memories of him on Martha's Vineyard fishing with his sons. He even talked about the different fish preparations they would do.

I was beaming. And I was also restless, knowing that I needed to pick his brain about business plans and loan applications. But before dessert, he was telling me that he himself would be interested in financing a small space. "How much do you think you'll need to get started?" he asked.

"I'm not sure," I said, "maybe $150,000?"

"Okay, call me. I might be able to help you figure out how to get that. But you'll need a business plan."

Family is everything.

BAGNA CÀUDA
Serves 4

DRESSING

6 anchovy fillets

3 cloves garlic,
thinly sliced

1 cup extra-virgin olive oil

¼ cup sherry vinegar

Belgian endive,
leaves separated

Radishes, trimmed
and thinly sliced

Baby turnips, trimmed
and thinly sliced

Cabbage, thinly sliced

Bell peppers, seeded
and thinly sliced

Scallions, trimmed and
halved lengthwise if large

Fingerling potatoes,
boiled, cooled, and halved

Bagna càuda is tactile and takes thoughtfulness to make and eat it the right way. When I read Johno's five-point plan on how he was going to chase down Gabrielle, this is the dish I thought about because the first time I ever had it was at Prune.—MB

For the dressing: in a saucepan over low heat, warm and mash the anchovies into a paste. Then, over very low heat, add the garlic and olive oil and cook for 3 to 4 minutes, being careful not to burn the garlic. Remove from the heat and add the vinegar. Set aside, keeping it warm.

Transfer the dressing to a small bowl and place it in the center of a serving platter. Assemble all the vegetables around the dressing and serve.

Store the leftover dressing, tightly covered, in the refrigerator for up to 2 weeks.

INFORMATION

PART II
THEN THERE WERE TWO

CHAPTER 6

By the second summer we were open, I began to feel as though we were starting to find our rhythm. One very hot evening that year, I was doing my best to keep buzzing around the main dining room until table 22's first course arrived. The gentleman in position two had been trying to get my attention since he'd been seated, but eighteen months into my life as a first-time restaurateur, I had learned a trick or two. One was that I usually waited until folks had a drink in hand and some food in their bellies before I approached them, particularly if I didn't know them and they looked at all antsy. Alcohol and calories worked magic on a guest cranky with hunger early on in their evening, and thus complaints that could set up small, negative interactions at the start of their dining experience would often simply dissipate as they began to eat and drink.

Since we'd opened The Grey, we had worked our asses off each day and night to provide our guests with a fulfilling dining experience. This, of course, was the typical story for any restaurant trying to be good at it, but no less all-encompassing when you're the people doing it. Since I was completely lacking in any restaurant-operation experience, I was on a steep learning curve. I mostly relied on past work and life experience and the numerous start-ups in which I had been involved prior to The Grey to help me figure out what I should be doing at any given moment on a busy restaurant floor.

It was hardest in the beginning, it's true. We worked in a diplomatic fashion. With Johno having no working knowledge about restaurant operations, he just wanted to be fair and sensible. As for me, from a restaurant managerial point of view, I was only a few steps ahead of him and thought it was a fair way to proceed. But sometimes you need to throw sensibility out the window and do what works for all the staff members, not just for the front or back of house or the guests. We were lacking a fleshed-out point of view on what we wanted to be. This created a vacuum. There were constant power struggles between me and the opening service director. While finding my voice as a partner, I needed Johno's support in those struggles. It took some time for him to see what I saw and for us to understand that we were ultimately the only two people in charge. The service director and I almost came to blows over a few issues while we were establishing the steps of service and how they affected the kitchen. We fought about staff drinks, table numbers, seat locations, and the placement of the damned iced tea brewer. He thought putting it in a front-of-house service area would be too crowded. It didn't work anywhere else. That iced tea machine floated around both kitchens, our main hot kitchen off the dining room, and our small prep/pastry kitchen upstairs, disconnected and taking up space, for nearly a month after we opened. Johno had no opinion and thought all these arguments were dumb, and so did I, but we had to do something about them as they were impacting the dynamics of the whole restaurant. Johno simply sided with the most compelling argument, which in his mind was to favor appearance over function. Not using the machine that we owned was a waste, and I would not let it go. I finally won that argument and we had it set up near the coffee station, but I lost the table-numbering fight—two examples of how we ran the place in the beginning. Too many opinions and not enough experienced restaurant leadership or confidence from either of us.

Even with age, wisdom, and a genuine love for food, wine, and making people happy, those first couple of years were rough. I was doing something that I had never done before. The skill of being a floor manager in a high-end, high-volume restaurant is not an easy one to acquire. It's completely experiential in nature. You absolutely cannot learn it by reading about it or by watching other people do it. Guests examine your every move. Their expectations are high and only get higher as you succeed. Most of them are demanding, some are unforgiving, and a few are even demeaning.

I was scared almost every night in the beginning. Cluelessness breeds fear, and while I could figure out how to refill a water bottle well enough, that was not the difficult part.

Counting open menus and then checking them against the ticket rail in the kitchen as people waited impatiently at the host stand was a touch-and-feel thing. Observing which servers were deep in the weeds and which ones were fine, which guests were easy and which were challenging, whether the greeter working the door was keeping up or being overrun by impatient people who wanted to be seated immediately regardless of their reservation time, and then processing all of that data, was akin to a rolling movie reel. Then you had your unexpected eighty-sixes, low counts, the undercooked duck at table 43, a bathroom pipe that has backed up into your server station, the porter who didn't show up, and, of course, the tray of expensive glassware the new back server smashed to the ground as he tripped his way up a flight of stairs, the crashing noise disrupting the experience of every single guest in the space. You turn all of that stuff around in your brain so you can make the necessary adjustments on the fly to ensure as smooth a night as possible for the two hundred guests coming through your dining room. Oh, and during nights like this, which are far more common than anyone might think, there is inevitably an incensed guest telling you how much you and your restaurant suck as you sweep up glass and shit simultaneously.

There are times when these evenings are actually paralyzing. So, typically, for that first year or two, I followed the lead of the other managers who had some experience, and I mostly faked it. As time passed, I got better. We all got better. And the night that the guest at table 22 was trying to get my attention, I felt like I was getting there.

Like waiting out the folks at 22; time to talk among themselves and look at the architecture of the space—the art deco design, the original Masonite walls and terrazzo floors, the stainless-steel fixtures and lighting, the chrome, the curves, the dark wood, the sea-foam-green leather banquettes, the horseshoe-shaped steel-and-wood bar that always seemed to me to be the most animated space in the restaurant.

While they looked around and settled in, I tried to remain on the move. It was easy to stay lost in The Grey if you wanted to, because the restaurant is a series of small spaces (other than the main dining room, which is housed in the former White people's waiting room) that resulted from our efforts to keep the historic footprint of the building completely intact. The space in the very front of the restaurant, the room that once served as the segregated lunch counter, is our Diner Bar, a sexy reimagination that, from the street, viewed through its long, curved plate glass window, gives you the sense that you may just have the ability to step into a painting by Edward Hopper.

In the back, where the "colored" entrance and bathrooms were, are server stations that are always a good place to kill time. Upstairs in the rear, in what was formerly the White women's powder room, is a private dining room that is usually full and always needs an extra set of hands to clear, drop food, or pour wine. Another private dining room exists downstairs in the space that was originally meant for White men to use the facilities, and we keep that room busy at least a few nights a week as well.

You can always camp out in the kitchen, too, but that night the guest I was temporarily avoiding was in the section we identified as the "20's," the three booths immediately across from our open-air kitchen in the narrow corridor that connected the front door, host stand, and Diner Bar to the main dining room. So instead, I kept circling through the other spaces, always seeming like I was in a rush to get from one room to the other.

No, way! I hate when people hang out in the kitchen during service. I'm so easily distracted that I always screw something up. Only free hands in the kitchen and no chatting during service. Thank you.

As they approached the end of their appetizer course, I finally looked in the direction of 22. As soon as I did, the guest in seat 2 caught my eye. I smiled warmly and, as anticipated, he waved me right over. He was casually dressed, had a ruddy complexion, and offered a welcoming smile of his own. He looked like someone I would have known growing up, a friend of my dad's, maybe. He was the blue-collar type who likely drank hard, smoked in spite of knowing it was killing him, and told great stories. I liked that kind of guy, and I let my guard down a bit as I approached him.

At that time, I found myself gravitating toward people of color in the dining room. I would send those folks a little something extra, like a second snack or some bread, in order to make them feel welcome in a room in which they were far from the majority. I clearly projected my insecurities on them. This guy was White, looked like a local, and appeared to represent the type of guest we always had at that point, so I wouldn't have noticed him.

As I reached his table, he greeted me by name. "You're that fellow Johno, right?" he said, in a slow and distinct Savannah drawl, pronouncing it John-ohhh, just as he put his fork down on his plate to free up and extend his right hand.

Since The Grey had opened, Mashama and I had achieved a level of minor celebrity in Savannah, so it was not surprising to me that he knew my name. "I *am* that fellow, Johno," I said as my hand clasped his.

As we shook, he continued, "I'm Tom and this is my wife, Nellie. We live on a square not far from you."

"Oh, so we're neighbors. Nice," I answered while shaking Nellie's hand next, not knowing the names of any of the twenty-two squares that defined Savannah's downtown geography or who lived where. "So, you folks are actually from Savannah?" I asked.

"Born and raised," Tom responded proudly.

"Well, that's great because there's nothing we love more than true Savannahians coming into The Grey and eating Mashama's food; so thanks for being our guests this evening," I said, sincerely.

They smiled brightly at me as they considered the concept that they were indeed our guests. This was a term that, to my knowledge, was not used regularly in restaurants in Savannah. Nearly every person we hired as part of our opening team, who had come from another food and beverage concern, referred to guests as "customers," and it almost seemed to shock Tom and Nellie that we referred to them and treated them as our guests.

We continued to make pleasant conversation, discussing Savannah, the summer heat, and the people we knew in common. They complimented our restoration of the old bus terminal and we covered all the bases people generally do in a polite conversation. It was convivial and easy—typical for Savannah banter.

After a bit, I began to feel that I was interfering in their dining experience and I started to inch away so they could get back to their evening. As I was doing so, Tom looked down at the watermelon salad and said, "Everything's been great so far tonight, John-ohhh. Really great."

Nellie nodded, offering agreement.

"Thank you. That's excellent to hear. I'm glad you're enjoying it."

"We haven't been here before, but we've heard a lot of great things about what you've done and your chef in there," he continued, gesturing toward our open kitchen. "This has been a real treat."

"I really appreciate that."

He paused another second, almost awkwardly. "But let me tell you one thing," he offered, again referencing his watermelon salad with a second downward glance of his eyes.

Here it comes, I thought to myself, *he hates something*. But that wasn't what he was thinking at all.

"Us crackers," he said matter-of-factly, surveying his plate and pausing for dramatic effect, "don't normally eat this shit." He chuckled as he continued, "But when one of them makes it," he said as he motioned toward Mashama, who was standing at the pass in clear view, helming the kitchen, "well, they know how to make it so that it's just so tasty."

He punctuated his thought by telling his wife rhetorically, "You know how they love watermelon," as he subtly waved an open hand across his face from forehead to chin.

Wow. That was really racist!

Maybe he thought this gesture was lost on me, but it was a move I recognized from the cop culture I grew up around. Guys who were on the job would sit around the bar inevitably talking about this perp or that perp who they had pinched the night before and rather than having to ask each other flat out, "Hey, was he a [insert any racial epithet for a Black guy]?" they would, instead, just wave a hand in front of their face combined with an inquisitive raise of the eyebrows and the question was asked. A near indiscernible nod would confirm the color of the skin of the perp in question and all of us sitting there were brought onto the same page. It seemed almost like progress to me at that time, like guys on the job were trying to tow the line and steer clear of using offensive language, whether out of conscience or to avoid trouble. Either way, their conduct was vastly different compared to the overt racism that was acceptable when I was a child, when my father was working in Lower Manhattan as a fireman.

But that gesture now, decades from the last time I had witnessed its use, no longer felt benign or anything like progress. It felt venomous. That and the crack of a smile on the side of Tom's wrinkled mouth as he glibly uttered the word "they" to his wife, and I knew that he was trying to gauge how his "compliment" registered with me. Tom wanted to know if I shared his view of Mashama's place in his world, in our White world.

He had caught me completely flat-footed, and if my face disclosed anything it was, at most, confusion. I processed his words and tried to speak, but could not.

By that time I had become used to the entitled guests, the few who tried to belittle our team or exercise control over us as a way to display their power, which mostly masked some insecurity or other shortcoming. These were the people who refused the first table offered, no matter what, even if it was the best table in the house. It was the person who demanded, not asked or politely requested, that you do something special for them because they felt they were "spending the money" or "the customer is always right" or, my favorite, "because I said so, and I am rich (or powerful or vindictive)."

Yeah, I had learned how to deal with those people by standing up to them, gently at first, and, if necessary, firming up my stance as things escalated. Thankfully, these were rare occurrences and by then I had gotten better at some things, including that. But dealing with a racist guest was not something I had prepared for.

I was saddened that this was someone who was eating in our dining room. This guy comes into my restaurant and thinks that I am going to bow my head down to him. He thinks that Johno is just like him. He was wrong. This Tom and all the Toms like him out there can kiss my ass! They no longer control my narrative. Those days are coming to an end. Men and women from Tom's era, who think like Tom, are dying and their old ways are dying with them. And the racist assholes replacing them no longer have a firm grip on the power structure; they will never control the narrative again. Sure, they are clinging to power wherever and whenever they can and we can't ever give up the fight—it is a monumental fight—but the field is leveling just a bit more every day. So, no, I didn't get mad. I got annoyed and I began to understand that, whether I liked it or not, I was going to have to deal with these jackasses and that on any given night there could be someone in my dining room thinking about or wanting to call me nigger.

What the fuck did you just say to me? is what I wanted to say, but silence continued to overtake my voice. I wanted to punch him in the face, but (luckily) paralysis took over.

After a few awkward seconds, I cleared my throat as effortlessly as I could. "I gotta go," I spit out in Tom's general direction as I walked away from table 22.

I made a slow yet deliberate march through the dining room forcing a smile at our other guests who sat happily at their tables. I, robotically and quietly reminded congregated servers, "Thirty-second rule," as I walked past them—our code for "Don't stand in one place too long."

My destination was the kitchen. I felt like such a rube for not having had a stronger response—or any response—to Tom's antagonism and overt racism. I exited the building out the rear door—what had been the entrance for Black people until 1963—into the parking lot and looped around the side to reenter through the kitchen door where Mashama was running things. *Fuck! As much as things change, they stay the same,* I thought.

Mashama was still at the expo station, calling out tickets and firing food so the cooks knew what tables were coming up next. The board was full, and the line cooks had nearly every burner covered with pans. She was in that don't-fuck-with-me-because-I'm-busy-but-still-happy part of the evening's service. She, too, was finding her groove and beginning to take ownership of her domain, our kitchen.

I hated to break her rhythm but this was important. I tapped her shoulder and pulled her to the side.

"You see that fucking guy at seat 2 at 22?" I said conspiratorially.

As she craned her neck around my head and looked through the window from the kitchen into the dining room, I recapped the interaction, telling her everything, including how he waved his hand across his face. I was in a full lather as I told Mashama about this racist asshole and his shitty remarks. The shitty, racist remarks that I let him get away with. I waited for her response.

When Johno walked into the kitchen I could see he was pretty pissed off. My first thought was, *What did we fuck up?* And then, as he started to tell me his story, I realized that we both had similar reactions to the same situation. Johno's manifested itself as anger and a little bit of outrage. I think he thought, *How dare this guy assume I am just like him?* For me, I took comfort in the fact that Johno was so pissed off. It was the moment I realized Johno had true empathy for my position and that together we were going to navigate our way through a sea of Toms.

But none came from her. In her crisp kitchen whites, her deep brown skin a sharp contrast, Mashama rolled her eyes and looked at me dismissively.

That man in our dining room would have nothing if it weren't for people like me. He needs to stand on my shoulders to make himself feel tall.

Her frustration was obvious, but it was directed at me for interrupting her flow at the expo station. She snatched a ticket from the rail and yelled across the line at her cooks, "Fire course two on 37" and then she took a barely discernible glance at table 22. "What do you expect from a redneck?" she muttered offhandedly but loud enough for me to hear.

I still wanted her to be angry. I wanted her to be angry at the South and American history. Along with me. I had let her down. I hadn't defended her.

Growing up Black in America, before you're old enough to read and write you are already being taught how to live among White folks. My siblings and I were told that Black folks are seen differently by White people. As African Americans we are already immersed in American culture. The world we grow up in doesn't always reflect—or protect—us. My parents never wanted us

to let White folks curb our enthusiasm for learning and being ourselves. For example, my parents learned that an elementary school administrator was willing to hold me back before even evaluating me for a learning disability. I was a happy and active child. I learned through working with my hands. Feeling stigmatized by my teachers had a negative (and lasting) effect on how I thought I should be learning and did not actually nurture the ways that I needed to learn. My parents stood up for me at that school and that taught me to stand up for myself. They also taught us that we have to work harder for our education, our career success, and to just maintain what we already have. We learned to behave a certain way around Whites in order to protect ourselves and what's ours because, if we don't, they have historically made things more difficult for us. Whites were all placed in the not-to-be-trusted category—until proven otherwise. Maybe that's what Johno feels when he says I'm guarded? It's the armor our parents placed on us to walk out into this White world. Our parents came of age in the 1960s and 1970s; that time was about Black Pride and breaking the world's opinion of what drove and motivated Black people. It was no longer about fitting in. It was about us establishing our own voice, and my parents instilled that in us.

But Mashama had no expectation that I would defend her. Or that defending her was necessary. She was fine. She had seen this guy before. She knew this guy. And now her point was, I guess, that I should know this guy too. That I should be able to recognize him when I see him.

As I went back to work, I thought about a cookout that Carol and I hosted at our house for Mashama's family—her parents; her sister, Zuwena; and Zuwena's son, Malik—before we opened The Grey. Mashama and I did the cooking. We cooked ribs and fish, steamed some crawfish, and I made a grilled vegetable ratatouille. We threw some clams on the grill and a few other random things—a real potluck of sorts. It was one of those days that solidify relationships.

I was excited for that day. My sister, who is a schoolteacher, had planned to move to Savannah when she heard that I was moving there. Zuwena is very much a Northern girl. She still carried her New York City accent, wore it like a badge of honor and refused to let the easy Southern drawl seep into her dialect. Me, I love saying "y'all," and "hey," and "fit'na." I like my lazy style of speaking. I think it makes me sound mysterious. (My sister thinks it makes me sound whiny.) Despite her Northern leanings, Zuwena was moving her family to Savannah from Charlotte in a few short weeks. With my parents in Denmark, South Carolina, and me and now her here, this move was going to

bring the family closer together. This was before The Grey opened, back when we had more time to spend together.

It was one of those days during which you realize that the people are your kind of people. It was one of those days when I started to really understand Mashama and where she came from and, I think, vice versa. Our differences began to fade as we fed ourselves and Mashama's family, and the two of us realized that our language about family was similar. We had shopped in the supermarket together that morning and gravitated toward the same foods. We chilled the wine and beer in a cooler on the porch, as we were both taught as children, and we chopped vegetables, happily bantering, with a shared focus on doing a good job for the guests. And when the Bailey family arrived, it was simple and easy, much like Mashama and me at our first meeting, like we already knew each other. I gravitated toward Mashama's parents, Cat and Dave, and spent the afternoon talking, sharing, and connecting with them—not out of obligation but out of sheer attraction and like-mindedness. That day was a moment in time. The moment when relationships cross a line into camaraderie and early loyalty. When you know that, if you were asked, you would do your best to drop everything to help each other.

My parents and Zuwena took to Johno and Carol as well. Malik especially took a liking to Johno. Actually, I think they were both taken with one another. It was the giant dog, Flounder, that most struck Malik, and his fear subsided when he witnessed Flounder's docile nature and the way that Flounder co-existed with everyone in the house. Malik's questions became almost an interview about how Johno had come to this point in his life; and, like a gracious host, Johno was patient in answering all of them. In that moment, I could see my nephew's world opened up a little bit more as he saw his aunt entering into a place that he had never seen before. I think he was like, *Oh, this could be nice.*

We all sat together on our side porch with copious amounts of food and wine scattered around the table in the late-afternoon Southern sun. We talked and debated and laughed, and the formalities of dining with people you do not know well never manifested. We reached over each other to get at serving plates and tore pieces of bread right off whole loaves. As platters filled with this and that made it from person to person, Malik, who was probably ten at the time, was not nearly as enamored with anything we had cooked as the rest of us were. Our plates were mounded high with fish, meat, and vegetables, but his plate housed one lonely ear of corn. His mom reoffered him everything he had already passed on: fish, clams, veggies, and ribs, with the rest of us egging him on to eat something. Everything offered was quickly turned down.

Mashama, Zuwena, and I took Malik into our kitchen and I turned to our less-than-busting-at-the-seams pantry and offered him the usual defaults—tuna fish, peanut butter and jelly, and even milk and cookies. He refused those as well.

Finally, I asked Malik, "What *would* you like to eat, because it doesn't seem like anything we are suggesting is doing it for you?" Without missing a beat, Malik responded, "Do you have any fried chicken or watermelon?" Mashama and Zuwena stopped dead in their tracks and looked at each other, both amused and entertained. Then they looked at me. I pretended to not have found anything about Malik's question out of the ordinary, funny, or peculiar but, truth be told, I was somewhere between tickled and startled.

I was a little embarrassed at first. I didn't know if Johno or Carol would find the humor in that. None of this food was familiar to him and, with all of us eating, I'm sure he was getting quite hungry. I didn't know my nephew even ate fried chicken. He was such a picky eater. I was just stunned when he asked. At that age, he ate foods that were only red, white, or brown. Now that I think about it, I guess fried chicken fits. Hell, I wanted fried chicken, too. In that moment, Malik made me more comfortable around these people. He showed them that we are Black and that this food wasn't all that familiar to us. And I was good with that.

Mashama responded first, "My God, Malik, can you be any more stereotypical?"

Zuwena just laughed out loud.

I tried not to miss a beat of my own. "Sorry, Malik, we don't have any fried chicken or watermelon," I responded, holding fast to my stance that there was nothing funny about his question, "but we can get on the bicycles in a little while and head down to Leopold's for some of their world-famous ice cream."

"Okay," he said, not really sure of what the adults were thinking, but satisfied with the offer of ice cream.

Out of the mouths of babes. . . Even after that amazing afternoon we were having, I was as unprepared for Malik's question and the unguarded responses from his aunt Mashama and his mother as I was for Tom-the-racist's. But in each case, in spite of the strength of the relationship we were forging, my own place in relation to the racial differences between Mashama and me was not terra firma. I was caught off guard both times, and my awkward responses were similar—silence and uncertainty about what would be an acceptable response in Mashama's eyes.

Our challenges in Savannah, as aspiring leaders in our adopted community and as the owners of a restaurant we hoped would have greater cultural influence, were far more complex than I had naively thought they would be. In those brief interactions, it was clear that while I might have an inkling about how to build relationships, I did not know jack-shit about the South or its social and cultural complexities—the benign ones or the malignant ones.

MOCK CAESAR SALAD WITH BROKEN ANCHOVY DRESSING
Serves 4

2 heads perfect romaine, Bibb, or red leaf lettuce

1 recipe Bagna Càuda dressing (page 76), chilled

1 wedge Parmigiano-Reggiano cheese, shaved

Cracked white pepper

We used to get these truly perfect lettuces from a farm that was called Canewater, which was down in Brunswick, an hour south of Savannah. Problem was that they were only perfect for a very brief period of time in the winter. When we did have them, I would make a simple dressing that enhances rather than hides the flavor of the lettuces. Once you find perfect lettuce, half your work is done. I'm not kidding when I say that Johno eats this salad just about every night as he sits by himself at the Gate 2 Bar at The Grey.—MB

Break off whole leaves from the lettuce and gently wash and dry them. Assemble a layer of leaves on each serving plate.

Drizzle with the bagna càuda and season with some of the cheese and a bt of pepper. Repeat with the remaining leaves, dressing, cheese, and more pepper, to form a lettuce "tower" on each plate. I like to stack my salads four or five layers high.

CHAPTER 7

The very first meeting I ever had with Mashama Bailey was scheduled for a Tuesday afternoon in November. This was more than a couple of years prior to Tom-the-Watermelon-Asshole-Guy setting foot in The Grey. Our meeting was at my office in New York, and it was set for 4:00 p.m.

At 3:50 p.m., the doorman rang my phone to tell me that I had a visitor. Mashama was early, and I took that as enthusiasm on her part.

I grabbed my blue sport coat off the back of my desk chair, threw it on, and headed out my office door. As I descended the grand old wooden staircase of my building, I was nervous. My palms were clammy, I was sweating through my shirt, and the butterflies in my stomach had reached flying-mammal size. I had such high hopes for this meeting. I was certain that it was as important for me to make a positive first impression on her as it was for her to make one on me.

The stakes were high for the project. I had run out of macho White guys—the archetypal kind who had been running professional kitchens since the beginning—or at least ones who were still interested in working with me. On top of that, my list of female, African American, fine-dining cooks to fill the role of chef and partner consisted of this one single, solitary person. As I reached the final stair, there was Mashama Bailey—waiting to size me up.

She knew right away that I was the person she had come to meet as she stood up from the small bench in the lobby. Her smile seemed to turn on. It was electric. Her energy filled the lobby, and she had an easy air about her, like I was in the presence of someone I already knew.

I always smile. I'm too tall not to smile. People are usually intimidated by my height. When I do I have found that I can relax the room. People seem to be drawn to me and let their guard down.

I wiped the sweat off my right hand inside of the pocket of my jeans as I approached her. She extended her hand confidently. As I shook it she simply said, "I'm Mashama."

Walking into this building in Gramercy Park, I was apprehensive and trying to be calm at the same time. When I arrived, I didn't know who or what to expect. My first impression of Johno was a bit of a contradiction. He seemed

to command his surroundings and wasn't afraid to make bold fashion choices with his blue eyeglass frames and colorful bow tie. But he was nervous. He had to stuff his hands in his pockets to keep from fidgeting. Standing there in the grand entryway, he stood out just enough to pique my interest in his back-story. I expected someone stuffy, someone older. But this guy seemed cool.

She was dressed casually but deliberately, looking relaxed and professional at the same time. "I'm Johno," I responded to her warm greeting, "thanks for coming to my office. I appreciate it."

"Yeah, no problem," she responded lightly.

I immediately felt good. I knew what to expect, but I was still almost surprised when it turned out to be true—she was the first person I had met during the entire process of seeking a business partner who did not look like me. She was a different gender and color. Hallelujah! This was the first time when, because of our obvious differences, I felt as if there was a chance that I was staring at my future business partner. And, I sensed from her smile and ease, that if today went well, she would be open to it. I almost could not contain my excitement about that first impression. Of course, I also could have been flat wrong about her but that was my gut in that split second. Time would tell.

I tried not to reveal what I was thinking, but I stood looking at her for a few sec-onds too long, taking in everything about her, relishing the excitement of where this meeting could lead us. My too-long gaze didn't seem to bother Mashama or make her uncomfortable—perhaps she was performing the same exercise in reverse.

I knew walking into that meeting that Johno had expressed a desire to talk with a Black woman about the restaurant in Savannah and yet I came anyway. I hadn't yet wrapped my head around why, but my antennae were up. It didn't bother me that he was White. I was more concerned that he was from Staten Island because my grandmother obsessed over Italian guys from Staten Island being in the Mafia, and her narrative was starting to creep into my train of thought. Also, I had just assumed that one day I would need to borrow money from a White-owned bank or take on a White investor to open a restaurant so that concept wasn't new to me. And, I was talking to cousin Sonny about all that kind of stuff anyway. Still, I was standing there, curious and wondering why he was so specific in what he was looking for in a partner.

"So," I finally said, "let's head to my office and talk for a bit. Cool?"

"Sure."

As we ascended the stairs and Mashama's eyes wandered, she was seeing a wood-paneled wall, a red velvet chair, an original Tiffany stained-glass window, and American masterpieces from the past century. The National Arts Club, the place that houses my apartment and, back then, a small office, is a Gramercy Park fixture. The NAC, as most people refer to it, is a place for its members to eat, drink, attend lectures, and generally support the arts. It is a cultural anachronism from the nineteenth century with the member spaces, the bar, and the dining room whisking members and guests back to another era. It was a lot to take in.

It was fancy as hell! What a first impression! I needed to know more. I wanted to know the story behind how this person, seemingly so down-to-earth and relatable, ended up living and working in a place so stuffy.

"This place is amazing," she said to me as we climbed the stairs.

"Thanks," I answered, a bit embarrassed. "It's really a privilege to be here. It's kind of a crazy place to be, and it's a long story about how we ended up here, but it's definitely been home for us these last few years. And it's not nearly as grand as it probably seems. It's actually, in a lot of ways, kind of homey and familial, a tad dysfunctional, but we're all pretty much a family here."

"Yeah, I can see that."

"Thanks," I answered again, and thought, *Well, that was probably too much information,* but I sincerely hoped, nearly every day of my life, that I would never lose sight of the values that I grew up with, the blue-collar values. In truth, they had to be tweaked a little as I moved into adulthood because those same values left a lot of gray area at times, but mostly, they were about hard work, integrity, humility, and loyalty. They were the values I tried my best to commit to but also the ones that contributed to me feeling that I didn't even belong in places like the NAC, and my discomfort with it makes me oversell the other side of it. I'm not sure why this embarrasses me, but it does—a lot—and maybe that's because I feel like one day someone is going to figure out I don't belong here, or anywhere for that matter. I decided to shut my pie hole for the rest of the walk up the stairs.

Walking into this office, I knew I was here to make a decision. I was here to decide if Johno was a person I could do business with. He was talking about partnership, but "partnership" was so new to my vocabulary that I didn't

register the true meaning of the word as it formed in my thoughts or came spilling from my lips. What I had to offer was not only talent as a chef but different forms of talent. Yes, I could cook, at least that's what some people told me, and I was starting to believe them. What remained to be seen was whether I had the skills to be a partner. But I knew I was intuitive, insightful, and a problem-solver, so for now I would fake it till I made it. At this stage, I simply thought of this as a job—a shot to start something new in a city that I only remembered myself in as a girl—but, there was also a shot for me to prove myself as something more than an employee. To do something new and different; it was a real opportunity to be a leader.

As we made our way up through the rental and administrative floors of the NAC, away from the member spaces of the club, the age of the building became more apparent and the trappings of a bygone era were exchanged for the trappings of a shabby, aging New York City interior that was insanely expensive to maintain and, as such, looked tired. I found this aesthetic shift a relief, as it was more reflective of who I am, and I wanted the initial impressions Mashama had of me to be accurate. By the time I opened the rickety, cracked door to my small office, I was more relaxed about our surroundings.

My office was old and austere. We sat at a stocky, glass meeting table, formerly adorning my dining room, now repurposed because it didn't fit in my current apartment. The table overwhelmed the small office. It never really made sense in that space, the way a hand-me-down flannel shirt doesn't make sense on the younger brother who is too small and fine-featured for its ruggedness, but it was what I had.

I offered Mashama a bottle of water and we began with the basics.

"So, tell me about yourself. I don't know much about you personally."

Mashama jumped into the conversation easily. "I was born in the Bronx," she said, "but I grew up in Queens—St. Albans, Queens. I'm the oldest of three. I have a younger brother named Dawud and a younger sister named Zuwena. My parents are social workers and live in South Carolina now." She took a sip of water and went on, "I live with my grandmother, still out in Queens, and take the train into the city every day to work at Prune."

We moved back into my grandmother Margret's basement in St. Albans, Queens, after six years in Savannah, the summer I turned eleven. She owned a beautiful red-brick, two-story home. She had a two-car garage and an above-ground pool. She kept a manicured lawn that ran from the front to the back of the house and she planted flowers every spring to enjoy all summer long. An iron banister, painted white, led up to her grand entryway, which was encased in stained-glass windows. When you stepped through the front door and into the foyer, you were greeted by brass chandeliers and African artwork. My grandma prided herself on her sun porch and large formal living room overlooking the shrubs and grass, with its décor and furniture from "the Orient," all covered in plastic. Right off the entryway were the stairs to the basement where we lived. Downstairs, long before my family occupied that space, was party central. My grandparents and their friends hung out, drinking gin cocktails while the children had the run of the rest of the house. It was a quiet, middle-class, Black neighborhood full of doctors and lawyers when my grandparents moved in. Jazz greats and soul artists, like Ella Fitzgerald, John Coltrane, and James Brown, owned homes nearby. My dad grew up in this neighborhood and, for a while, my siblings and I did too. My folks worked two jobs, finished college, and earned master's degrees while we lived in that basement. As the oldest of their three children, I was in charge when they were working and at night school. I would walk my brother and sister to school, or to the babysitter's, and pick them up after. My parents also put me in charge of our daily snacks. I would bake peanut butter cookies from scratch, grill cheese sandwiches with lots of butter, and make stacks of ham sandwiches with Swiss cheese, lettuce, and tomato. I often threw in a handful of Cheez-Its on the side for good measure. If my siblings didn't finish their snacks, then I would—I was a greedy kid.

"I'm a Staten Island boy," I said, commiserating that we were both from the outer boroughs of New York City. Manhattanites would call us the "bridge and tunnel" crowd because on the weekends, folks from the outer boroughs would come into the "real" city, Manhattan, by train, bus, or car, and descend upon the restaurants, museums, clubs, and bars. It's a small commonality, but a shared experience nonetheless. We both noticed, and I think Mashama was relieved to hear, that my roots were not what I thought she had assumed, given the fact that I was currently residing in Manhattan.

"Staten Island? I don't know much about it," she said.

Only the Mafia! And Wu-Tang Clan.

"Most people don't," I answered. "I grew up in a neighborhood that was mostly Italian families. Lots of firemen and cops. My father was a fireman, so we fit right in."

Now I took a sip of water and continued. "I'm the fourth of five kids. Three older brothers and a younger sister. My three older brothers all went into civil service following my dad's footsteps. Cop, fireman, and cop. That wasn't for me. I had the benefit of watching all of them go down that road and while I respect the hell out of it and them, life on a civil servant's salary in New York City just seemed too hard. So, I decided that I needed to do something else."

"College?" Mashama asked.

"Yeah, Pace University, in Lower Manhattan." I laughed at a memory that I then shared. "I remember sitting and talking with my mother one day. I guess I was a senior in high school. I had been dating this girl for years and it was really serious. As far as I was concerned, both of our families expected us to get married—at least that was my perception—but I knew deep down that getting married so young was the absolute wrong thing for me to do. At the same time, the pressure of trying to conform to the Roman Catholic expectations of our upbringing was so strong that it was hard for me to see my life any other way than marrying this girl I'd been dating since I was fourteen."

I paused to make sure I was not boring Mashama, but she was staring right at me, listening thoughtfully.

I continued, "So my mother says to me one day, 'What are you going to do next year after you graduate from high school?'" It was an odd question by the standards of that time, as there was no one we knew who didn't know, almost to the minute, what their children were going to do at any given point, let alone something as important as what they intended to do with their futures.

"I thought about my girlfriend, and I thought about my mother and father. They all wanted me to be a fireman. The girlfriend wanted that because it was the quickest way to money and a semblance of independence so we could get married. We had talked about getting married almost since we met," I said, mystified that I had supported those ideas at such a young age. "My parents wanted me to do it because it was what they knew and felt was the safest option for me once I got out of high school. My parents were very big on doing safe things when it came to life and money.

"And after I thought about them, I thought about me. I think I dreamed up a plan, even though I didn't know it at the time, to go for genuine independence—independence from Staten Island, my girlfriend, and my family. So, I answered my mother. I looked at her, and almost surprising myself, I said, 'I think I'm going to go to college.'"

"My mother looked up at me, more surprised than even I was. 'College?' she asked rhetorically and to no one in particular.

"'Huh,' she grunted. Then she turned back toward me, looking right at me for a second or two and she asked, very seriously, 'Can you afford that?'"

Mashama laughed.

That's brilliant! I loved this woman and I'd only known her son for ten minutes. This was good. Very good!

I laughed too.

"So, I went to college and became an accountant."

I took a moment and looked out the window of my office into Gramercy Park across the street. The talk of college and the outside greenery got me thinking about sitting in my brown 1976, Chevy Nova with my best friend, Cap. We would drive up Snake Hill to the parking lot of the Latourette Golf Course, late at night, drinking an eight-pack of Rolling Rock ponies between us. It was probably the summer after high school. We sat there for hours and hours, just talking. Talking about how we would get out of there—away from Staten Island. Away from fathers who were as volatile as they were generous. Fathers who worked harder than men should have to work, only to still feel so up against it. We fantasized about what life would be like with a job that wasn't blue collar, one where the only gunk on your hands was ink from a pen. A job where you weren't busting your hump all day, every day, and still broke as soon as you cashed your paycheck, bought the groceries, and paid the bills. What other girls were out there? What other women? What were they doing with their lives? What did other places out there look like, feel like? I had no idea where "there" was, but I knew that's where I wanted to go. During those talks, I just remember thinking, it must be better, better somewhere else. Easier. Richer. Prettier. Happier.

And, almost thirty years later, after a career of "better," here I was talking to this woman Mashama, about similar themes, the same themes. I needed something more. Happier. Better. And now I was again seeking rebirth, seeking reinvention. I think I may have sighed audibly.

Mashama took it as a cue to talk. "It was never a question in my family. The only way I was going to college was if I paid for it, so I did. I went to college to be a social worker. Just like my parents. That's why I didn't start cooking until I was a little older. Right after college, I moved to Jacksonville."

I was interested in the sciences in high school but I found them too hard. I loved culture and the arts. I wrote poetry and enjoyed working with my hands. When the time came to apply to colleges, my parents couldn't afford it. They were just finishing their own educations; there was no money set aside for their kids to go to school. So, I enrolled in Sullivan County Community, a SUNY school in upstate New York. The tuition was affordable, paid for by student loans that I would pay back. The entire student body lived off campus. We had our own little apartments with full-size kitchens and electric stoves. On any given night, someone was playing music and cooking dinner. Sullivan was attended by kids from all five boroughs, and I gravitated to the ones from the islands who grew up in neighborhoods like Washington Heights, Flatbush, Bushwick, East New York, Harlem, Spanish Harlem, Concourse, and Parkchester. It was there that I tried delicious foods from all over the Caribbean. Sure, I was from the city, but this was a different level of exposure to these cultures and foods—it was up close. I started using Goya seasoning, cilantro, hot sauces, and curries. We ate spicy baked chicken with tomatoes and onion, saucy rice and beans, homemade beef patties, and fried sweet plantains, all with cheap and easy-to-get ingredients. The flavors were robust and diverse. When I would visit home, I'd replicate those meals for my parents. I was nineteen, and after eating some stewed chicken wings I cooked for dinner, my mother suggested that I should think about being a chef. *Too hard,* was my response to that. After Sullivan, I moved back home and attended Brooklyn College, where I finished my education the quickest way I could and earned a degree in psychology, following in my parents' footsteps.

"What for?" I asked, interested in her having mentioned that she had already moved to the South once before.

"A guy," she said, "but that didn't work out."

There was no great love for me in high school or college. I moved to Jacksonville shortly after I graduated to be with family and that's where I found my first real love and he is why I stayed.

"Never does," I offered cynically.

"I was living with my cousin Danielle down there but I wasn't getting anywhere. So, I came back to New York City, moved to East New York, and got a job as a social worker. I was working with children and families from some of the roughest neighborhoods in the city." Now she laughed at an old memory, adding, "God, that was a hard job. That was the only job I ever got fired from."

I may have gasped a little.

"Why did you get fired?" I asked. Being fired seemed to me to be almost the worst thing that could possibly happen to a person in life. I was dumbstruck.

She smiled her enormous smile, completely comfortable in her response: "Because I was a really bad social worker."

I was working in a family shelter. I didn't have the patience or empathy to help people. I was just frustrated with the system. So, getting fired was good for me. It forced me to make a decision about my life path, one that I thought was too late for me to make. It was the best thing that could have happened to me.

Another laugh exchanged.

The more we talked, the more we both relaxed. No longer were we sitting rigidly in our chairs; we were leaning in now, the posture of people talking—not people on a professional first date.

"That's when I really thought about cooking professionally. When I was in East New York, I was making food at night and bringing it to work for staff parties the next day. I wasn't reading case files. Every time I had a free moment, I cooked something. I was finding I was good at it, and people were responding to it. They were telling me I was good at it, and I really liked that—that people were complimenting me on the food I made. I started to realize that I wanted to be good at something, and it made me feel really good when people told me how great my food was. I kind of need that in my life—the validation."

I was driven by two things: the ingredients and the praise. I craved the immediate gratification that cooking provided. I knew right where I stood with people when I cooked for them. Nothing had held my attention like that before.

Candidly, Mashama's honesty befuddled me. It even frightened me a little. I had all of those feelings of insecurity and needing validation but would have never said them out loud—not to a stranger. I had never met someone who was so confident and secure that they could share something so revealing about themselves after having just met. It made me feel special, like we had instantly formed this unique connection.

After a bit more chitchat, four o'clock turned into six o'clock and the bar at the NAC was open. I suggested we continue the discussion over cocktails. Mashama agreed easily and we made our way back downstairs.

I'm a sucker for a cocktail. A year or two prior to this, I had begun to learn more about classic cocktails, like Negronis, Corpse Reviver Number 2, and Daiquiris, because I loved how balanced they were. I was moving away from drinking like a college student and becoming more interested in flavor profiles, spirits, and mixers.

With drinks in hand, we sat in one of the club's parlors that overlooks Gramercy Park. Like she had the first two hours of our meeting, Mashama settled into the nineteenth-century room with ease. She did not have the awkwardness of someone who was in a new environment. And while the NAC is one of New York's most egalitarian and accessible social institutions of its type, truly committed to culture and working artists as the people it supports, its interiors can be intimidating to first-timers.

Oh, I felt awkward. But the trappings of old New York City money were not completely new to me.

But Mashama, the only Black person sitting in the parlor, was, well, Mashama. She was relaxed, interested in the art and the architecture, and soaked up the environment. "How'd someone who grew up on Staten Island end up in this place?" she asked bluntly.

I had been dying to ask this since he talked about his mom asking him how he was going to pay for college. I wanted to know if we had anything else in common. I wanted to know if he struggled at all and if he felt like he belonged in his current surroundings. Staten Island is primarily a working-class suburb, like Queens. His family worked like my family worked, so how did he get here?

"Dumb luck," I said, laughing out loud. "This is not the kind of place that I would have dreamed of being a part of in a million years when I was growing up." I continued, "But my old business partner was involved here, which is how I was introduced to it. I think his grandmother had been involved here for, like, fifty years or something. As we were splitting up our partnership after a long run, he moved all of his business stuff across town, but I decided to keep that little office we were just in. As time went on, I became more and more involved in the club's operations because it started going through a difficult period. That was right after my wife, Carol, and I moved into an apartment here in the residential building in the back. So, I became part of a small team that helped get the club back on its feet. There was all kinds of legal shit going on; we had to do a bunch of restructuring and other admin things. It was hard, very combative at times. After a few years of lawsuits and stuff, we finally were able to settle everything and we felt like, 'holy shit, did we just do all of that?' Now, I feel like a piece of me is part of the history of this place and it'll always be that way. That's kind of surreal because I *am* this kid from Staten Island, I guess I'll always be. I'm not sure if I'm here because of that or in spite of it, but I know we did something good for this place and that feels good."

This was really refreshing to hear. It was nice to be in a conversation with someone discussing building something new while also preserving what was there.

"Interesting," Mashama said, seemingly satisfied with my explanation.

"Where do you eat in New York?" I asked; a complete change of subject.

"To be honest, I work all the time, so it's hard to get out to eat. But I went with friends to Marea a few weeks ago and we balled out at lunch. Champagne, wine, the whole thing," she said. "It was a going-away party for someone."

"Was it good?" I asked.

She considered my question for a second or two and then responded, "Yeah, it was good. The food was prepared right. It was thoughtful. I had a Dover sole and it was so delicious. It tasted just like Dover sole."

"Huh. That's an odd way to describe food. What do you mean?"

I love simple foods that aren't hidden by other ingredients. I once worked for a chef who said, "If it's oversalted, you suck. If it's undersalted, you suck." This is a very silly thing to remember and not the most exacting way to explain the nuances of cooking technique and seasoning food, but it was a simple way of checking yourself if you are doing too much. Finding the balance among the ingredients, textures, and the seasoning—the salt, aromatics, and spices—is as close to perfection as a chef can hope for.

She seemed perplexed by my perplexedness. "I mean, it tasted like what it was—this incredibly delicate and perfect fish that you can only get in one part of the world. It didn't taste like butter or herbs or sauce almandine. It tasted like Dover sole, and that's what made it delicious. The fish itself really stood out."

"How about you?" she asked, "where do you eat in New York?"

"Me? I'm a creature of habit. Carol and I eat at a lot of Italian places no one has ever heard of but are just simple and delicious—Ecco in Tribeca, Emilio's Ballato down on Houston Street. We also love Indian food, and Carol is a freak for Thai."

I thought for a second about a meal we just had. "Carol and I went to this Italian place way over east in Chinatown a couple of weeks ago—on Division Street. I had never even heard of it before, but it had this super-cool wine bar in the basement. Like you were in Europe and not New York City."

"Oh, wait, I think I know that place," Mashama said immediately. "Starts with a *B* or something. I've been there."

"Yeah, that's it," I agreed. "Bacaro, I think it was called. I really liked it."

"Yes," she said, almost clapping, "Bacaro is right."

That's the thing about New York. There are something like 13,000 restaurants in the city, but mention one joint that is unique because of where it is or some feature, and you are one second away from someone saying, "Oh, wait. I know that place."

"I'll tell you," I began, recounting my evening at Bacaro, "they made this pork shank. It was as big as my head. I'm not kidding—it was this giant plate of food. And it had this deep, rich reduction on it, with some root vegetables and risotto. My God, it was good. You just forked the meat right off the bone." And then I added, "And the best part of it was the reasonable price for this giant plate of food. We took half of it home."

"That sounds amazing," Mashama said. "Braising meats like that is my favorite way to cook. That's how my grandmother cooked, and shanks were one of her things."

"Really? That was my grandmother too. She'd put a pork shank, or any kind of shank for that matter, in a pot of gravy, you know the Italian kind, and cook that shit until it completely disintegrated and it just became part of the sauce. I've never seen a pork shank on a menu anywhere before this place. It was like being a kid again," I said, almost unable to contain my glee.

"Well, my grandmother didn't cook it in tomatoes, but same idea. She braised it down, low and slow. Threw some good vegetables in there and just let everything work its magic. You have to love food up," Mashama said, thinking back to her own childhood meals.

"You have to love that thing up," my grandmother would say, referring to just about every dish she cooked. She was the queen of condiments and she loved food. In the mornings, while eating breakfast, she wanted to talk about what we were having for dinner. She was a petite woman who was ruled by her stomach and quick to invite people into her home for a meal.

"Huh, that's weird."

"What is?" she asked.

"That pork shank is a thing for us. That we both have memories of stuff like that. Who would have thought that a White, Italian kid from Staten Island and a Black girl from Queens grew up on the same food? Cultural appropriation be damned, I guess."

"Yeah, but food's food, right?"

"Yeah, food's food, but pork shank, pig's feet, and stuff like that, that's poor people food. That's what my grandmother bought because that's what she could afford to feed us. I bet you your grandmother did the same thing."

"Yup," Mashama said, "she definitely did."

Food was a symbol of wealth for Grandma Margie. She took pride in her stocked fridge. That was how she invested in her family and how she showed her love for us. Providing this constant in our lives was her way of making her family feel like we had a safe place to feed our souls and lay our heads.

As we sat for a while more, Mashama asked me, "So what do you eat in Savannah?"

"Not a lot of ridiculously delicious pork shanks, I can tell you that," I responded. "But, don't get me wrong, there's some good food there, but you have to kind of search for it. I did have a really good pork chop at this place, Local11Ten, when Carol and I first drove through town, and it was the kind of meal that made us think we could live there—it was straight-up good. Cooked perfectly to medium-rare so it was super-moist and flavorful."

Mashama was shaking her head disapprovingly at the concept of a dry pork chop. "Remember when pork had to be cooked to death because it had bacteria in it?"

"Do I? Trichinosis! It was all my father talked about. I think he used to buy pork just so he could tell us about trichinosis. He just liked saying the word."

Mashama laughed. "Yeah, I remember that too." Then she asked, "How about seafood? Can you get good seafood in Savannah?"

"You know, for a place right on the water, there isn't a lot of it. Shrimp and grits is served everywhere, but that's not really my kind of food. The only oysters they have are the warm-water ones—Apalachicolas from Florida—also not my kind of food."

After a few hours into our first meeting, I was starting to get excited. We seemed to like the same type of food even down to cold-water oysters. He had my attention and now I was really curious about Savannah.

"So, what *do you* eat?" Mashama asked again.

"Well, we get sandwiches and burgers at this place called the Crystal Beer Parlor. That's our local joint, just around the corner from our house—simple bar food, and the people are nice. So much of a place to me is the people working in it. Most of the places are geared toward tourists, so I find one thing I like at a place, like steak frites at Circa, and I go there for that. I have a couple of places around town like that."

Mashama was nodding at me, listening intently.

"Part of the opportunity I see is to build a place that is a complete package. One that as soon as you walk in, you know you're in for something good," I said, as I finished my thought.

"That's the thing about Prune," Mashama offered. "It's small but the dining room is so Gabrielle that as soon as you walk in you know that Gabrielle is going to be in every plate of food that you get, and that's special. Everything about the place comes from her."

Now I nodded. "Yeah, I feel like that's the type of thing that can be created in Savannah," I said, supporting Mashama's theory. "Someplace that's completely personal."

"Problem is that I don't really remember the food in Savannah. When we lived there, we didn't go out to eat much."

My mother, Catherine, was born and raised two hours outside of Savannah near Augusta. She is one of nine children, the middle of three girls. My Aunt Matt would say that my mom grew up marching to the beat of her own drum. Being from such a small town, she had the desire to leave it from a young age. After meeting my dad, who was friends with my mom's older brother, Uncle Wille C., my mom moved to New York City when she was eighteen, lived with Willie, and began dating my dad. They were both young and quickly fell in love. Shortly after, they had me and they have been together since. They lived between New York and Georgia until just before I turned eleven. Settling in New York after that, they built their careers and family until my mother's father, Willie C. Jr., passed away in 1995. That was the catalyst for my parents to return to the South and why they now reside in Denmark, South Carolina. Sometimes things were coming full circle.

Wait.

Stop the presses. Did I just hear right?

"You used to *live* in Savannah?"

"Yeah," she answered with the same ease she had employed all afternoon. "I thought you knew that. We went when I was five and stayed till I was about eleven. That's why I don't really remember anything about the food."

"But you lived there? Don't you find that an amazing coincidence?" I asked, truly baffled by the news.

"Yeah, I guess I do," Mashama responded. "Hadn't really thought about it, I guess. My mother's family is from Waynesboro, which isn't very far from Savannah. It's near Augusta. So my parents moved there for a while to see if they could find more work. Actually, better work might be the right way to put it."

"Wow, that's amazing. So, you have ties to the South. To Georgia and to Savannah. Huh. Did you like Savannah?"

"I was a kid, but, yeah, I remember liking it. I went to school at Charles Ellis, and that wasn't far from the house we lived in. We lived on Ott Street, by Daffin Park. And I remember these things called Thrills. Women in our neighborhood would make them by freezing juice in Dixie cups and they would sell them to the kids in the neighborhood for a quarter. I loved them, and I remember always trying to get a quarter so that I could get a Thrill. They were delicious, and that damn place is so hot that the cold was instant relief in the summertime."

New York summers were not as familial as Savannah's. You couldn't just go to someone's house to get a treat, whereas in Savannah that was normal. Where and when we would go to the Thrill lady's house is how we would plan our afternoons. That iced, sweet Kool-Aid stimulated hours of easy, lazy summer conversations. In New York, we had only the corner candy stores and the neighborhood ice-cream truck. Going back to New York was a real culture shock for me because I had come to love living in the South.

"A Thrill?" I asked, not completely sure I grasped what this thing was, while at the same time, her description sparked a memory of my own. "I remember as a kid waiting for my grandfather to get home from work. He was this little old Italian guy who worked as a tailor in Manhattan. He always wore a tie and a fedora. I'd wait for him to get home each night, because he had to walk past our house from the bus stop on the way to his own house, which was just a few doors down from ours. I would stop him and I would ask him for a quarter. 'Hey, Uncla,' I would say—that's what we called him, Uncla—'Uncla, can I have a quarter?' He'd dig into the front right pocket of his trousers and fish through what sounded like a sack of loose coins. He amazed me, because no matter how much change he had in that front pocket, pennies, dimes, nickels, quarters, he always came up with a single quarter on the very first try and he would give it to me. We definitely didn't have anything like Thrills, so I would go to the little hardware store on our street that had a candy counter for us kids and buy a Snickers or a Milky Way with my quarter."

Maybe I was seeking connection where none existed, but the idea of the quarter being the thing we each sought as children to satisfy our sweet tooth felt like another coincidence in a series of them. I laughed to myself and asked, "These women would freeze juice in a cup, and you guys would buy them for a quarter? Just frozen juice in a cup?"

"Yup, that was it. Just Kool-Aid, frozen. It was sugary and sweet and tart and cold. I haven't thought about Thrills in a long time. I definitely liked our time in Savannah," she added as I watched her cycle through that memory bank.

"Why did you guys leave?"

"Work, I guess. My dad's family, my other grandmother, they were all in New York, and my parents couldn't make a good life in Savannah because they couldn't make enough money. So, they went back to New York. They both needed jobs, as there were three of us kids by then. It was just about work, and Savannah didn't have enough of it."

It was nearly eight o'clock in the evening at this point. Our one-hour meeting had turned into four. We were well into our third drink and hanging out like two old friends talking about life—the past, the future, and the food.

"No matter what," I said, "whether we want to pursue a relationship or not, you need to come visit Savannah at least once and see it again. You need to see the bus terminal and where we live. How we live. It's different down there than New York City. Not better. Not worse. Just different."

Visit Savannah! Sweet! I was so caught up in the moment, in Johno's warmth and hospitality. I remember thinking to myself, this was the best meeting I'd ever had. I also remember thinking it was the first real business meeting I'd ever had.

"Okay, I'll do it. I'll come down and see the bus terminal. But while you're in New York, why don't you and your wife come to Prune and have dinner. I'm cooking Thursday night," she said, thinking about her schedule. "Just come in and I'll try and snag you guys two seats at the bar. You'll have a view right into the kitchen and you can just watch me cook and see me doing what I do."

"Yeah, we can do that," I said, jumping at the idea. "That'll be fun. We'll see you then."

Going into that first meeting with Mashama, I expected us to be different. I expected our common ground to be food, but I just assumed that she would have a somewhat rarefied view of it, given her chef background. And I fully expected that our childhoods as they related to food, upbringing, culture, and everything else would be dissimilar.

I was so wrong.

After seeing Mashama out, I went back to the bar, got one more glass of wine and considered the future.

I had to admit it, meeting with Johno was disarming. He was nothing like I had expected, which was a good thing, but fear began to creep into my brain after we talked. This business opportunity could actually happen and I had to start to wrap my head around that and figure out if opening a restaurant in Savannah with a White man was something that I wanted to seriously pursue.

After having spent four hours together, talking about so many things, my plan seemed less hairbrained than maybe it had just a few hours prior, before I met her. Race, my views toward it, my inherent racism had been topics of introspection for me, in some way, for as long as I could remember.

Since my days as a child when I would sneak into my brother's bedroom, a brother who is ten years my senior, and secretly and incessantly listen to his Richard Pryor album titled *That Nigger's Crazy*, I became completely fascinated by the comedian. Particularly, I was fascinated by his takes on race. I was fascinated by his language, his carefree use of the "N" word, a word that was used in my own orbit with venom, his depiction of White people as bumbling, soulless nerds, his jokes and bits and, what I realized much later on, all of these things amalgamating into his social commentary on our society and its foundational inequity. The subject of race, in its rawness, the way Pryor delivered it, was, in retrospect, game-changing for me, and I was ten or eleven years old. Words matter, I guess.

As time passed, I came to realize that Carol's and my move to the South had something, maybe everything, to do with my mounting desire to understand the greater social context of Pryor's words. I was the one who pushed us toward our move to the Deep South. I was the one who became the owner of a formerly segregated bus terminal, its history a factor in my decision to invest in that particular building. I wanted to connect with a wider community to, maybe, make amends for my own sizeable shortcomings. These could not all be coincidences, could they? Clearly there was some path that I was traveling, even if it was an unconscious one, that almost compelled me to seek a Black woman as my partner, a woman just like Mashama Bailey. It just seemed like that had to be the next move, the move that would animate all of these questions I had, give them life and, maybe, just maybe, provide an answer or two.

Wanting to explore race in the South by creating social and racial awareness could be noble, but we were talking about starting a restaurant, not a movement. Neither of us said it at the time, but we saw an opportunity in each other. I knew that was why I was there. I wanted to have my own restaurant and Johno wanted to partner with a Black woman to help him create a distinctive business.

What Johno was likely not sensitive to is how African American women are historically unprotected in society. Black men and women have been stripped and robbed of their dignity in so many ways, each not knowing where they stand and having to go it alone in this world. Black women are especially vulnerable, so Johno "seeking one" meant he was putting himself in a position from which he could not begin to understand the historical and cultural ramifications of the endeavor.

FRIED OYSTERS

Serves 6

1 teaspoon
cayenne pepper

1 cup buttermilk

2 cups corn flour
(or Wondra, if you
can't find corn flour)

24 oysters, shucked

3 cups peanut oil

Fried oysters always remind me of club food. Even though they were not a staple at the National Arts Club, all of the private clubs in Savannah serve a version of them. It's one of the most basic Southern Gulf dishes around. You can do anything with them once they're fried—put them on a sandwich, dip them in some tartar sauce, or throw them on top of a salad. One source for oysters is Rappahannock Oyster Company, which has operated in the Chesapeake Bay since 1899. They sell their Barcat Shucks on their website.—JOM

Combine the cayenne and buttermilk in a small bowl. Place the flour in a shallow bowl. Drain the liquid from the oysters. Dip the oysters in the buttermilk, dredge in the flour, and place on a plate. Line a baking sheet with paper towels.

In a deep-frying pan, heat the oil until it registers 325°F on a deep-fat thermometer. Carefully place the oysters in the oil, not crowding them, and fry until golden and crispy. Using tongs or a slotted spoon, transfer the oysters to the paper towels to cool and drain. Do something cool with them and eat 'em up!

CHAPTER 8

My parents moved back to the South in the late 1990s. My brother and I were out of the house, but Zuwena was still in high school. She was going into her senior year, which isn't the best time to move, but my mother needed to go home. Her father had recently passed away. Her mother had fallen sick with diabetes and was in the process of losing one of her legs. After a few years, they made it permanent by purchasing their very first home in Denmark, South Carolina.

Before Savannah, I had spent a lifetime in New York City and a couple of other big cities, Los Angeles and Paris, along the way. A smaller, rural city like Savannah was never really on my radar screen. But life has a funny way of moving you along if you let it, and for Carol and me, we have allowed it to move us along more than most do.

Our vagabond ways, maybe, are rooted in the fact that we never had children. We tried to have them for years, but we just couldn't. After a pragmatic doctor at New York University Hospital, having treated us for a year or two longer than guidelines would have indicated, advised us that we should no longer come to his fertility clinic and that an adoption agency might be a better use of our time, we decided to settle into the roles of aunt and uncle to the eighteen nieces and nephews that our siblings had amassed at that point in our lives. We learned, over time, that there's a place in the world for the childless, which was a difficult concept for us at first as it is so antithetical to our family backgrounds.

I'm sure that each of us would have benefited greatly from being parents. However, once we were dealt that blow—and it did seem like a severe blow at the time, particularly for Carol—our decision was that we would ensure that our lives were fulfilled in other ways. Work, food, travel, dogs, and, most importantly, friends and family all became central in our lives. Embracing the mobility that our altered life plan afforded us came naturally.

This turning point, combined with a natural disaster, was likely most fundamental to Savannah becoming such an important locale in our lives.

The natural disaster was a volcano. Yup, a volcano. Eyjafjallajökull was the volcano . . . in Iceland. How does an Icelandic volcano have anything to do with Savannah? Well, it erupted constantly for four months during a period when we were to go on a long-planned a trip to Italy. The volcano virtually shut down the air-traffic lanes between the United States and Europe for a good portion of those same four months.

Carol had a corporate job, so she could not risk traveling and being unable to return. We were forced to cancel our dream Italian vacation. After exploring a number of domestic options over a bottle of wine one night, we concluded that neither of us had spent any real time in the Deep South. Carol had attended college in Virginia but had never explored the South beyond that.

And me? Never, in spite of it always having held a great fascination for me.

A drive around the Southern United States became our new plan. Charleston, Savannah, Thomasville, Magnolia Springs, Gulfport, New Orleans, Natchez, Clarksdale, Greenwood, Chattanooga, Memphis, and Asheville were just some of the places we stopped, stayed, ate, and drank on our two-week Southern sojourn.

I had considered moving to the South when I returned from Europe. Denmark is a very small town but fairly central. In 2008, I paid an extended visit to my parents and toured nearby cities that I thought I would like to live in. I really thought about two cities at the time: Atlanta and Charleston. Charleston was attractive because it was right at the center of the Southern food explosion that was happening with restaurants like F.I.G. and McCrady's. But it seemed too preppy for me, too *Gone with the Wind,* and I couldn't relate. Atlanta was also booming! It was growing at a fast rate. Darryl Evans, Scott Peacock, Anne Quatrano, and Linton Hopkins, who were solidifying the roots of Southern food there, made the city very compelling but, frankly, the traffic and construction reminded me too much of home. So, I thought, overall, it wasn't the right time. I returned to New York City and restarted my restaurant career.

Upon returning to New York, of all the places we visited, we agreed that Savannah had made the greatest impression on us. It was, of course, all of the things that we had read about the city. It was the *Gone with the Wind*–era architecture, with rows of beautiful three- and four-story 1850s attached homes. There were stand-alone mansions on picture-perfect green spaces—Gothic, Federal, Italianate, Greek Revival, and Victorian were only some of the architectural styles on nearly every street of the Historic District. The enormous live oak trees, dripping with Spanish moss, allowed you to laze away hot summer days in a park or slowly wander the streets, icy cocktail in hand, thanks to a law that made to-go cups a completely legal, and often, a seemingly obligatory accessory for any stroll. Under the shade of those trees, we walked the famous, perfectly manicured town squares, each with a monument, gazebo, or fountain creating its distinct personality. We toured ancient cemeteries, visited the beach, and admired art in more museums than a town of Savannah's size should offer. We ate well, drank well, and truly enjoyed the city's charms.

What struck us most about Savannah, after its cultural offerings and all of its physical beauty, both natural and man-made, were the people. They were Southern in a different way than those in some of the other towns through which we had traveled over the course of our two weeks. The people in Savannah were more open and transparent with us and not at all obsequious or defensive, unlike the residents of some of the other places we visited.

In Charleston, for example, the backdrop of the Civil War seemed to still loom large in even the most cursory interactions when people discovered we were from New York. In our first evening in that town, we were quickly informed that there, in Charleston, the Civil War was referred to as the "War of Northern Aggression" by a fellow patron as we made small talk with him in a crowded bar over predinner cocktails. City Market, the centerpiece of Charleston's downtown, housed a Confederate Museum in a building of elevated stature that seemed to trump all else around it. The stalls that made up the remainder of the market's elongated structure were filled with vendors selling Southern souvenirs that seemed, to me at least, to trivialize or obfuscate rather than enhance the town's history. Seersucker and Lily Pulitzer prints were almost government-issued gear. Kids dressed like their parents. And while I have come to truly enjoy and admire Charleston since moving to the South, on that first visit, the city culture felt forced to me—almost like an amusement park.

The reprehensible part of this conversation is that they are not talking about how horrible and inhuman slavery was or how the North came down and righted this wrong. They are still talking about how the North came down and fucked their shit up. Why don't they start talking about the division between classes, which is just a euphemism for "race" in the South, and how it is so damned stark that there is a pervasive hopelessness in it all? Because, I think, they like it like that. The sad part is that the line of division is literally right in front of our faces. You can look to the other side of the street and see how badly people are living and yet the people who are supposed to lead change don't seem to be affected by seeing it.

In other places, the smaller rural towns of, say, Alabama and Mississippi, people were cordial and easygoing. They received us pleasantly and were gracious in their hospitality. But these towns move slowly. It is one of the elements that makes them so freaking charming, but it was also too big a breach for us to bridge as New Yorkers for longer than a quick stop or an overnight. The heat is part of the reason for this, but there is more to it. When push comes to shove, people don't like change, and if there are no outside factors forcing change on people or a town, well, things stay the same.

Inertia is a powerful force the farther you get from epicenters of activity. There is no shortage of small towns, Southern or otherwise, that have been cut off from growth through shifting economics and industry. The corporatization of agriculture has passed many of them by. The promise of manufacturing, long ago dried up, has been traded in for the service-based economy of the modern United States—a service economy that takes place elsewhere in the midsize and larger cities. The lunch places where we ate in the South had the trappings of old, with Formica tabletops and vinyl chairs that had likely been there for fifty or seventy-five years. The sense of history and nostalgia was real, but just as real was the Black waitress who took our order or the Black cook who made our food while the cash register was nearly always operated by a White person. Is that inertia? The way things are?

I've always wondered how White people took notice of things like that—the on-display division of race and class. Some people like to pretend that these divisions are normal—as if where Black folks live and work is by choice. I've never asked a White person for his, her, or their opinion about Black folks doing the cooking and White folks tending to the money, but maybe I should start.

In Savannah, just as in the smaller rural towns, the slow Southern greetings were seemingly honest—people actually wanted to know how you were when they asked. They remained engaged throughout small talk, and sometimes their interest would almost make me uncomfortable, as if they were getting close to that line of intrusion. The only downtown market we saw was the Farmers' Market in Forsyth Park, and while that park had its baggage from the era of segregation, it did not have any of the foreboding of a Confederate Museum sitting higher than the buildings around it. When people asked us where we were from, it was with a genuine curiosity, and no mention of the War of Northern Aggression was made as a means of poking us. The first place we ate lunch was a local burger joint, the previously mentioned Crystal Beer Parlor, and it was one of the only restaurants we had frequented during our trip, outside of a few very rural places, where Blacks and Whites were both represented in the guest base and the staff.

When we walked the streets of downtown Savannah, the Historic District as it is known, there was a youthful energy to it. There were straight kids, gay kids,

Black kids, and Brown kids. They were pierced, dyed, and tattooed. Their unique outfits—one person was wearing tight-fitting Daisy Dukes with a green taffeta top that looked as if he/they had borrowed it from a ball gown—indicated that fashion and self-expression were, if not encouraged, at least tolerated in Savannah. (Over the years, I would come to learn that such self-expression was indeed encouraged.) There were kids painting, taking photos, and shooting films in almost every square, capturing the city's physical wonders in a variety of mediums.

This is all because the campus of Savannah College of Art and Design (SCAD), one of the country's premier art schools, is scattered throughout Savannah's downtown area. SCAD owns dozens of buildings in the Historic District. Its impact on the city's character is incontrovertible. SCAD not only helped restore much of the downtown architecture through its preservation of all of the buildings it owns, but that work effectively set the bar for what the Historic District could and should be through its ongoing preservation efforts.

Preservation efforts in Savannah really started in the mid-1950s after the original city market building was destroyed. It was replaced with a parking lot and the Historic Savannah Foundation (HSF) was formed in response. Union Station, which was located in Frog Town, and the original Desoto Hotel were both also destroyed just before the Savannah downtown area could be declared a national landmark. HSF's early grass-roots work quickly established the basis for the city's tourism industry and, in some respects, shaped the downtown into what it is today. The preservationists realized that visitors wanted to see the city's historic homes and there was money to be made. The Historic District was the attraction. The old homes, tours, customs, and even clichéd food defined the experience of visiting Savannah. Staying in the past made the city a lot of money. The tourism industry set the tone not only for visitors' expectations but for locals' too. In the efforts to promote tourism, communities around the downtown areas, which were and are primarily Black, were forgotten. Destroying the Union Station to add an I-16 extension is what cut off and killed one of the oldest Black financial areas in the city. The African American community, post-segregation, was actually further segregated—all of the city's resources were focused on the Historic District and not on the surrounding areas. This resulted in the breakdown of businesses in these Black neighborhoods leading to these communities, it seems to me, becoming violent and unprotected. The people who could afford to leave the downtown did so and moved to the Southside where there were newly developed homes and safer communities. It seemed as though Savannah wasn't interested in growing as a whole. This left the many of those who remained downtown, just

outside of that one-mile-square area where all of those tourists were spending their money, broke and broken.

Incorporating such an inclusive cross section of creative students meant that Savannah was the beneficiary of a genuine injection of one of the only places true progress comes from: idealistic, youthful thinking.

The Savannah residents with whom we spoke were proud that SCAD had helped transform their city into something beyond a typical Southern town. Yes, there were the various friction points between residents and the school about such things as students taking up all the parking or the idea that SCAD's preservation efforts had caused real estate prices to rise beyond what was affordable for the average homeowner. And yes, SCAD is the 800-pound gorilla in the room and doesn't always play nicely with everyone else downtown by taking a somewhat siloed approach to its business rather than a more actively communal one. But, even though those things are almost stipulated in the organization's words and behavior, its effect on the city's personality and how that is received by visitors like Carol and me is overwhelmingly positive and compelling.

With SCAD right downtown, there is a transient way about Savannah. Some of that is because of the student population, and some is due to the lack of industry and opportunity for young, working-class people. Many folks move away, looking for opportunity to succeed that their hometown does not offer. Those who can afford to buy real estate stay put, but that is not the regular, working-class person. So, this is not a throwaway point or something to be regarded lightly. Savannah is transient, and unless real working opportunities are created, giving higher-education students and homegrown people a reason to stay, they will continue to leave to seek opportunity elsewhere.

Churches were another thing we noticed as we strolled the streets of downtown Savannah during those first thirty-six hours we spent there. As anyone who has been in the South knows, churches abound. You can't really spit without likely denigrating some house of worship. Additionally, they make up the social and political backbone of any self-respecting Southern enclave. I think that's a verifiable fact.

Some of Savannah's churches are even famous. For instance, there's the Independent Presbyterian Church, its steeple appearing high in the sky as a feather sails by it in the opening credit sequence of the film *Forrest Gump*.

There is weightier notoriety for Christ Church Episcopal, situated on Johnson Square. During the first twelve or so years of the current millennium, it served as ground zero in a theological, social, and political battle over gay rights that had a worldwide ripple effect. The vitriolic fight ultimately split the Savannah congregation in two, with the pro–gay rights half of the congregation keeping the original, hallowed structure on Johnson Square after a bitter lawsuit. This was widely, and rightfully, seen as a national victory for gay rights within the ecumenical community.

The most amazing thing about Savannah's religious community was to us, however, the fact that within less than one mile of each other there were three other houses of worship sprinkled among all of that White Anglo-Saxon Protestantism typical to the South, which included Temple Mickve Israel, the Catholic Cathedral of St. John the Baptist, and the First African Baptist (FAB) Church.

The FAB is arguably the first Black church in this country. The congregation was founded in 1773 by George Leile, a slave who was the first licensed Baptist preacher in Georgia. He had delivered sermons in slave labor camps along the Savannah River before this church was built.

If houses of worship are the social and political backbone in the South, well then, what in God's good name were these Jewish, Catholic, and African American centers for social and political power doing right smack in the middle of Savannah's downtown? A coincidence?

It turns out it's no coincidence, no accident, that all these different congregations sit side by side. Savannah has a long history of diversity of religion. It has a long history of diversity of ideas. Savannah has had a prominent Jewish community dating back to the year of its founding in 1733, making Mickve Israel one of the oldest congregations in America. Its Catholic community began to thrive only a few decades after that, and Saint John's now serves as the seat of the Diocese of Savannah, which includes all of the counties in the Southern half of the state. Finally, freedmen and enslaved people began the building of what would become the FAB in 1788, a church that would go on to be a shining light for African Americans throughout the South and an important stop on the Underground Railroad.

Buildings and churches like these, that helped protect enslaved people as they moved north toward freedom, became popular in the 1830s and 1840s. Due to the increase in escaped enslaved people, the Fugitive Slave Act of 1793

was reinforced in 1850. This strengthening of the act held Whites accountable for harboring or even ignoring runaways, with high fines and imprisonment if caught. It also allowed Whites to capture Blacks and enslave them, even if they had already been freed. This law was highly controversial in the Northern states and became one of the catalysts for the Civil War.

As we explored the history of these churches and the roles of the various religious and social communities in Savannah's long history since its settlement in 1733, it became more and more clear that Savannah was unique. Very few cities throughout the United States, let alone just the South, had so many ingrained attributes as Savannah: the strong urban planning of a grid system built around the twenty-two squares that defined the topography; the foresight of providing an urban tree canopy; a humble populace that grew up in the shadow of the much wealthier Charleston; a world-class institution of higher learning situated downtown that promoted a strong dose of progressiveness in its students and faculty; and, finally, strong and disparate religious, social, and political groups vying to promote their values, methods, and traditions, resulting in a broad diversity of viewpoints. Yes, Savannah was attractive beyond its postcard image.

Of course, the requisite challenges that come along with some of these attributes are magnified by the history of the South and the small-town nature of Savannah—the dividing line between rich and poor being almost entirely the same as the division between White and Black. There are subpar schools delivering subpar educations. There is drug crime, gang violence, stalemates in local and regional government because the various power bases clash, and a long-established old-boys' network that makes real change nearly impossible. These things are not truly discoverable until you have actually lived in Savannah. And discover them we did.

These things are most noticeable to the people they affect. I don't think you need to live in Savannah to get a feel for this division. Just drive around the bordering neighborhoods and you can discover a lot about the city that you won't find in the tourist books.

CRYSTAL BEER PARLOR-INSPIRED GREEK WINGS

Serves 4

I rolled into town on May 6, 2012, dropped my bags in my new apartment, and walked around the corner to meet Johno at the Crystal. These wings are the first thing we ate together to commemorate my moving to Savannah. When we need to talk shop, we still meet at the Crystal for wine and wings. For the record, we always drink a Spanish Garnacha blend with our wings.—MB

For the marinade: Combine the oil, lemon zest and juice, garlic, oregano, black pepper, and salt in a container large enough to hold all the wings.

Add the wings to the marinade and stir to coat. Marinate overnight in the fridge.

For the dressing: Combine the oil, lemon juice, cayenne, salt, black pepper, parsley, and garlic in a quart-size canning jar and shake the hell out of it.

Preheat the oven to 375°F.

Lay the wings on a wire rack on a baking sheet lined with foil and roast until golden brown and the skin crisps, about 50 minutes.

Transfer the wings to a platter and pour the dressing over them. Dump the feta on top and you're good to go.

MARINADE

½ cup olive oil

Zest and juice of 1 lemon

6 cloves garlic, peeled and crushed

2 teaspoons dried oregano

1 tablespoon cracked black pepper

1 teaspoon kosher salt

12 chicken wings

DRESSING

1 cup olive oil

¼ cup lemon juice

1 teaspoon cayenne pepper

½ teaspoon kosher salt

1 teaspoon cracked black pepper

½ cup chopped flat-leaf parsley

1 clove garlic, grated

½ cup feta cheese

CHAPTER 9

On the ground level of a tenement building at 54 E. First Street is Prune, the restaurant at which I spent nearly four formative years of my career, comes alive at dinnertime. Tea lights set at the centers of the white marble tabletops twinkle magically like fireflies in the antique mirrors lining the walls. The wainscoting makes you think of Granny's dining room. You sit shoulder to shoulder on the pew-like benches. In the warm glow of the room, with pink-topped servers enticing you with cocktails as you settle in, you know you're about to have a unique experience and that a very good meal is coming. You will have communion with fried chickpeas and poppadum—a crispy, salty, boozy, happy, and playful deliciousness.

The next several months after first meeting Mashama had been a whirlwind of a professional courtship between her and me. It all started that night with her suggestion that Carol and I come to watch her cook.

As Mashama had promised, when we arrived, there were two empty seats at Prune's small, four-seat bar, which is positioned on the right side of the restaurant. When you enter the space, you are immediately transported to a neighborhood joint on the outskirts of Paris; marble and wood bistro-size tabletops on metal bases, dark wood and mirrored finishes, and people enjoying each other, all added to the effect. Given the tiny dining room, it was not more than five or six paces to our stools from the front door. The restaurant, just thirtyish seats in total, was in full swing per its perpetually busy nature. Every chair was filled with a smiling diner. The servers, exclusively women, were dressed in signature pink T-shirts and long white aprons. Food was delivered to guests via a large pass window at the far side of the room, through which you had an unobstructed view into the kitchen where there were three or four people, again primarily women, cooking the evening's provisions. Mashama was front and center, her presence dominating the restaurant with that kitchen window perfectly framing her (and whoever might be running the kitchen on any given night) as if she were the star of a television show.

When I returned from France, I knew that I wanted to fully immerse myself in higher-echelon kitchens. I wanted to further my French training and continue my education from culinary school. With these honed skills, the plan was to own my own restaurant where I could continue to pay that training forward. I also knew that I wanted to do this in the South. That was it. Those were my goals.

I worked for three years around the city in male-dominated kitchens before arriving at Prune. And I sought out those kitchens. There is something baked into this business that is clear to everyone who works in it: if you want to cook at a certain level, you need to enter the boy's club. The club is a lot of fun at first. The energy is high all the time. It's competitive, sometimes the nature of it is good and sometimes it is not. As a woman in these kitchens, I learned quickly that I had to establish my boundaries, protect my personal space, and set what I believed to be acceptable standards of personal behavior from my male colleagues. These things were non-negotiable for me. Since this was my second time around the entry-level positions within this club, I intended to move up rapidly. When I left restaurant kitchens the first time to personal chef, I hadn't yet arrived at a higher level than where I found myself currently. I knew that I needed to start over, which I was willing to do. The work was hard and I was always up for the challenge of matching or besting my counterparts but, at the same time, I mostly felt overlooked by the men around me.

After a few years in this environment, I wondered if there was a different way to achieve my goals. A different path that was smaller, focused, prestigious, and, possibly, a little kinder.

I found Prune to be that place. Very early in my career, and I think also during the early days of Prune, I remember reading an article about a woman chef who was doing these Sunday suppers at her restaurant. She created these menus by looking to see what was left in her walk-in from the week, and to me that was fundamental to running a smart business. But it also seemed like something that only someone who really wanted to feed people would do. Look in your fridge, see what you got, and use your creativity to come up with something people want to eat. I never forgot that. And as I had cooked and worked through my career, I had constantly heard good things about the way Gabrielle Hamilton ran her kitchen, the respect she was earning from her cohorts and what her cooks got out of working for her. For me, this was the kind of untraditional way that I needed to plug into this industry as someone who didn't look like most of the people you found in these types of kitchens. I knew I wanted to work with someone like her to help me find my own voice.

The staff seemed to be aware of our presence as soon as we checked in. Some greeted us while others just glanced in our direction, leaving me with the feeling that first impressions were being registered by Mashama's friends and colleagues.

As we sat at the bar, the bartender, who was one of only two men on staff in the dining room, the other being the general manager, poured us each a glass of Cava, which I quickly sipped to calm my nerves a bit. We looked in Mashama's direction and she politely, albeit subtly, acknowledged our presence, remaining mostly focused on the tasks in front of her. In that moment, I thought she was being cool, maybe even aloof, but I have since learned that when she's cooking, that's just how she is.

As we sipped the bubbles in our glasses, we perused the menu and settled in, striking up some small talk with the bartender. He gave us some advice on what to eat, but it turned out that we didn't really need to look at the menu or heed his advice as we ordered almost everything available.

The bartender acted as if people did this all the time and he suggested that we let "Chef [Mashama]" course it out for us. Carol and I were happy to think as little as possible after a long week, so we took his suggestion and sat back to have a simple evening out together as there was not much left for us to do but drink some wine and enjoy the food at one of New York's favorite restaurants.

We rarely, if ever, held seats at the bar for people in the restaurant. I knew that this was an overstep on my part, but during our meeting Johno mentioned that his wife and he loved to eat at the bar whenever dining out. When I suggested that they come and eat at Prune, I didn't hesitate to offer them seats at the bar. The problem was that I wouldn't know if I could really pull it off until that night. So, I promised the seats anyway and hoped for the best. Serving a splash of Cava when someone we know sits down at Prune is classic, the bartender calling me "Chef" was icing on the cake. We were laying on the Prune vibe thick.

Taking a look at the wine list, I went for a bottle of Chateau Musar Rouge—a Bordeaux-style blend from the Bekaa Valley in Lebanon. With Lebanon not being one of the world's more famous wine-producing countries, you don't see Musars on a lot of lists. It's just smart wine. While they ain't cheap, they are great value for what you are getting. *I knew I liked this place,* I thought. I also made a mental note to get some Lebanese stuff on our list when we opened.

In the first few months of our getting to know each other, Johno's wine knowledge really shone. That was a relief, because I could barely afford to drink the stuff.

As the dishes started to arrive, we were immediately immersed in the joy that delicious food, super wine, and great service can bring. While my collective memory of all of the food I have eaten over the years is not very accurate, I seem to recall crispy sweetbreads in some kind of bacon jus, anchovies or sardines (or something of that sort), a rabbit confit, and, I think but am not positive, a whole roasted fish and charred eggplant.

It was all great. Except for two items. There was a crab bisque–type soup that came out with an uncracked, giant blue crab claw in it and another plate with some whole chicken livers skewered on a stalk of rosemary.

I didn't remember ordering them, but we had ordered so much. And when we were talking to the bartender, we kind of said that we were going to eat our way through the entire menu, so maybe we had unintentionally.

Immediately after leaving our first meeting together a few nights prior, I couldn't have been more excited about Johno coming into Prune to eat. As I was heading to the subway that night, I stopped into a restaurant called Maialino that I had been wanting to try since it opened. I sat at the bar and ordered a glass of wine and a couple of small plates. One of the snacks was chicken hearts skewered on rosemary sprigs that permeated through each tiny offal. There was a simplicity to that dish that I really liked. *This was quite an idea*, I remember thinking to myself. When I arrived to work the next day, anticipating Johno and Carol's visit the following night, I convinced myself that this would be a great opportunity, and possibly the only opportunity before Johno went back to Savannah for a couple of months, to express myself creatively while showcasing Southern flair. Ha! Possibly overstep #2 . . . and, a little ballsy.

The first two ingredients that had come to mind were crab and chicken livers. I couldn't stop thinking about that heart and rosemary dish from Maialino. We had chicken liver mousse on the menu and thyme was one of the flavors. So, I thought replacing that thyme with rosemary would be a seamless transition from the dish that inspired it and would ring as something someone would eat in the South. I thought it was really clever and it tasted pretty good. I also made a small batch of she-crab soup, running around and having everyone in the kitchen taste it to make sure it was good. I then put some of that up for family meal and even splashed an earlier table with it before Johno and Carol had arrived.

Foolishly, I felt good about these non-vetted dishes. What the fuck was I thinking? I didn't even know this guy and I was cooking "my food" in Gabrielle's kitchen. I think the pressure and excitement of this possible opportunity had me not thinking straight. If I'd taken a step back, I'd have realized I wasn't being respectful of Gabrielle.

These dishes also stuck out because they were different from the rest. Everything in front of us to that point was elegant in its simplicity and fully practical, but these were clunky.

As Carol and I tried the crab soup, she commented, "This is good, but it's too strong for me. A little too fishy."

"I like the flavor," I commented back in a low voice so the staff in the small dining room couldn't hear me. "I just don't get this crab leg and why it's in here. There's no crab cracker, so I'm not exactly sure what to do with it."

And, as we were eating the chicken livers, which I usually love however they are cooked, my reaction was similar, mentioning to Carol offhandedly, "Huh, I don't really get this, you know? What's up with this rosemary? You can't eat it. Livers are tasty, though."

As Carol nodded her agreement, I noticed over her shoulder that the owner and chef of Prune, Gabrielle Hamilton, come through the front door.

I jumped up, probably overenthusiastically, with a signature awkwardness that shows when I am nervous (and Gabrielle's stature in the industry made me very nervous). I was excited to see her again, to introduce her to Carol, and thank her for introducing me to Mashama and . . . I wanted to do all those things simultaneously.

I tried to get her attention as she made her way through the tight restaurant, pleasantly greeting a few of her guests who were equally anxious to say hi, to no avail. Instead, wrestling with her scarf, coat, and bag, she passed by our seats, directing a brief glance in our direction and the food in front of us, then rounded the bar and made a quick right, descending the stairs into Prune's basement where, I guessed, an office was likely housed.

Gabrielle had been gone for about a week to cook at an event and had just returned to town. I had been texting with her over the course of the last day, telling her that Johno would be coming in for dinner with his wife, but she hadn't responded. I wasn't sure if her lack of response was because she was traveling or there was more to it. There was no real turning back from the evening at that point, so I figured I would deal with whatever later but, as soon as I saw her, I got anxious.

I shrugged in Carol's direction and looked over toward my new friend, Mashama Bailey, in the kitchen, who seemed to have taken notice of the interaction.

I received the first of what would be many an eye roll from Mashama that night for being awkward and geeky.

As I sat back down, Carol said, "I take it that was the owner?"

"Yup," I answered.

"She moves fast," Carol observed.

"Yeah, she looked busy."

We turned back to the food in front of us.

No sooner did we get fully repositioned on our barstools again than did Gabrielle return to the main dining room, her fall accessories having been discarded somewhere belowdecks. She approached Carol and me with a smile, introducing herself to Carol with an extended hand.

After she and Carol exchanged some pleasantries, I recall that she asked me if we could have a brief word together. We took a step away from where Carol and I were sitting at the bar toward the center of the room. Then she calmly and quietly told me, in very certain terms, that performing an audition in her restaurant was not acceptable regardless of whether she had introduced Mashama and me. I got the impression that she was not interested in a response, which was very lucky for me because I was struck, at that moment, by and large, speechless. I even had to take a second to process the word "audition." I wasn't auditioning Mashama! We hadn't even decided at that point if an audition was in order because we had only met two days prior. Our conversation had not progressed beyond agreeing to get to know each other, and when Mashama suggested that I come to Prune, she did so saying that it would be nice for me to see her working in her environment.

I don't remember the entire interaction with Gabrielle taking more than sixty seconds before she left us to finish our meal after saying an equally warm goodbye to Carol.

As I sat back down, Carol paused a moment and then asked, "What was that about?"

"I'm not sure what it was about exactly, but I *am* pretty sure it wasn't good."

We turned back to the food in front of us, finished our meal quietly, and then paid our check and left. The walk to our apartment was cold. The brisk New York City fall air was a welcome countermeasure to the effects of the red wine and the sting of my first lesson in the protocols of the restaurant business. The next morning, as we had previously planned, Mashama and I met again at my office before I was scheduled to head back to Savannah.

I immediately dove in and asked Mashama what the hell had happened the night before.

It was awkward.

Mashama was somewhat defensive about the evening and other than assuring me that all was fine, she seemed to not want to have a discussion about it at all. I pressed her on it, firing off a series of questions to which her answers came out almost as if she were distracted.

I was nervous and defensive. I had not processed what happened and I was concerned that I had damaged my relationship with Gabrielle. Johno was anxious about the evening prior and implied that he felt set up, that I had set him up. He also told me that he didn't want to sour his relationship with Gabrielle or his reputation. The way things ended the night before had left a pit in my stomach. I was the sous-chef and I had command of the kitchen, but I had gone too far. That was not my restaurant and I had treated it as such. I had to take responsibility and I did not know where to begin. This wasn't Johno's situation to deal with, it was mine and, as I sat across from him, all I wanted to do was to jump up, run to the second-story window of his office, and leap out. Prune has always led with the spirit of generosity and I had thought that was what I was doing, but I was actually being self-serving—the craziest part is I thought I was totally within my rights until I saw Gabrielle walk in the door. Because I had not yet really spoken to Gabrielle, I had nothing to tell Johno, so I just sat there and watched him until he was done freaking out so that I could change the subject back to the two of us (if there could still be a two of us).

I felt kind of fucked over at first. I had been under the impression that my visit was fully sanctioned by everyone involved, including the owner of the restaurant. Being dressed down for being there, mid-meal, struck me as if there were something going on and that I didn't know about. Mashama continued to maintain that I should let it go. But that was difficult for me to do because Gabrielle was a leader in the industry that I was trying to break into and I had clearly, regardless of my lack of intention to do so, offended her. My only expectation for the evening was to be around Mashama as much as possible before I returned to Savannah for the next almost two months. She had invited me and I was so excited about the possibilities of this relationship that it never occurred to me to do anything but accept her invitation. Doing this over a nice dinner with my wife and maybe impressing her by being able to introduce her to renowned chef Gabrielle Hamilton were added bonuses.

As I continued to think it through that morning in my office, with Mashama sitting across from me, I realized she was probably right. I needed to let it go. I respected everything I had learned about Prune and its owner through that point. Things got fucked up somewhere and I didn't know where. Whatever it was, my showing up at Prune was probably a mistake because it put an enormous amount of pressure on Mashama given the weight of what we were discussing. Mashama, however, remained resolute throughout the morning that this was something that she needed to deal with and that I needed to trust her to do so. So that's what I did and I finally dropped the subject. Watching me sit silently and turn things over in my head, Mashama finally cleared her throat and changed the subject. "So what did you think about the food last night anyway?"

"The food," I said, forcing my brain to change gears, "I loved the food. Everything was delicious. Just like I remember Prune from the old days. I thought it was all great."

"Great," she said. "Gabrielle's food is so good. She just gets what makes things delicious and what people like to eat."

"I agree. The only two dishes that I didn't love were that crab soup and the chicken livers."

Mashama perked up and inquired why, with a nod and a raised eyebrow.

"The soup was good. It was a little thin, I thought, for me, but flavorwise it was good. I also didn't understand the crab claw in the middle of the bowl. There was no way to crack it or eat it so it just seemed to be this tempting little treat that you couldn't have. Just felt weird."

Mashama smiled, waiting for me to continue.

I obliged. "Same thing with the fried chicken livers. I loved them. Simple. Delicious. But I couldn't understand why Gabrielle would skewer them on a rosemary stem. It made them really hard to eat because you had to eat around the rosemary. If you just bit them off the branch and you snagged some of the rosemary it would overpower the liver. Just seemed like another weird choice."

"She wouldn't," Mashama said.

"She wouldn't what?" I asked.

"Skewer chicken livers on rosemary—Gabrielle wouldn't do that. I did that. The crab and the chicken livers were my two dishes. Those were the ones I think Gabrielle got pissed about because they weren't from her menu. But I wanted to send you a couple of ideas I had for dishes from the South. I have been thinking about Southern food for a long time, and I felt like this was a chance to try out a couple of things."

I could've struck out here and lost the chance to run my own kitchen, but I had to tell him that those dishes, the ones he didn't like, were mine.

"Ah, sorry," I said, not embarrassed that I had issues with them, but more that I was so blunt as to what those issues were.

"No, it's good. You're right. I was just thinking about how they would look and taste. I was only thinking about the creation part and not what happens when you put the food down in front of the person who is going to eat it," she said, pausing for a second.

"Okay. Sorry for being so direct. I didn't know those were your dishes." I began to backpedal a little. "But they were good. The flavors were good. I liked them."

"Really, it's fine," she said, flashing a moment of slight frustration for my pandering. "You were right. Everything you didn't like about them is right. If you gave it to me, I would have said those same things. I like the way you talk about food," she added sincerely. "I can hear what you're saying because you keep it simple. You're not being critical to prove you know something about food, flavor profiles, ingredients, and shit. You just say something is delicious or not delicious, or what's wrong with it or what can be more right with it without any bullshit. I can hear that kind of feedback."

This was an important experience for me, having to sit and listen to someone who I didn't know critique my cooking without taking it personally. That was hard.

I smiled broadly at receiving such a nice compliment from this person, with whom a shared future was starting to seem like a possibility. "Thanks. I do like food that's delicious and simple. It's what I was raised on. It's what I can taste. It's what my grandmother cooked—like potatoes and eggs. Or mozzarella and eggs."

"What?" Mashama asked, unsure of what I was talking about.

"When I was a kid, if my grandmother had potatoes lying, around she cooked them in a cast-iron skillet and then mixed them with eggs and put it on a piece of Italian bread as a sandwich for my brother Glen and me. Or, if she had mozzarella in the fridge, then she would do that with the eggs in that same skillet and that would be the sandwich."

Mashama nodded, unsure of where I was going.

"But she never did both. It was always either potatoes and eggs or mozzarella and eggs. Doing all three would have been one ingredient too many to her, I think."

"Your grandmother knew how to cook," Mashama said, seeming at ease for the first time that morning.

DIRTY RICE
Serves 4

I staged for Donald Link in New Orleans while I was working at Prune and got a chance to eat at his most refined fine-dining restaurant, Herbsaint. I knew I was going to blow my entire paycheck but figured it would be worth it. (His dirty rice stays with me to this day.) When it was time to get my check, the server informed me that Gabrielle had paid for my entire meal. Her generosity moved me and has stuck with me ever since.

You can add a protein to dirty rice and make it into a one-pot meal. We have served it with fresh crab, cooked fish, or roasted duck and it's always delicious. It's kind of a Southern version of fried rice.—MB

9 ounces chicken livers

1 cup milk

2 tablespoons butter

¼ cup finely chopped yellow onion

¼ cup finely chopped celery

¼ cup finely chopped green bell pepper

2 teaspoons minced garlic

2 tablespoons brandy

2 teaspoons gumbo filé

4 cups cooked long-grain white rice

Kosher salt

Cracked black pepper

½ cup finely chopped flat-leaf parsley

Soak the chicken livers in the milk overnight in the refrigerator. Remove the chicken livers from the milk, chop finely, and set aside.

Melt the butter in large sauté pan over medium heat. Add the onion, celery, bell pepper, and garlic and lightly sauté for 3 to 5 minutes. Add the chicken livers and sauté for 1 minute. Deglaze your pan with the brandy, scraping the bottom with a wooden spoon and cooking for 3 to 4 minutes. Add the gumbo filé and fold in the rice.

Season the rice with salt and pepper and cook while tossing, making sure to heat it all the way through. Taste and adjust the salt and pepper as needed. Transfer the rice to a serving bowl, garnish with the parsley, and serve. Store leftover dirty rice in the refrigerator for up to 3 days. Reheat gently in a skillet.

CHAPTER 10

In the dead center of The Grey's dining room, on the south wall, is table 34—a semicircular booth that seats five people. If The Grey has a best table in the house, this is it.

From opening day, above 34 has hung a painting by Marcus Kenney. Marcus is Savannah's best-known artist, locally and nationally. He is a multidisciplinary talent who paints, sculpts, photographs, and works with neon and found objects—and he does all of them well. When we were in the run-up to opening the restaurant, Mashama and I visited Marcus in his studio and asked him to make a piece for us that would inject a big splash of color into the middle of a dining room that is otherwise restrained. Marcus, a Louisiana native, is a SCAD alumnus and received his master's degree in photography in the SCAD building next door to the bus terminal (long before it had become The Grey). He has a long history with the bus terminal building because it had been a restaurant briefly at the end of the 1990s, owned by very good friends of his. That restaurant was a Savannah favorite and a Marcus favorite.

When we arrived at Marcus's studio, the first thing I noticed was the neighborhood. His studio was in a house, a two-family home near the Thomas Square section of Savannah, about a mile from downtown. At first glance, you could see that this was once a thriving, middle-class neighborhood. But upon closer examination, it had deteriorated since. Not a lot of love had been put back into the houses around there and I was curious why Marcus, a White guy from Louisiana, was making art in the middle of the 'hood, but I guess I figured it was because it was what he could afford. He probably bought that house fifteen, twenty years ago, before "gentrification" was a word in neighborhoods like these. Back in the neighborhoods where I lived in Brooklyn, having guys like him move in meant change was coming—some White guy rolls up at the bodega and it's like *poor people, get ready cause you may have to move soon.*

When we walked into his studio, I thought we were in an episode of *Hoarders* because Marcus collected things from *everywhere*—off the street, from the land, at the seashore, and from abandoned houses—to use in his art. Our second visit was less shocking for me. The house was more organized and artworks in progress stood out. He was working on this life-size bejeweled horse in the kitchen. Its mane was soft and colorful and it had a coat of pearls, crystals, and stones. I thought it was beautiful.

Mashama and I gave Marcus no real instruction on the piece other than telling him to tap into his knowledge of the history of the space, his time in Savannah, and his budding relationship with Mashama and me to create a work of art that we could hang over table 34 and anchor our dining room.

A few weeks later, we went back to his studio to see what he had created. It was indeed a big splash of color—on a few levels. The image portrayed, 1950s postcard-style, a multiracial family disembarking from a Greyhound bus that had traveled from New York City to Savannah. In the front of the bus rode the Black passengers, and in the rear were the White ones. Various imagery of the South's ugly past, (potentially) bright future, progress, and inertia were incorporated throughout the piece.

Mashama, after taking it in for a minute, reacted first. "I love it," she said. "It's perfect."

I really thought it was perfect for the space. Smart. Very smart. The postcard feel, made with old trading stamps and stickers, was not a collage like I had ever seen before. As I was taking it all in, I could feel Marcus staring at me almost as if he didn't believe that I liked it or that my initial reaction was my true reaction. At that time, he didn't know me very well, but we'd get past all that.

"Thanks," Marcus said. "Yeah, I'm happy with it."

Marcus, a tall, skinny, pale guy with dark curly hair and a perpetual five o'clock shadow, looked toward me. He touched the wide brim of his floppy felt hat nervously with one hand, repositioning the love beads that hung around his neck with the other, and asked, "What do you think?"

"I need to look at it some more," I said, offering no reaction at all.

I looked at it for what felt like a solid five minutes before I said a word. It concerned me. It was provocative. At first glance it was difficult for me to interpret it as racist or hopeful or both. "I don't know," I said honestly. "There's a lot going on in there. I'm not sure people will get it."

"That's what's great about it," Mashama offered. "The Black people in the front of the bus? All you have to do is see that to know what this thing is about. The rest of it is kind of a mind bend, I agree, but isn't that what art is supposed to do? Makes you think a little bit. I like the fact that you have to really look at it.

If someone's first conclusion is that it's racist or saying it's something it's not saying, I think we can deal with that. Fuck 'em if they can't take a joke. Right?"

Marcus laughed. I laughed. I stood a few minutes longer.

"I do think it's perfect, Marcus," Mashama repeated.

Finally, I came around, "I love the piece. I do," I said. And I did. "I would definitely hang this piece in my house. But I have to defer to you on this one for the restaurant, Mashama. If you think people are going to get it, I'm down."

"I think most people will get it. Not all people though."

A few weeks before seeing Marcus's piece, Johno and I had dinner at Local11Ten, a beautiful restaurant housed in an old bank, just south of Forsyth Park. Johno was sitting at the bar when I arrived, chatting with people who looked familiar to me but I couldn't place. We were still excited to be together and a little nervous around each other, as you are in a new relationship/partnership. I sat down, right next to him, greeting the bartender and asking for a glass of whatever Johno was drinking. Not paying attention to his conversation, I sipped my wine as I waited for him to say his good-byes. Shortly after settling into my seat, Johno turned to me and asked if I realized that I was a Black woman in Savannah opening a chef-driven restaurant. I was surprised, maybe even a little shocked, by his phrasing and then wished that I had paid attention to the conversation he was having as his question seemed to be a result of it.

Where was he going with this? "Johno," I said calmly, "Do I realize that I'm a Black woman? And a chef? Is that your question?" I asked, taking another sip of wine.

He went on to say, "Do you know what that will mean to people here?"

I wondered if this had to do with my food or my gender or my race. I was confused and I bet those people had put some sort of doubt in his mind about one or more of those things. I was wondering if that was the first moment that he had been confronted with the power of stereotypes or the racism that might confront The Grey. I wondered if he was truly up for the challenge of opening a restaurant with someone like me. I wondered if we would be up for the challenge of changing the stereotype of business relationships in this city. Changing someone's ideas about race was a challenge that I was not up for. I was here to cook food and I wanted to say my peace that way.

"It's provocative, and it is definitely going to illicit reaction. We'll just have to be ready for that. I guess most people 'getting it' will have to be good enough."

"Let's do it," Mashama said emphatically.

It is a very good piece. It's hopeful about the future and honest about the past. Had Mashama not been there with me, I don't think I would have had the guts to take the piece and hang it in The Grey. And it has proven to be a risky bet. That painting, titled *Collected Stories,* has caused enough people—mostly White people—to walk out of The Grey that we finally had to ask Marcus to write an artist's brief explaining all of the imagery and symbolism. We then had his write-up laminated so we could keep copies of it at the server stations. This way, when people start to ask a member of the team about it, we'd be at the ready to diffuse the situation before it got heated. Once most people read Marcus's statement, they ultimately seemed a little embarrassed about whatever their initial thoughts had been.

The painting is about a collective future full of change—change that I hope that the world is ready for.

The discussions that painting has started about a South that is in motion, however, have been worth it. There was a prescience in Marcus's work that was eerie. How I reacted to it, how Mashama reacted to it, turned out to be the general reaction of our respective racial counterparts. I saw in it something that might offend, maybe because I sort of live my life worrying about offending someone, and Mashama saw something powerful. Just the conversation that Mashama and I had about hanging it was eye-opening. Growing up in a house where drawing the attention of my father, even in the most benign circumstance, often resulted in negative consequences, I learned to try to keep my head down in certain situations and, in a lot of ways, that is how I am wired. But Mashama's parents taught her to find her voice as a person, a woman, and an African American, and she was almost surprisingly practiced at it. It was simple to her. It was hopeful and that was that.

About eight months prior to that visit with Marcus in his studio, Mashama came to visit Savannah for the first time since her childhood. She arrived on a Tuesday afternoon in January. Because of Mashama's work schedule in New York, I only had about eighteen hours to show her the abandoned bus station that I hoped would become our first restaurant, as much of Savannah as possible, and to eat some food so she could get a sense of the food scene. Time was definitely going to be tight.

It was a bright blue Savannah winter day—cool enough that a sweater was welcome. I came to learn that you put up with six to eight hot, stinky, humid months in Savannah for four to six months of temperate perfection, and this day exemplified the latter.

As we drove through Savannah on our way to the bus terminal, I made sure to take the route that would offer Mashama the highest volume of eye candy. I drove the streets that had the largest live oak trees and the drippiest Spanish moss. We carved our way through a few of the most beautiful squares with tourists, students, and locals completing the idyllic backdrop. I drove past ornate homes and downtown mansions with peaked dormers, white columns, wrought-iron fences, and balconies. I made sure to include several restored SCAD buildings on our brief tour that showed Savannah's past and its potential in the architecture, restorations, and the school's student body.

Johno also mentioned an African American gentleman named Dr. Walter Evans. Dr. Evans, he said, was from Savannah but left to practice medicine somewhere in the Midwest. He came back when he retired. Johno told me that Walter was an avid art collector who had the largest Jacob Laurence collection in the world, he had a huge library of African American historical documents dating back centuries, and owned buildings on the section of MLK that once partly housed the Black business district. I think Johno told me this because he wanted to say something relatable and he wanted me to know there were Black people thriving in Savannah.

Right away, I could see that there was so much potential in this sleepy city linked with so much sadness. The neighborhoods that make up the city seem so detached from one another. I was impressed by Savannah's beauty but intrigued by its past. The more I learned, the more its history opened up to me. The downtown is so different than it once was. So many once-thriving neighborhoods seem not so thriving any longer. But, there was something going on, it felt to me, and I thought this moment may help to change some of that.

I stole glances at Mashama to gauge her response to it all. It was hard, frankly, for anyone to not find Savannah compelling. It was gorgeous and old and sentimental.

Her pleasant smile and head swiveling from side to side indicated that she was eating it up with a spoon.

The bus terminal was not located in *that* Savannah, however. It was located between the Historic District and the other Savannah—the Savannah where the stately homes are no longer and the tourists visiting to ogle the trappings of old Southern wealth and charm do not venture. Public housing projects, where the physical segregation and relocation of the poor and minority classes has taken place over the last seven or eight decades, encircle the Savannah we drove through to reach our destination. The old bus terminal backs up right onto the other Savannah and one of the city's most well-known public housing developments, Yamacraw Village. The Grey, since it opened, has had a mostly benign détente with Yamacraw. We employ some of the residents from time to time, but otherwise, our interactions are few. Occasionally one of our staff, who parked on the fringes of the neighborhood, has had their car broken into, the contents taken. And there have been more than a few nights when the sound of gunfire could be heard just around the corner from the rear door of our restaurant, sometimes the bullets a little too close for comfort, but never injuring any of us. Our relationship with that community has never progressed beyond one of caution and we know we should try to fix that, as we are neighbors, but we haven't yet figured out how to do it. It is frustrating.

To me, the building was in the middle of nowhere on a busy main street— Martin Luther King Jr. Boulevard. The Historic District is one block to the east and the projects start two blocks behind it. Most people, whether they are walking or driving, use MLK to either head north to River Street, the epicenter of the tourist area, or south to Liberty City, a poorer, African American suburb. It is ironic to me that the name of this street, which was changed from West Broad Street to Martin Luther King Jr. Boulevard in 1990, to commemorate a man whose ideals were equality and justice for all, remains a stark dividing line between historic Black and White neighborhoods.

Modern-day Savannah is certainly progressive and diverse by Southern standards, thanks to its history as an outlier, the variety of religious groups that occupy it, and SCAD. However, its past is also rife with, at best, indifference and, at worst, overt and covert racism. It is the South, after all. Even its diverse religious base was born of intolerance. When James Oglethorpe settled Savannah for the Crown in 1733, the trustees of the colony had three distinct rules: no Jews, no Papists, and no slavery. These were prerequisites for the "Utopian" society Oglethorpe, a trustee himself, was trying to create in Georgia (named for King George II). But fate, not enlightenment, would intervene over time, eliminating all three of these rules.

The Jewish ban ended quickly when, in the summer of 1733, five months after Oglethorpe settled Savannah, many of his original group took seriously ill. He badly needed a doctor to tend to his settlers. It just so happened that right at the same moment, a ship carrying a contingent of Ashkenazi and Sephardic Jews, who were seeking their own freedom to worship, had just arrived from England, and one of them happened to be a doctor. Oglethorpe, pragmatist that he was, let them into his utopia, and Mickve Israel, the congregation they founded, is now a stalwart of Savannah society.

The slavery ban, the only one of the trustee's three directives that actually tended toward true enlightenment, had no real chance of survival. Economics would not allow it, and, in 1750, people did what people in power do and placed their own well-being ahead of the needs of those in positions of weakness or vulnerability. In this case, the weak and vulnerable were the chained Africans who were bought and sold regularly in the slave markets throughout the South.

It is recorded that nearly 400 enslaved lived in Savannah since its inception in 1733. The slavery ban that was set in place by James Oglethorpe and the other trustees was unenforced when labor was needed during the city's initial construction. Rather than building their new city themselves, they brought in "help"—in the form of enslaved people who were shipped in from Charleston.

White farmers and landowners availed themselves of the free labor to plant, grow, and pick rice, among a plethora of other crops (the cash crop of the Low Country was rice, not cotton). It quickly became clear that it was economically prohibitive for Georgia (and Savannah) to actually pay people to do the same work. Basic laws of supply and demand meant that Georgia couldn't compete with other agricultural communities of the South that had embraced slavery, and so Georgians reversed their founding morality on the issue and succumbed to market pressures, incorporating slavery into their economic model with a vengeance in the 1750s and onward.

With slavery, America had established itself as one of the richest countries in the world. By 1750, there were 16,000 enslaved in the state of Georgia. In 1793, the invention of the cotton gin by Eli Whitney fueled the slave trade by revolutionizing the cotton industry and radically increasing cotton production and the demand for field labor. At that point, the Savannah market was setting the world's price for cotton and, according to the census of 1810, the number of enslaved people in Georgia exceeded 100,000.

The Catholics were admitted to Savannah as a result of the Revolutionary War because a group of 3,500 from France, Poland, and Ireland—including the famous general, Casimir Pulaski, who is credited with organizing the American cavalry—fought on behalf of the colonies at the Siege of Savannah. It is believed that Pulaski was wounded by cannon fire during that battle and died a couple of days later from his injuries. Pulaski is revered in Savannah; a fifty-five-foot monument to him adorns the center of Monterey Square, Savannah's most famous of its twenty-two squares. The reward for the Papists who fought alongside Pulaski? Not being kicked out of Savannah after the war (although more time would pass until they actually got equal rights and could vote).

And so, it was those three foundational rules and the breaking of them that brought a diversity of race and religion to Savannah. The Jews and Catholics assimilated over the next two and a half centuries, and are important sub-communities within Savannah. However, it has been a completely different story for African Americans. Their subcommunity, which played the most vital role in building the city and creating wealth by virtue of their forced and free labor, has remained segregated since Savannah's inception, even after receiving their freedom in 1865. The public housing projects that encircle Savannah's Historic District, which are literally on the other side of the streets that serve as the Historic District's borders, are just a twentieth-century invention, created under the guise of progress, to perpetuate segregation and oppression. The building that served as the bus terminal and would become The Grey was also on the other side of that Historic District border to the west, on Martin Luther King Jr. Boulevard. The restaurant's only adjacent residential neighbors are the folks who live in Yamacraw Village, just behind—the people with whom we still have no relationship of which to speak.

When we pulled up to 109 MLK, the scenery was markedly different from what we had driven through to get there. It was more urban and seemed somewhat forgotten. There was an oversized and under-frequented art store serving SCAD students to the left of the boarded-up bus terminal, a couple of small restaurants, and a trash-filled vacant lot. Yamacraw was visible from the street next to the building. I stole another glance to gauge Mashama's reaction to this part of Savannah, but she was poker faced and just waited for me to continue the tour by taking her inside the abandoned bus terminal.

Granted I hadn't been to Savannah in years. I hadn't been in downtown Savannah since I was a child. This part of town didn't seem familiar. I remember thinking as we drove in from the airport and through the city streets, *if Savannah's population was more than 50 percent Black, where was everybody?*

The interior had been cleaned out since I'd toured the building last but remained in the very same condition structurally and aesthetically—dilapidated. I was concerned, reasonably so, that once Mashama soaked in the location and then realized the scope of the undertaking necessary to restore the building and turn it into a restaurant, she would spin around on her heels and get right back on the plane to New York City, never to return to Savannah (at least not at my invitation).

We entered the building through the same makeshift door that I had come through that first time I'd looked at it. I stepped in ahead of Mashama and quickly turned to get a full view of her as she entered the space. Her head tilted up, drawn toward the large skylight that ran the length of what was formerly the bus station's main waiting room. Was that a smile on her face? Hard to tell. She looked at me and said offhandedly, "This place is cool."

I consider myself to be very intuitive. I trust my gut more than anything else. When I walked in, the whole building was warm, even in winter with no glass in the window frames and no heat. The bones were good and the energy of the space was happy. *This building has a lot of good memories,* I thought immediately. It was the right place for me.

Whew, I thought. "Yeah, it is," I agreed.

I began Mashama's first tour of the space by walking through the building to the front entrance on MLK. This part of the structure was completely sealed off from the street by a large, plywood wrapper concealing its long, curved facade. Because all of the glass had been removed from the building's defining feature—the enormous paneled window that ran the length of that structure—the plywood wall was necessary to protect the building from the elements. It also served a secondary, unintended purpose, completely hiding the building from all who passed by it on busy MLK—likely depressing interest in it and making it possible for me to ultimately buy it.

As we began to walk through, I pointed out all of the architectural spaces and details of note as I have now done for guests and media countless times since. The first was the original, segregated lunch counter directly to the right of the entrance that was consigned to the Union News Café in 1938 and operated until 1965, two years after Savannah had desegregated (and four years from when Savannah decreed lunch counters were no longer allowed to be segregated). Mashama walked into that room and looked at the bar that was the only remaining fixture. "That's not original," I let her know. "I'm thinking that this is going to be the cocktail area. We would build the new bar in the exact footprint of the original lunch counter that occupied this space. We'll do booths similar to the original ones along the window. It'll be very retro."

"Cool," was her only response.

Walking toward that front area was beginning to feel and look different. It was dark and very dusty. I had to really focus and use my imagination when it came to what Johno was saying to me. I stayed quiet because I didn't want to start talking myself out of any future plans before they had gotten started.

Making our way deeper into the building, we passed the ticket counter and a worn-out spot in the rose-colored terrazzo floor where White riders waited in line to purchase their tickets to someplace else. I explained each detail, and Mashama took it all in, quietly.

We made our way back to the main waiting room, where we had entered the building.

Mashama pirouetted once or twice to soak in the entire visual of the large rectangular room. A streak of chrome here and there. A curve. A flash of glass covered in decades of grime.

"The Masonite on the walls," I said, pointing to the rust-colored faux wood panels that had become another minor obsession of mine, "has a thick layer of tar and nicotine on it because everyone smoked back in the day. David Bloomquist, our general contractor on the project, has done a couple of cleaning tests with some SCAD preservation students, and he thinks that coating has actually helped preserve those panels all these years. We're going to be able to save them."

She nodded, absorbing with all of her senses.

We continued on, walking to the back of the station and down the stairs. I showed her where drivers slept to freshen themselves for an early morning journey. This space also contained the boiler and the bathroom for the White men.

We walked back upstairs and then up another flight to a grand space (by the era's standards) on the mezzanine level. Graffiti-covered mint-green tiles lined the way and encased two rooms at the top of the staircase. As we entered the first, I said, "This was the White women's powder room and bathroom." Pointing at the first wall we encountered, "This was mirrored and had a counter and chairs so that women could fix their makeup."

"*White* women," Mashama said pointedly.

"Yeah. White women," I mumbled.

Entering the second room just behind the first, "This is where the toilets were. If you look at the floor, you can make out the outlines of the stalls and where the sewage lines were."

Mashama, her face expressionless, noted, "White women sure needed a lot of room to pee."

I was amazed by the intention behind it. The beautiful green tiles that lined the walls, the gorgeous light pouring in through the windows, *these women were on top of the world,* I remember thinking to myself. This room suddenly represented to me White women being put on a pedestal, peeing above everyone who was allowed into the bus station.

This was the deification of White women. Those women being such a prize that, if Black men tried to "possess" it, their murders were easily justifiable by their White counterparts. Emmet Till being a prime example—and he was just fourteen years old.

Back down on the main floor, we crossed a threshold into a small five-by-ten-foot space near the rear entry.

"This is where the colored folks waited, right?" she asked me.

"Yeah, this was the colored waiting room, and back in here, the two little bathrooms were the colored his and her restrooms."

That space was as big as any apartment I'd ever lived in. But, compared to the 24-hour diner in front, the ladies' room upstairs, the men's room downstairs, and the large waiting room, this area was tiny. I was excited to see *this* space, and, as I stood there, I thought that I would feel sad or humiliated after I had seen all of the other parts of the building that I would not have been allowed into. I mostly felt pride, though, because there was a very strong chance that I would have an opportunity to alter the building's historic narrative by possibly being a partner in the next business that would occupy it, adding an element of hope to a changing city.

Mashama took a few steps into the middle of the colored waiting room and stood perfectly still, her eyes the only things moving. Suddenly, I felt like an intruder in her moment. I hesitated for a second, unsure what to do. Then I quite literally stepped over the threshold out of the colored area, back to the White side. The building was completely silent as Mashama took it in.

I'm not sure why, but I was humbled. Black people have been through some shit in this country, and we continue to go through it with our heads held high and full of pride.

After a bit she turned, her back to me, looking toward the colored bathrooms and the rear door. "Was that the colored entrance?" she asked.

"Yes, I think so."

More silence and stillness. She walked farther back and looked into the bathrooms. They were mostly still intact. Finally, Mashama turned again, and walked toward me back into the center of the main waiting room—the White waiting room. "It's good," she said.

I did not realize that I was ready or prepared for this challenge until I stood in that building. As we walked through the vacant parking lot, leaving the site, Johno stopped me: "Are you ready for this? Are you ready for a true partnership? Something that could last twenty years?" *He's gone nuts!* **I thought. But, really, I was flattered.**

That afternoon we sought nourishment to help grow our burgeoning friendship. Mashama and I ate charcuterie and drank red wine at Local11Ten. We snacked on wings and fried things at the Crystal Beer Parlor and had a cocktail and more to nibble on in the form of a fried green tomato salad in the subterranean, haunted tavern in one of Savannah's oldest restaurants called The Olde Pink House. As the night drew on, I did my best to cross us over from eating to drinking, as I have a rule when making decisions about picking people with whom I want to work. If at all possible, I go out of my way to get good and drunk with them. That's when you really get to know someone.

We got good and drunk, indeed!

We were making our way back toward my house when we ducked into a local tourist spot for martinis, the proverbial "one more" drink. The liquor had loosened the mood considerably and the chitchat was getting deeper with each sip of gin and vermouth.

"What are you thinking?" I asked.

"About?"

"About Savannah? The bus terminal? Me? Life? You? Cooking? Food?"

"Okay, okay. I get it," she said, laughing. "I think I can do it."

"Do it? Do what? What do you mean?"

"All of it," she said flatly, with the confidence and optimism that would, for me, become two of her most defining characteristics. "When you were describing the building to me and showing me blueprints in your office, it all sounded so big. I've never been an executive chef before. It sounded scary," she said, sipping her martini. "I was worried it was too much for me for my first restaurant. But, being there, being in the space, I feel like I can do it." One more sip from her glass, "I know I can do it."

"So, you're interested in coming down here?"

The level of commitment that Johno was asking for with this partnership had my head spinning. He was intense, not in a weird way, just in a very excitable way. I was playing it cool, but of course I was interested in moving to Savannah, and now, as we neared the end of the day, I felt reconnected to this city and thought maybe it was exactly what I was looking for. I had loved Savannah as a child. I was open to loving it again.

"Yeah, I'm interested."

"Well, Mashama Bailey, I guess we should get a real audition together when we get back to New York."

"Yeah, definitely. You need to eat my food. We need to know that we are on the same page when it comes to food."

"Agreed. And, if you're going to make crab again, let me know and this time I'll be sure to have claw-crackers on hand. Wouldn't want that meat to go to waste."

She smiled at me. We were getting along, expanding our common ground.

"By the way, what does your name—Mashama—mean? How'd you get it?"

Mashama laughed a little bit, explaining "My dad was definitely a little bit Black Power in the 1970s. My parents gave us all African names—Mashama, Dawud, and Zuwena. 'Mashama' means 'surprise,' because I was, well, you know, a surprise when they had me."

"That's cool," I said, admittedly not having any real understanding of what Black Power was.

And then, Mashama added, "Johno, you should know something as we get into this."

"What's that?"

"I'm a little Black Power too."

I wasn't trying to scare this White man. I just wanted him to know where I stood. This was my way of letting him know that it was going to be important to me to support other Black people going forward, recognize the contributions of Black people in the past, and acknowledge all of the sacrifices that Black people have made. This was my way of letting him know that bringing Black people along and amplifying their voices to help shape and mold our culture would be very important too.

I nodded, "Okay, noted."

"No, really. That's how I was raised and it's in me."

I nodded a second time, too ignorant and embarrassed to respond, as I truly did not know what, if anything, it would mean for me, for us, that Mashama was "a little Black Power."

CARROTS IN HARISSA FOR MARCUS KENNEY

Serves 4

We barter with Marcus Kenney for artwork, partially paying him in the form of what we affectionately refer to as "Grey Bucks." He and his wife, Sarah, are regulars in the Diner Bar and in our dining room. Marcus is a great eater with a real Southern palate and he loves spice. These carrots are perfect for him.—MB

For the paste: Place all the chiles and the tomatoes in a bowl and cover with boiling water. Set aside to steep overnight.

The next day, drain the chiles and squeeze out the extra water. In a small skillet over medium heat, toast the caraway and cumin until fragrant. Char the bell peppers over a gas burner or under a broiler. Transfer to a bowl and cover tightly. When cool enough to handle, peel, stem, and seed the peppers.

Combine the chiles, tomatoes, caraway, cumin, bell peppers, garlic, coriander, and 3 teaspoons salt in a food processor, pulsing until everything is evenly chopped. With the food processor on low speed, slowly drizzle in the olive oil until fully incorporated. Add more salt to taste. Transfer the paste to a bowl.

Preheat the oven to 350°F.

Wash the carrots and remove and reserve the tops. Put the carrots in a baking dish, coat with ¼ cup of the oil, and sprinkle with salt. Cover the dish and cook in the oven for 30 minutes. Pierce the carrots with a fork to see if they are beginning to soften. When they are cooked half through, spread with 3 tablespoons of the harissa paste and cook uncovered for an additional 30 minutes, or until fork-tender.

HARISSA PASTE

3 ounces dried ancho chiles, seeded and stemmed

3 ounces chiles de árbol, seeded and stemmed

3 ounces guajillo chiles, seeded and stemmed

7 sun-dried tomatoes

1½ teaspoons caraway seeds, ground

1½ teaspoons ground cumin

2 red bell peppers

6 cloves garlic

3 teaspoons ground coriander

Kosher salt

1 cup olive oil

8 same-size carrots, with their tops

¾ cup olive oil

Kosher salt

Zest and juice of 1 lemon

1 tablespoon finely chopped capers

CONTINUED →

CARROTS IN HARISSA FOR
MARCUS KENNEY (CONT.)

Put the remaining harissa in a canning jar and store in the refrigerator for about 2 months. (Use on other roasted vegetables, eggs, chicken, and what have you.)

Finely chop the reserved carrot tops, add the lemon zest and juice, capers, and the remaining ½ cup oil, stirring to mix a salsa verde. Salt to taste.

Transfer the carrots to a serving plate and top with the salsa verde. Feed the artist in your life (or yourself, if you are the artist.)

CHAPTER 11

Gathered at our apartment on the evening of Mashama's audition were Jeremy and Andrew from PLD; my buddy Ed and his girlfriend, Kim; my friend Chris; and, of course, Carol and me. (Oh, and Flounder and a new ten-week-old puppy we'd named Otter.) Also, because I wanted Mashama to feel more like she was at home rather than on a performance stage, which just sounded horrible to me, I asked her if she would like to invite someone as her guest so at least there would be a person familiar to her in the room in case she was in need of a supportive smile. In my parents' home, our friends were always welcome around our dinner table and I had carried that same sense of hospitality into my own life. I wanted Mashama to feel comfortable in our home and to create a sense of us doing this together—throwing a party of sorts. She invited her brother, Dawud, who came with a friend. Ironically, this ended up working against her a bit, as Dawud's buddy turned out to be a vegetarian and Mashama hadn't planned for any non-meat-eaters. It was a small and kind of funny (at least to me) wrench in her plans.

Actually, Johno, the man was a vegan!

I have always suspected that Mashama chose Dawud to attend the dinner not simply to provide support but, rather, to spend some time with me so that she could get a second opinion on whether I could be trusted as a long-term business partner or if I might be just a big bag of wind.

I had other friends and family in mind to invite to Johno's that night, but these invites were so last minute and unexpected, none of them could make it. When I mentioned it to Dawud, I think he was intrigued. We were both raised around some good home cooks and he always cleaned his plate and often asked for seconds. I had never done a tasting before. I wanted an honest grade or a genuine reaction to the meal and the experience whether I got the job or not. I knew Dawud would be honest with me. This was an opportunity for him to see me in my element and, not completely knowing what to expect myself, I told him to bring a friend. Scrambling around at the last minute, the only person he could come up with was a vegan? Way to up the ante, Dawud.

Carol and I have a duplex apartment with two small bedrooms upstairs on a small, mezzanine level. The downstairs consists of a living area and a galley kitchen with a four-seat counter that literally extends from the cooking range, allowing perfect sight lines to whoever is doing the hard work. To the right of that, slightly behind the eat-at counter, there is an extendable wood dining table that can seat another six people if everyone went to the gym that morning and holds their breath that night. My suspicion that Mashama did want to get Dawud's read on me gained traction as the night progressed because even though I made the seating arrangements and had put Dawud and his friend at the table and me at the counter, Dawud, mysteriously, ended up seated right next to me at the counter throughout the entire dinner.

Mashama spent much of the afternoon in our kitchen, prepping, roasting, and chopping various foodstuffs. It was the biggest workout our kitchen had seen in some time. While she did that, I got the apartment ready to receive guests by breaking out the fancy dishes and glasses, setting up candles in the nonworking fireplace, and generally sprucing up the joint.

Johno jumped right into the front-of-house work. Throughout the day, he hung in the kitchen on his laptop or phone, he set tables, and he cued music. I remember feeling relieved that he kept himself busy, but I also wondered if he was just there to keep a close eye on me.

Mashama brought three young ladies, co-workers of hers, to assist with the heavy lifting for the night. One helped Mashama cook the dinner, of which there were five or six courses; another was there to clear, reset, and act as a bartender for a very thirsty group of attendees; and Paola, who would ultimately move to Savannah with Mashama as her first junior sous-chef, acted as server for the evening.

I'm so thankful for this group of ladies!

Truth be told, I don't really remember much of what we ate that night without going back and checking the menu. What I do remember was a very nervous chef. Oh, and that I was really nervous too. What if she sucked? What if Mashama Bailey couldn't cook? And what if I discovered that in front my friends? God, that would have been an awkward scene with me reverting to blowing a call into the pizza place around the corner.

Of course I was nervous! I was taking a big leap of faith, not only for myself, but with Johno. What if he were a crook! What if he had zero vision? What if I had zero vision? And worse, what if we didn't see eye to eye or if he didn't like my food? I am nervous all over again just thinking about it. But that night, we both had to put on our best faces and hope to get through the evening.

Jeremy and Andrew were the ones most connected to the project on a day-to-day basis besides me and cared the most about the chef who would cook in *their* space. It was by far their biggest undertaking since they had started their young design firm a couple of years earlier, and they were hoping that this restaurant would launch them into the sphere of elite designers in the industry (the year after we opened, they would become first-time finalists for a James Beard Foundation Award for best-designed restaurant in America for The Grey). They were already on the record with me stating that finding the best cook as fast as possible should be my priority over everything else. I knew if Mashama's food did not knock their socks off that night, I would be addressing it the next day, and rather than having supporters in my closest advisors, which I really needed from a momentum perspective, I would have active naysayers—possibly even lobbying for a return to Sloppy Plates McGee.

My good buddy Ed had become a successful guy on Wall Street, which I swear was just so he could eat and drink everywhere and anywhere. Ed, the nicest guy you could meet, made me look like a guy who didn't give a hot damn about food. The guy lived to eat and he had developed this informal grading scale for chefs and restaurants that went from A+ to F-. Most places never exceed a B and the only places I can think of that earned the rare A from him are helmed by chefs like Éric Ripert and Joël Robuchon (only in his most pure incarnation) or are time-tested institutions, like Raoul's in SoHo or Emilio's Ballato on the outskirts of Little Italy.

Chris had a palate like a chef's palate. He could taste every ingredient in a dish, and he knew if someone was making bullshit food or if they knew what they were doing. He understood the technicalities of flavor profiles and combinations. He understood balance in a way that allowed him to articulate it easily. While my food vocabulary mostly consisted of "delicious" and "not delicious," his was expansive. He talked of dishes that "needed to be brightened" or that were "missing a textural element" or that would "benefit from some fat to help balance" a certain spice. Sure, he was an advertising guy by trade and his cooking career was limited to his own kitchen, but his palate was professional-grade.

This was a small crowd and to Johno, a room full of heavy hitters. I'm glad I didn't know any of these details at the time. I had met Jeremy and Andrew prior to this evening and, frankly, that night, they seemed relieved that Johno was close to finding someone to partner with.

As people began to arrive, Mashama set out a whipped chicken-liver mousse. It was a hit. Small talk ensued over cocktails and noshes as Mashama worked feverishly in the kitchen. The vibe in the room was great from the get-go and it really did feel like Carol, Mashama, and I were hosting a dinner party together with an interesting group of guests, who, for the most part didn't know each other. That part of the plan was coming off without a hitch as people mingled.

I had to redeem myself with the chicken livers, but I had decided to opt out of the rosemary skewers this time around. I was pleased with the result.

Then it was time to sit down and start to hit the food. The opening course was a pickled shrimp dish—a first for me. It was pretty good.

I got these to just about where I wanted them. I wished they were more acidic.

Dawud's a handsome, solidly built guy. At six feet tall, around the same height as me, he took up some space but nonetheless plopped himself right down next to me in one of the four snug seats at the counter near where his sister was cooking. His hair was closely cropped and his complexion was a bit lighter than Mashama's, almost the color of peanut butter. But his smile, which was more broadly horizontal than turned up at the sides, like Mashama's, made it easy to identify them as siblings.

We began to talk. "My sister says this'll be the first restaurant you've ever been involved in," he noted.

"Yeah, that's true."

"Why a restaurant?" he asked. "Why now? Why Savannah?"

All fair questions. "I grew up in an Italian family. Food was everything for us. I've just always loved it and really, it is in all of my best memories from when I was a kid straight through now," I started answering. "The only times that I can remember that my family was both calm and all together was around the dinner table. Because my father was a fireman, even that wasn't a normal occurrence. I remember everything about it—the brown Formica table with the folding side leaves. The high-backed chairs my mother ultimately replaced with these wood chairs she bought when a local restaurant went out of business. She recovered the seats in vinyl, flower-print wallpaper. I remember the order we all sat in. It's been almost forty years since one of those dinners happened because two of my brothers were much older and they were out of the house by the time I was eight or nine. My mother was at one end, by the stove. My father parked at the other end near the door to the steam room. I sat on his left with my brother Glen between my mother and me. Across from us, were my brothers Frankie and Anthony. When our sister Maria came along, she got the added spot right next to my mother. That was our family unit, the seven of us for a very brief period in my life. You can't shake those kinds of memories, right? Because of the food of my childhood, I'm that guy who's asking Carol what we're going to eat for dinner in the middle of eating our breakfast."

Dawud laughed in acknowledgment, "That sounds like something my grandmother would say."

I went on, "Then Carol and I decided to buy this house in Savannah as an investment. For the future, you know, maybe when we got a little closer to retirement, we thought we would start to spend some time down South to get away from the long New York winters."

And that was the truth about our original plan.

"But," I continued, "one thing led to another, you know? A couple of things happened that accelerated stuff for me. My long-term business partner and I had been splitting up over the last few years, and the idea of starting over again in New York City just didn't seem appealing."

"It takes a few years to break up a partnership?" he asked genuinely.

Yes, brother! This is why, I realized later, I needed him in my corner there and then. My brother has challenged me his whole life, and I've never understood why. In this moment I gained some perspective about our relationship. I never thought he was interested in ANYTHING I did. I was the "little momma" growing up. I minded my sister and him after school and on the weekends during their formative years. I enforced the house rules, I disciplined them, and sometimes, according to them, made their lives a living hell. But here he was, looking out for me and keeping my best interests at heart. It felt really good to have him there.

"I guess. We were in business together for a long time. It's hard. Depressing, even, to unwind shit. We spent a career together trying to build stuff, and here I am now, just sort of unbuilding it. I'd basically had it with New York City, so I said to Carol at some point, 'now that we have this place in Savannah, what do you think of me looking for opportunities to do something down there?' Carol was, like, 'Why not?' So, I did."

What I left out of my conversation with Dawud is that I was pretty shot at that point in my life and career. My old business partner and I had a very rough relationship those last few years, and our breakup, as many are, was exhausting. We had been involved in a number of projects and companies over the course of our business life together. Those companies were mostly focused on content, media, and the arts. As our relationship expanded and wore on, I had become almost mercenary in my approach to doing things. I had lost focus and passion, and it all became primarily about money. That fucks with your judgment.

Our fate was likely sealed immediately after September 11, 2001, when the most promising company we had ever put together failed to get its second round of venture capital financing. That was a giant turning point for us, as we had invested nearly all of the time and resources we had in that one entity over the prior couple of years. It was doing everything it was supposed to do. We had raised millions in our first round of financing for it and all was going according to plan. But we needed another round of financing to continue to grow.

And then September 11 happened.

Being from Staten Island and the child of a family and a community filled with cops and firemen, combined with my own white-collar career in Lower Manhattan, the effect of that day was devastating to just about every person I knew. There was a seemingly unending stream of funerals and memorials to attend. At that time, Carol and I were living in Tribeca, just a few blocks from Ground Zero, which made it difficult to think of anything else.

The firehouse across the street from the front door to our apartment building was where my dad spent most of his career as a fireman. That afternoon, after the Twin Towers had already collapsed, I sat with a bunch of those firemen and we smoked cigarettes while my dog, Barnacle, ate and then vomitted American cheese from the deli next door—the only provisions they had left by the time I remembered he had never eaten breakfast. They took me into their fold as they waited to account for their one missing guy because firemen are families and thanks to my dad I was, in that moment, part of theirs. I needed their comfort and tried to give them mine. As we sat there and the afternoon dragged on, a buzz started mounting. A voice came over a walkie-talkie one of them was holding and squawked, "building number seven is about to collapse." The firemen and I nonchalantly walked to the corner of Church and Duane Streets and stared south. Number Seven World Trade Center collapsed soon thereafter and it was anticlimactic compared to what we had all already witnessed earlier that day. We lit our cigarettes, I am sure, and silently walked back to the firehouse, its enormous, double-garage doors open, and we sat back down quietly facing the street and my apartment building. Their missing guy returned at some point along with a French camera guy who happened to be filming him that day. I honestly can't remember when they showed up in that series of surreal events—or if I was even there when they did—but just like that they were back. Relief was the only emotion.

Thankfully, and this is weird to say, my brother Frank injured his ankle very badly years earlier, while he was a fireman, and he was no longer on the job. This turned out to be lucky because many of the men from his old firehouse, his best friends, were killed that day. My brother Anthony had also, thankfully, traded in his life as a policeman to be a lawyer, which kept him safe as well. My brother Glen was still a cop and we were able to account for him late that afternoon, and he was also unharmed. Although a back injury he incurred while working on "The Pile" (the name for the rubble from the fallen Towers) has been debilitating to him ever since.

And with all of that going on, my partner and I still needed our next round of financing for our company or it would go under and sixty people would lose their jobs. So, yeah, we beat the pavement in the weeks following the terror attacks.

It's difficult to describe how dreamlike the days and months were following that attack. As if trapped in a nightmare, the acrid smell of death and destruction filled our lungs each day when Carol and I returned home from work. We had to present identification at a military checkpoint just to walk into our neighborhood. And then there was always a piece of intermittent news of how a body part of a friend or an acquaintance was found in the rubble and matched to their DNA so that their family could finally plan a funeral.

The financing markets had gone completely dry. My business partner and I couldn't even get people who had been fully supportive of our deal before the attack to answer our phone calls. We failed at securing financing and the company went under.

We had to terminate everyone and wind it down. Tanking the company we had been working on for several years as a follow-up to and consequence of September 11 continued the nightmare.

After a while, we dusted ourselves off, preserved our remaining resources, and chased deals. But it was never the same for me. It was no longer about passion and creation. It had become transactional. I felt like I was beginning to lose sight of who I was personally and professionally over the next several years; and as months passed, I felt that it was time to move on. It was subtle at first and took several more years, but eventually we started the formal process of slowly unwinding things.

I was at my apartment in East New York when the terror attacks happened. 9/11 didn't push me out of New York City. The aftereffects of death and mass destruction couldn't quite reach as far as the border of Brooklyn into Queens. I heard the news just before a wave of radio silence went rippling through many New York neighborhoods. A few hours later, my grandmother and cousin were at my door to take me to the comfort of my family in St. Albans, Queens. We all stayed together for the next few days. I was working on Spring and 6th at the time, just a few blocks north of Canal Street. Our restaurant reopened about a week after that day and I returned to work, like many other New Yorkers, to restart our community after such a horrific act. I remember once we got together as a group that there was a moment of silence for all of the workers at the restaurant, Windows on the World, that had been at the top of one of the Towers. Those people were part of our extended restaurant family and we also knew that there would have been a whole group of undocumented people working in that kitchen whose names may never be known.

It hit me hardest once I got to Savannah—I knew I needed to fundamentally change my life. I focused on reclaiming my identity and rediscovering my passion for the things that brought me joy and pride. I needed my focus back, my motivation, and my sense of self.

When I found that building on Martin Luther King Jr. Boulevard and decided to make it a restaurant, I had begun to take that next step in listening to the voice that centered me. I was back to my childhood in a way, with food being the thing that gave me peace, comfort, and completeness.

I left all of that out of my conversation with Dawud, instead boiling all of the emotion I felt down to this: "I come from a place where family and loyalty are everything. That's how I was raised and I strive to be that person each day. I'm not always successful, but I think about it and I try. Food represents those ideals to me. So, building a restaurant with community and family at the heart of it—that means that I get closer to achieving that; to connecting completely with the values I was raised on."

Like the way his sister caught me off guard in my office during our first meeting, maybe I caught Dawud by surprise by showing my vulnerability. Or, maybe he just thought that I was full of shit. His face displayed no emotion, so I would never know if he believed me or not.

Dawud then asked me a question that I was not at all prepared for: "Do you think you're going to be good at it?"

That was it, in a nutshell—we all ask ourselves that question. Am I going to be good at it? In this case, "it" was made up of a lot of parts: the food, the service, the complete experience.

I hesitated for a moment to make sure I heard him right and then I answered, "Yeah. I think I'm going to be good at it. A lot goes into it, like any start-up, but I think I'm going to enjoy it, the making people happy part. I'm a pleaser and if I can please people through food and wine, the things I love most, yeah, I'm probably going to be good at it."

I don't really recall much of the rest of the night in terms of what else Mashama served. I focused on the guests and my conversations with Dawud.

I served:

Main
Pickled Shrimp and Celery Salad
Roasted Oysters with Parsley and Arugula
Market Salad
Chicken Schnitzel with White BBQ Sauce
Pan-Seared Trout with Pork Belly
Spicy Collards
Burdock with Oyster Mushrooms

Dessert
Apple Charlotte with Crème Anglaise
Chocolate Pudding and Pretzels
Cheese Plate

I do remember that at the end of the evening, Mashama finished by giving each person a Bit-O-Honey candy in its yellow-and-red wrapper.

I love penny candies because everyone has a favorite and they invoke strong childhood memories.

People were surprised by this because they didn't expect a fine-dining chef to offer them something so humble as a piece of nostalgic candy. They didn't expect Mashama to be able to connect them so simply and so completely with their childhoods.

And that is Mashama's genius. She's a chef who feeds people in ways that conjure memories while, at the same time, transporting them. This is a gift, almost magic.

But we didn't really know how people liked the food. I knew I mostly liked it. There were a few hiccups, but for the most part everything was good to really good to delicious.

If there was one dish that could have screwed up this whole thing for me, it would have been the burdock root. I was looking for salsify and had never even heard of burdock, but they looked very similar, like they were in the same family. I gave it a try without testing it. The burdock was starchier than I thought and didn't cook as evenly as I wanted it to.

The next morning, I talked with all of the guests from the night before. I started with Ed. He gave the evening's menu a solid B and a couple of dishes, including Mashama's chicken schnitzel with white barbecue sauce, a B+. I felt good about those grades, considering it likely took a Michelin star (or three) or being in business for a hundred years to get a higher mark from Ed.

Chris, minus the grading system, had the same take on things as Ed. He thought some dishes were off-the-charts good, the chicken-liver mousse being one, the pan-seared trout being another, and the apple charlotte, which utilized store-bought white bread as its crust, had taken his breath away.

That wasn't just any store-bought white bread. That was Arnold's, Brick Oven, PREMIUM, White Bread. My Nana's favorite.

Jeremy and Andrew were becoming flat-out smitten with Mashama as they were exposed to her more than anyone else in the room. They were never against her, but they held the design of the space in such high regard, I am not sure they would have thought any chef was really, truly good enough for this restaurant, the first preservation project in their young firm's life. But the draw of Mashama was undeniable and after eating her food and seeing the potential, even with some of the hiccups, they were completely on board and the four of us started to become a unit.

Carol loved everything about Mashama and that night.

Me? I thought the entire evening was a huge success. The food won me and everyone else over. The chicken liver mousse, chicken schnitzel, collard greens, apple charlotte, and the penny candy showed everyone that the person who had crafted their meal was a true talent. But more than that, it was Mashama's grace that was the clincher. It was the way she handled a kitchen full of strangers who were there for the express purpose of judging her skill as a cook, by not only feeding them but hanging out with them. By the end of the evening, we were all acting like a group of new friends, who had just spent a particularly memorable night together.

Yup, I was on board.

All that was left to do was to put together a deal between us that was tempting enough for Mashama to change her entire life to do it.

CHICKEN SCHNITZEL WITH WHITE BBQ SAUCE

Serves 4

WHITE BBQ SAUCE

2 cups mayonnaise

2 tablespoons apple cider vinegar

1 clove garlic, grated

1 teaspoon cayenne pepper

CHICKEN SCHNITZEL

8 boneless, skinless chicken thighs

Kosher salt

1 cup all-purpose flour

1 cup panko

3 eggs, beaten

2 cups clarified butter

1 lemon, cut into wedges

This was the dish that blew everyone away the night Mashama auditioned. She made it again for our first tasting with some of the New York City media and they were equally knocked out. It briefly showed up on the Diner Bar menu in the form of a sandwich, but I will always remember it as the dish that made me certain that Mashama's cooking was as good as I had hoped it would be.—JOM

For the sauce: In a small bowl, whisk together the mayonnaise, vinegar, garlic, and cayenne and set aside.

For the schnitzel: Season the chicken thighs with salt and set aside to rest at room temperature for 1 hour.

Place the flour in a shallow bowl. Place the panko in a separate shallow bowl. Dredge the thighs in the flour, then the egg, then the panko (this can be done up to 2 days in advance and kept in the fridge).

Line a baking sheet with a brown paper bag.

Heat the clarified butter in a deep, cast-iron skillet until it registers 325°F on a deep-fat thermometer. Add the thighs to the skillet and fry until golden brown, approximately 10 minutes per side. Using tongs, transfer the thighs to drain on the brown paper bag. Immediately salt the thighs. Let rest a few minutes, until cool enough to eat.

Serve the chicken with a wedge of lemon and the bowl of sauce for dipping.

CHAPTER 12

Back in Savannah, we had just started construction on the restaurant. Overall design was nearly finalized. Because Mashama had not yet started, this meant that I was finalizing the kitchen plans in the vacuum I had been trying to avoid. I started getting her on the phone with PLD and Larry, the kitchen consultant, to at least get some input from the person who would most likely be running all things food, even though we hadn't yet tied up deal terms between us.

Mashama, I would learn over time, is an eternal optimist, and just a little bit frugal about certain things. This means that when confronted with questions about costly pieces of equipment, she would often look for an alternative way to overcome whatever challenge we were facing rather than just saying, "We need this" or "We need that." This is not a bad trait. But sometimes, you just need the equipment.

I don't think of myself as frugal or an eternal optimist even though I often find myself wanting or even hoping for the best-case scenario. In my mind, the best-case scenario was to steer this kitchen design ship into port without veering too far off the course that had already been set. I knew I could cook the food with what they had already laid out; so I tried to not say too much even though I did a lot of research online and had become very partial to the European equipment, including the layout. But it was too late for that; so I figured French tops, burners under a flat cast-iron cooking surface, could get me pretty far, so I just made sure we got those.

I was having a conversation with Larry about an oven and whether or not we should invest the extra money and go for a "combi" oven, with a steam component. This was a decision that would affect several of the tradespeople on the job—the electrician would have to run different amperage, the plumber would need to install a water line and a drain, HVAC folks would have to account for the equipment in the hood design—and with me not knowing anything about the necessities of steam in Mashama's cooking, I brought her into it.

"Mashama," Larry said, framing things, "do you think you'll be cooking with steam at all?"

Mashama considered the question and her cooking experience to date and the different cooking lines on which she had worked. "No, I think I'll be all right, Larry. I can't really think of anything I would cook with steam."

BLACK, WHITE, AND *The* GREY

"Well, you know there's a trend toward clean cooking of fish and vegetables, so I just want to make sure you're considering this now, while we still have flexibility in how we are laying out the hot line and what equipment will go on it," Larry said, prodding her to consider it a bit longer.

I really didn't think I would do any steam cooking at the time. This question had me thinking that I wasn't in touch with the overall practices of the industry. Which maybe I wasn't. Sous-vide and hearth cooking, also big trends at the time, were not in my wheelhouse either. You can make good food without it. But Larry kept bringing up that damned combi oven.

"Yeah," she said, taking another moment, "for fish and veg, huh? Nah, I can just rig a steamer for that stuff if I need it. We don't need to pay for that."

I chimed in with a lilt in my voice, "Rig a steamer? What the hell does that mean?"

"You know, couple of hotel pans, hot water. We'll figure it out. It's just steam."

I laughed. "Okay, Larry, we'll figure out how to rig a steamer," I said, continuing to attempt to relieve a little of the tension I thought was building between Mashama and Larry. "You know," I joked with Mashama, "if you can figure out how to rig an oven, we can really cut the equipment budget in half. You know, a couple of hotel pans, some wood, a match. . ."

"Don't tempt me. I would love to cook like that," she said, laughing in return.

At this point, I was thinking *fuck these guys,* and I wasn't going to order a combi out of spite. Then, I thought of one key element that I hadn't considered before. I was there to lead a team of people, a team of people with different levels of experience and with different needs. Through this banter, I realized that everyone wanted the same thing: the most effective kitchen. We ordered the damned combi and now we all love working with it.

As we got to know each other better through conversations like this, we also began the work of trying to piece together a deal so that Mashama could get to Savannah. During this time, we got into the habit of getting together over dinner and drinks whenever I was in New York City. We would alternate picking the restaurant. This served to not only allow us to learn about each other, in a relaxed way, but to create greater shared experiences around food and drink. I usually picked an old New York City standard, the kind in which I felt

166

comfortable and one that likely served Italian or French food. Mashama, on the other hand, usually chose based on a chef whose food she wanted to try or a style of cooking that she thought we should try together.

Over these dinners we noticed we had a very similar sensibility in the food we liked and how we ate it. We liked to touch our food, so we would go to eat the pork buns at Momofuku Ssäm Bar. We liked simplicity on our plates, like the fresh anchovies and olives at Casa Mono. We liked the flavors of Mediterranean cooking and almost everything we ate at Estela.

During that period, I think the dish that I remember the most was something we ate at Pig & Khao, a spot on Manhattan's Lower East Side where the chef serves her version of Asian street food to a never-ending supply of hipsters and serious food lovers.

Mashama, of course, picked this restaurant; I had never even heard of it. The combination of the facts that Pig & Khao was Asian (a favorite fare of Mashama's), that it was located on the Lower East Side, a neighborhood she knew well, and that it was headed up by a young woman who was cutting her way through this crazy world of restaurants, made it a natural choice.

Carol and I arrived at the restaurant and Mashama was just a few minutes behind us.

The place was cool. An open kitchen filled by cooks wearing backward baseball caps was situated in the back left of the room with an eat-at bar in front of it. Dark wooden banquettes with lighter wood two-tops dominated the right side of the room. Guests practically sat in each other's laps to maximize the space. A white tile floor, Asian-style latticework on the walls, and the sound of hip-hop filling the room completed the transportive, energetic effect of the environment.

We quickly placed our order for predinner cocktails.

This was a sharing place and Mashama's pick, so she took to ordering for the three of us. This is dangerous, as Mashama and I suffer from the same affliction, which is, when a menu looks really good, we order everything—and this menu looked really good.

We were still getting to know each other and most of our interactions were somewhat awkward because we tried to download as much information to

and from each other as possible. We felt the most comfortable when we were eating together. I was very excited for this place. I had heard good things.

As we settled into our cocktails, I pulled a two-page document that was folded down the middle from the left breast pocket of my blazer and handed it to Mashama.

"What's this?" she asked as she took it.

"It's a letter of agreement. I sketched out a proposed business deal, you know, if you moved down to Savannah and decided to do this ridiculous thing with me. I figured it was time to see if we were on that same page too."

"Okay," she said, a bit surprised. "Should I read it now?"

"Sure. It's really short. It only goes on to a second page because I couldn't fit the signature lines on the first page," I said, smiling but not joking.

As she read it, the first of our food arrived.

I *was* surprised by this and I felt put on the spot. We had not discussed contract terms at all. I knew we were getting closer to making a deal, but I didn't think I was going to have to decide anything right now. The food was a welcome distraction as I collected my thoughts.

Our server, setting down the first dish, explained it as we listened to him. "This is the Sizzling Sisig," he said, with a wave of the hand over the plate in question. "Chef cooks the pig head forever. Then she takes all of the bits you would use to make a head cheese and combines that into this kind of Asian barbecue with some chiles. Then she picks it up in this cast iron at a really high temperature," he said, pointing out that it was quite literally sizzling loudly on the table, "and then we crack an egg into it." He made a semi-dramatic show of cracking the egg with one hand and dropping it into the middle of the sizzling plate. "Let that sit for a minute, because the meat is cooking it.

"Then," he finished, "you can just kind of stir that egg around it and start eating."

We were all mesmerized. As we waited for the egg to cook for a minute, Mashama finished reading the document, and when she was done she put it down in her lap. Silently, she grabbed her fork and with an easy deftness began to work the sunny-side-up egg into the auburn, glistening hue of the sizzling pig head meat.

Her touch was expert and light, and for a brief moment, she was finishing that plate of food just the way *she* thought it should be cooked.

Once Mashama was satisfied with her work, we got right in there, forks first.

That was one of the best things Johno and I had eaten together to date. We both acted like overeager children pulling out toys from a toy box to play with our favorites as we dug in.

On the first bite it was easy to know that it was heavenly. Ethereal, even. It was warm and spicy and fatty and chewy, and the egg coated everything in this sultry glaze. A second bite let you know the heat level of the chiles was right on.

I looked at Mashama and asked the obvious question. "What do you think?"

"I like it," she said, without hesitation.

"I was talking about the deal," I answered, smiling.

"So am I," she said, smiling back.

That sizzling pig was something special. But we remember how we came to terms on our agreement a bit differently. When we left dinner that night, we were still in negotiations. What Johno presented to me at dinner was a type-written letter that laid out the things we would have to settle, but I needed help. I wasn't sure if he wanted me to sign it right then and there. There was no way I was signing anything on the spot. The next day I called up my cousin Sonny for his business advice. I also called my Aunt Matt, who was a paralegal. They gave good advice on tightening up certain details and adding language that protected me in case it all went wrong. I sent this stuff to Johno, he made the changes I requested, we addressed all of the most important terms—profit-participation, equity participation, salary, provisions for mutual decision making—and we reached a deal.

SIZZLING SMOKY PIG
Serves 4

PORK RUB

1 tablespoon
black peppercorns

1 tablespoon
mustard seeds

8 ounces
dark brown sugar

½ cup kosher salt

2 tablespoons
hot paprika

2 tablespoons
garlic powder

2 tablespoons
onion powder

2 tablespoons allspice

1 tablespoon
cayenne pepper

We love pig. Who doesn't? We cemented our partnership deal over a dish similar to this recipe and it was put on our first menu. It was also our first "riot dish," meaning that if we took it off the menu, people would riot. Ultimately, we did take it off. (There was no riot . . . but it was close.) —MB and JOM

For the pork rub: Grind the peppercorns and mustard seeds in a spice grinder. In a small bowl, mix the ground pepper and mustard with the brown sugar, salt, paprika, garlic powder, onion powder, allspice, and cayenne. Set aside.

For the jelly: Combine the pepper scraps with the apple cider and white vinegars in a saucepan. Bring to a boil over high heat, turn off the heat, and let steep for 30 minutes.

Place the red chiles in a blender or food processor and blend into a paste. Strain the vinegar mixture through a fine-mesh strainer into a pot and add the chile paste, sugar, vegetable stock, and apple juice. Bring to a boil over high heat, decrease the heat to medium-low, and reduce by one-third.

In a small bowl, dissolve the pectin in the water. Add the pectin to the hot mixture and stir vigorously for 1 minute. Then add your diced bell and jalapeño peppers. Refrigerate until set.

For the pig: Rub down the pork butt. Let rest overnight, wrapped in the butcher paper, in the refrigerator.

Preheat the oven to 300°F (or prepare a smoker, if you have one).

Wrap the pig in foil. Bake (or smoke) that sucker for 8 hours. Check to see if the meat is fork-tender. If not, continue to cook until it is falling off the bone. (You ultimately want to be able to shred it with a fork.) Set aside to cool, reserving the liquid. When cool enough to handle, shred the meat.

Preheat the oven to 325°F.

Heat the oil in an 8-inch cast-iron skillet until it smokes. Add 2 cups of the pulled meat and cook for 3 minutes. Create a hole in the center of the meat. Crack your egg into the hole and pop the skillet in the oven for 3 minutes, or until the egg white is cooked through.

Remove the skillet from the oven and dollop the red pepper jelly around the sides of the pan. Garnish with parsley. Serve in the center of the table, inviting people to break up the runny yolk. Serve with slices of white bread to mop up the juices.

RED PEPPER JELLY

1 green bell pepper, seeded, stemmed, and cut into small dice, with all scraps reserved

1 red bell pepper, seeded, stemmed, and cut into small dice, with all scraps reserved

1 yellow bell pepper, seeded, stemmed, and cut into small dice, with all scraps reserved

1 jalapeño pepper, seeded, stemmed, and cut into small dice, with all scraps reserved

¼ cup apple cider vinegar

½ cup distilled white vinegar

20 fresh red chile peppers, stemmed and seeded

1¼ cups sugar

3 cups vegetable stock

1 cup apple juice

2 teaspoons powdered pectin

¼ cup water

THE PIG

1 (6-pound) bone-in Boston pork butt

1 tablespoon peanut oil

1 farm-fresh egg

Chopped parsley for garnishing

White bread for serving

PART III

HARD WORK, HEARTBREAK, AND HOPE

CHAPTER 13

"Hey, it's me," I said into the phone. "We're on for ten this morning. Right?"

Mashama, true to her life as a cook (they're more often than not, nighttime people) answered a little groggily, "Hi. Yeah, ten is still good. I just have a lot to do trying to plan for the weekend. Yeah, so ten is good. This way I still have the afternoon. I have to clean my apartment, go to Target, the liquor store, and a couple of other things."

"Okay. I think that's fine. We should be able to get through the list I have and settle on some things in an hour or two. Where do you want to meet?"

"Can you come to my place so I can clean until you get here?"

During this period, leading up to the opening, Johno and I spent all of our time together. We saw each other during the week and ate dinner together on the weekends. I didn't have any friends in Savannah, my spare time was very limited, and often my personal life and work life felt like the same thing.

I looked at my watch. It was just shy of eight in the morning. I still had to go to the site, which is what we called 109 MLK after construction got underway, and check on a few things. "Yeah, I can come there. I may be a couple of minutes late, but I'll be there."

I looked out the front window of my house to see what kind of day it was, but all I could make out was the opaque green of the outdoor foliage as the condensation that had formed on our windows obscured the square in front of our home. This was an accurate weather report, as it told me everything I needed to know about that Savannah morning and the day ahead: it was already oppressively hot and humid.

Flounder, Otter, and I steeled ourselves and headed out into the early morning soup. As soon as we stepped out the front door, the summer air blanketed us— my glasses fogged up, my ears were filled with the deafening buzz of the cicadas, the humidity instantly triggered my sweat glands, and what little breeze that existed carried the unmistakable odor of the paper mill—yes, it was summertime in Savannah.

As I began to walk the one-mile distance to the site, I started stressing over Mashama's fixation on her fortieth birthday, which was only a few days away.

She was throwing herself a birthday party over a long weekend and had invited about a dozen friends and family to come to Savannah and spend four or five days celebrating with her. As she had only been in Savannah a couple of months, she was using the occasion to also show everyone around her newly adopted city and spend some time out at Tybee Island, Savannah's beach community, where the main party would take place.

Having had my sister recently relocate to Savannah was a godsend, but it made this weekend more than just about my birthday; it was about her too. She was getting married in Savannah in a few short months. She was planning her wedding during the same time that the bus terminal was being reconstructed. My newly engaged sister was also finding her way in a new city. She expected me, her older sister, to help her along the way. She wanted me to be involved in the wedding planning and the timing couldn't have been worse for the new turn in my career path. She saw my birthday as an opportunity to invite family from the surrounding area and both sets of future in-laws to meet each other. It turned into an EVENT—an engagement party/fortieth birthday celebration and it needed my attention.

By now, we were fairly deep into construction, and our projected opening day of Memorial Day weekend had long come and gone, so the financial pressures had me feeling well beyond stressed out; freaked out was more of an appropriate descriptor. I spent each day not only physically sweating but also sweating all the details, small and large, my mood typically a millimeter away from turning from fretful to foul. I woke up each morning and went to the construction site. We were missing deadline after deadline and while many things felt as if they were going too slowly, the actual construction for example, other things seemed to be blasting along quickly because of the amount of money that was going out the door each day with no revenue coming in to offset it. Every rushed decision seemed like life and death to the successful completion of the project. I didn't mind working, that's not what had me so frazzled. I always have had a job to do, beginning with the newspaper route I inherited from my older brother when I was eleven. After that, I worked at a Carvel ice-cream store when I was fifteen, then a gas station, tire store, and car dealership. Next was valet parking, followed by roofing with my brothers in the summer, and then I was an accounting clerk at an independent film company, which was the job I took to work my way through college. Going to work is who I am.

But when Mashama finally arrived in town, after months of spending time together in New York City and negotiating a deal for her to come on board as a partner, I viewed it as the cavalry arriving. Finally, some of the pressure would be lifted from me because I would be sharing the load with her. But I never felt any less pressure. In fact, I felt the added pressure of having her professional well-being on the shoulders of the project, on my shoulders. I felt the additional pressure of having her draw a salary so she could afford to live. We honestly didn't have a clue about when we'd be able to open the restaurant because the schedule was so fucked up and it just felt to me like *everything* was added pressure and nothing seemed to relieve it. I was, quite simply, going crazy.

Mashama needing a week to plan, execute, and recover from her fortieth birth-day celebration added insult to injury. I couldn't relate to that or understand it. I was completely indifferent to celebrating my own birthdays and preferred for them to come and go as any other day did.

I needed to let off some steam, considering all of the changes I had made in my life over the past several months. Surrounding myself with my friends and family was going to help me do that.

Another emotion was beginning to surface in me around my relationship with Mashama over the course of that summer: frustration. Maybe because I was forcing the issue, I noticed a passivity in her around the tasks in front of us that I was, at times, reading as a dismissal of some of her responsibilities. She never said, "No, I'm not doing that," but there were things that we had talked about that were just not getting done.

In addition to the layout of the kitchen, our menu was a great concern for me. It was definitely proving to be Mashama's biggest challenge. Opening a brand-new restaurant required a brand-new menu, and she had never even written one before. I worried about this constantly, because though we talked about menu development over and over and over, progress, the actual development of recipes and the testing of them, seemed elusive. To me it was simple—think of a dish and cook it until it tasted good. Mashama, however, clearly saw the menu development process differently, and it didn't look to me like she was testing or cooking much of anything in those first few months. That was hard for me to watch without displaying some of the frustration that was creeping up in me.

Johno's anxiety and nervousness toward this process was starting to manifest itself in his attitude. He was mostly a level-headed thinker, but I was seeing a different side of him that I had not seen yet—the business side of him and his emotional investment in this project. He expressed himself the same way

no matter the size of the problem, with a degree of passion and seriousness, the intensity of which was slowly increasing over time. The man was working around the clock. And he expected the same from me. My view of the project was still fresh, so fresh in fact that I thought I could still change layouts, paint colors, and fixtures but those days were long gone.

And now this damned birthday party. As my frustration mounted, I was beginning to feel as if Mashama was not taking our partnership or this project seriously enough. And she was starting to have feelings, I suspected, that maybe I was a little more like a stereotypical business guy than I had let on during our courting period. Maybe she thought that I didn't actually want a partner as much as a subordinate. Maybe she thought that all of my talk of wanting a business partner, a strong female voice, a strong Black female voice, someone completely different from me, was more form than substance, just rhetoric.

I didn't understand this partnership and my role in it. I felt like a sidekick who was being brought up to speed on so many things that my head was often spinning. I was being bombarded with information and decision-making requests that I was not equipped to make, so, for the first few months, including right at that moment in time, I just kind of was being dragged along by it all. I needed a break in the day, the week. I needed another person to talk to other than Johno about this new phase in my life. This was one of those times in my career that I needed to seek out my support system so I could work out my fears and express my gratitude. I wasn't focused on the timing of it all because the restaurant wasn't close to being ready. With everything so new and tenuous, I wanted to celebrate all of the new challenges and changes I had made over the past eight months. I thought 2014 was going to be a good year.

As Flounder, Otter, and I continued our walk to the site, me stewing over Mashama's fortieth birthday break, my shirt darkened conspicuously with perspiration. With each step, I was being increasingly drained by the humidity and my own thoughts.

An unwelcome thought passed through my mind as the dogs and I entered the side yard of 109 MLK: *I hope I didn't screw up by partnering with Mashama.* A chill passed through me and I immediately shooed it away as I unhooked Flounder and Otter from their leashes and made my way toward the building.

As usual, I entered the building through the same side door that we had been using since my first visit. I immediately noticed something was very wrong in the old waiting room as soon as my foot landed inside the four walls. I took a second to soak it in.

And then I blew.

"Who the fuck told you guys to plaster that fucking soffit?" I shouted.

The place fell silent, and every one of the dozen or so workers who were in the building froze in place.

"WHHHOOOOOO?" I screamed louder, my voice breaking with rage while my dogs scooted back outside to take cover. "Who-The-Fuck. Told-You-Guys. To-Plaster-That-Fucking-Soffit?"

I just snapped. It was too much for me—all of it. I looked around and there was nobody in that space who was on my side. I had that streak in me, an inherited one, and I raged like I had done only a few times in my life.

When I was a child, probably the age of ten or eleven, we hunkered down a lot. My father was erratic, often angry. He would be a normal, blue-collar guy one moment, struggling to make ends meet, working two jobs, supporting five kids. It was the common story in my neighborhood. Then, suddenly, on another night, my house would explode into alcohol-fueled violence with my dad providing no way out of an altercation with one of my brothers, usually the oldest. An unbreakable desk chair, it was painted red, slammed across my brother's back as he went to the ground. Then from nowhere, blood spilling from my father's head as my brother Frank saved my oldest brother by slamming a thick, wood walking stick onto the top of my father's head. A policeman came, a friend of our family, and the mess was cleaned up. Hospitals were visited. Stitches were received. In the following days, it was chalked up to just one of those nights and we went back to normal, our dad also back to "normal."

During these nights, when my father would be angry at the world and at us, I began to develop a skill at processing what was going on and then reasoning it out, maybe rationalizing it. As my brothers got older and went out on their own, when my father tore through the house my mother and I would sometimes wait him out in a front room where she had her sewing machine set up, or in a foyer by the rear door that doubled as our laundry room. I quietly spoke the language of an adult to my mom, telling her that she needed to get us all out of that house to safety. When she refused, because she had no place to go, we would talk about how we might do the things differently in the morning to prevent this from happening again, ignorant to the fact that those moments had nothing to do with my siblings, our mother, or me.

As I got older, my reasoning and rationalization turned to frustration and then . . . extreme frustration. My father confronted me more, the last and youngest of the boys to make the crossover into manhood. I was confronted in our backyard one morning because I grabbed the wrong wrench as we worked on fixing the engine to his beloved fishing boat. I ran to my room and grabbed a baseball bat, a copper-colored aluminum baseball bat, and came back outside. He laughed at me, dismissed me.

In my late teens and early twenties, my father and I rarely, if ever, spoke. My own frustrations and anger grew. Unlike my dad, I was not angry at everything, but I was angry at a lot—at him, my mother, my limitations. My mother and I argued as often as we got along, the topic usually my father or my kid sister. I was shutting down, desperate to leave the place in which I was formed. All I could think of was finishing college and getting as far away from Staten Island, New York, as I could.

As soon as I graduated Pace University, a commuter school in Manhattan, I began sleeping on the couch of work friends of mine on the Upper East Side. Within a couple of years, I took a job a little farther away, in Connecticut, and then six months later I moved to Paris for another job. Finally, it felt far enough from all of that anger and angst that I felt was all around me.

But, the anger wasn't around me, it was in me. When I returned from Paris, after spending some time in Los Angeles with the same company, Carol and I got our first apartment together in Tribeca. On a morning waiting for my brother Glen to pick me up to go to a Knicks game at Madison Square Garden, Carol and I had a heated argument, about what, I honestly don't remember. As I was yelling, I punched a closet door in our apartment to punctuate some ridiculous point I was making. My hope was to create damage and I did. My hand fractured. Carol was scared to death. We were in our twenties.

I had never felt such intense loathing for myself as I did after that morning when I frightened the person who meant more to me than anyone. I swore to Carol that I would never do anything like that again, just as my father told my mother on so many a morning after. I feared who I was becoming, where I came from—from those same people who taught me about the comfort of family and food and loyalty. Luckily, I was so scared of it, that I began on a road to do better, to understand what had shaped me and to filter all of these emotions through a cleansing sieve. Luckily, also, Carol did not offer me a choice. Unlike in my own family, this was a nonnegotiable turning point and since then we have learned—I have learned—how to live and argue, sometimes with gusto, in a way that has sustained us for nearly three decades.

But that morning of the soffit, I regressed to the anger, the screaming.

Was I a fool? Was this the folly of a middle-aged guy who, again, did not know his own limitations? Was the anger directed at the guy responsible for this mess? Me?

But now this historic soffit, the one that envelops the room that was slowly becoming our main dining room, the very first architectural element that drew me to the building, was being plastered over, the original finish lost forever, because some shit-for-brains subcontractor just decided, on his own, to plaster it.

It was too much for me to take that morning.

"Nobody do another second of work to that fucking soffit," I shouted into the room.

I wasn't there the morning of the soffit debacle. I wasn't on the receiving end of Johno's rage until a few years after we opened. On New Year's Day, every year, we do a traditional Low Country oyster roast at the restaurant. It comes with other traditional New Year's Day fixin's, like hoppin' John, collard greens, and ham hocks. We mostly do a good job with controlling the crowd and providing good food and service. That year, we partnered with a local brewing company and we were expecting the largest turnout we had ever seen. But there was a problem. My sous-chef, who opened that morning because the majority of the kitchen staff had worked New Year's Eve service the night before, called, blurting out "Chef, we have no oysters." *WHAT? HOW? SHIT!* After a couple of phone calls, it became clear that we forgot to order oysters. I could feel myself starting to panic. It was New Year's Day, so all normal purveyors were closed. I didn't know what to do and it was too late to cancel the event. I called our major oyster supplier who was just down the road in Darien, Georgia, and, after pleading with him, he told me he would do his best. He showed up with about 800 oysters just as we opened. I located a few hundred more at a local seafood market for a grand total of 2,100 oysters. I threw my Greyhound, Daisy, in the back of my car and raced to The Grey. I was making progress under not the best circumstances for progress, and by now I was in full panic mode.

When I arrived back at the restaurant, the tension level was high. At first, I wasn't sure if it was me projecting tension or the fact that we actually had no oysters. The staff was frantic, setting up, everyone was moving quickly. I dragged the oysters to the backyard area where they would get washed and grilled for later that day. As I reentered the restaurant, standing a few steps inside was Johno, and he lost it. He was screaming and cursing and shouting and pointing his fingers and waving his hands at how fucked up this all was and how he couldn't see how we would open without any oysters. I was stunned at first. I wanted to snap into *my* finger-pointing and hand-waving mode right back because I had found a way to mitigate the situation, and unless we were closing, that behavior isn't helpful, so I didn't do that. He wanted an explanation, and when I spoke he seemed provoked. I knew we needed to just get back on track. But when I looked into his eyes, I saw rage—rage directed at me—and that rage affected everyone else in the building. The responsibility for not having oysters fell to me, but I turned on my heels and walked right out the front door. He wasn't going to yell and point fingers at me like I was a child in front of anyone, let alone our staff. I also wasn't going to let this service go up in flames without a fight. So I drove the two miles home, dropped off Daisy, and walked back into the restaurant without saying a word. I needed to pull us out of that crazed state. The kitchen was way behind and wasn't ready for service at that point, oysters were still being washed, our only bartender was late, and the fire for the oysters kept going out. No one was in control and all we could do was muddle through. We ended up 86'ing oysters with over an hour of service left to go. The most disappointing part of this for me was that we just went into survival mode. We focused on the parts that were broken about that day and not the parts that worked. We all ran around during that service trying not to look each other, and everyone ended up blaming themselves for such a terrible day.

The construction crew remained frozen, not daring to utter a word.

"Do you hear me?" I said, only slightly calmer. "Do you fucking hear me?" A couple of guys on a scaffold nodded.

I walked outside, shaking, near tears.

I waited until I was calm enough to dial the general contractor's number. "David," I said as politely as I possibly could, beginning to tamp down one of my weaknesses, "did you know that one of your subs is laying plaster over the entire soffit?"

Silence.

"David?"

"I'm around the corner. I'll be right there," he said, hanging up abruptly.

As I waited for David, I thought about all of the complicating factors of the project: The fact that the federal government was overseeing the preservation because I had applied for tax credits, resulting in the need to retrofit all of the functionality of a modern restaurant into the existing interior spaces of an old, old building. And, that Jeremy and Andrew had designed an interior that may have been easy enough to build in New York City, but in Savannah it was not at all easy because we just didn't have the local craftspeople to do complex steel, glass, furniture, and interior builds. We were also attempting to drive a rigorous schedule so that revenue would start coming in, but all of these circumstances were competing and causing delays, frustration, and, in the case of the soffit, a possible design catastrophe.

I was having the worst morning of the entire project. My wife was on the road for work constantly, my partner was distracted with planning her fortieth birthday party, and it seemed to me that our build team just did what they wanted.

As I looked down at the dogs, who were back, dutifully sitting next to me, seemingly trying to calm me with their presence, tears began to well up in my eyes. I was as low as I had ever been since starting the project. The need to cry began to overwhelm me and my vision blurred as tears collected, my lids the sidewalls of a pool.

I was turning to walk toward the back gate and just let it all out when, a gray Honda SUV pulled into the front of the yard. David, a tall, thin, gentle man with a shock of white hair, emerged from the car and walked toward me. I dragged my forearm across my face and opened my eyes to dry the newly forming tears.

"Hey, what's going on?" he asked.

I just forced a smile at him, preferring not to speak as I feared that my tears would again flow freely had I uttered a word. Instead, I nodded toward the interior of the space.

We walked in and he craned his neck, looking up at the soffit and the work that had been done to it.

"I will find out what happened," he said calmly.

"Okay," I managed.

"But that's your new soffit now. We can't change that."

"I know," I answered emotionally exhausted.

"I'll call Brian," David said, referencing our preservation architect, "and Jeremy and Andrew, and find out what happened."

I nodded.

"I don't think we would have been able to save that old finish, so I am pretty sure we would have ended up in this same place anyway," he offered.

"You're probably right," I whispered.

I looked at my watch, exhaling deeply, thankful that David showed up when he did, interrupting my mounting breakdown. I leashed up the dogs with an hour to get them home and then get myself to Mashama's for our ten o'clock meeting.

As the dogs and I walked, the temperature had easily climbed into the 1990s and the sun was high enough in the sky that there were fewer shadows to offer protection from its relentless glare.

We entered our house, and Flounder and Otter quickly stretched out on the hardwood floor to let the coolness lower their body temperatures. I ran upstairs to shower away the morning's sweat and grime and, maybe, some of the sadness I felt for a project that was officially sideways.

The shower worked, a bit. Donning a fresh shirt and pair of pants, I headed back out the door to slowly walk the couple of blocks to Mashama's, breathing deeply the entire way. I knew I only had her for a few more hours and I wanted to get my mood as stable as possible so that our time together was productive. Productivity was a great healer for me.

I knocked on Mashama's door at ten sharp and waited for her to answer.

Because we were seeing each other nearly every day, although our relation-ship was relatively young, we were quickly learning each other's habits. Not only were we working together on the project most of the time, but because Mashama was so new to town, we had also become fast friends, dining companions, and drinking buddies. So, when Mashama answered her door, I noticed right away that she was dressed in different gear than she would normally wear to meet about work. Her clothes didn't telegraph "let's meet about the menu, wine, tabletop, service, inventory, construction," or any of the million other things that were constantly rattling around in my head but more like, "I got a lot of shit to do today so let's make this fast." It seemed like meeting with me was not the top priority of what was certain to be a busy day for her.

As soon as I opened the door, Johno looked upset. It was all in his body language. I instantly became defensive.

This meeting *wasn't* a priority for me that day. Honestly, I didn't even know why we were having a meeting. I wanted to get it over with because I had a laundry list of things to do. I am sure I was a little standoffish because of it. If this were going on now, I would have just told him that I couldn't meet, but back then I wasn't sure how to establish boundaries.

"Hey," she said as I walked into her apartment.

"Hey," I responded, noticing that Mashama's sister, Zuwena, was also present for our meeting. While this caught me by surprise, Zuwena and I greeted each other warmly with a kiss on the cheek and hug, as we had gotten to know each other over the previous few months—particularly during that afternoon she spent at our home with her family and son, Malik. Obviously, Zuwena was there to kick off the upcoming weekend's festivities.

Zuwena showed up about twenty minutes before Johno got there. She had strict instructions to go upstairs and leave us alone once we settled in.

"Zuwena and I are going to have lunch and do some of the things I mentioned this morning to get ready for all of the other girls arriving," Mashama said, doing a bit of a dance, knowing that our to-do list was long.

This meeting started off very awkwardly. The more I talked, the more agitated Johno got. I wanted to just sit down and get into our agenda to avoid the situation getting any more uncomfortable.

"Do you want to meet later this afternoon then?"

"No, I think now is better. I don't know how long it is going to take once we leave and start running errands."

"When do the rest of the girls start arriving?"

"My cousin comes in tomorrow morning and then everyone else tomorrow night and Thursday morning."

It was becoming clear to me that the birthday weekend was starting as soon as I left Mashama's apartment.

I stood silently for a minute and all of the raw emotion I felt earlier that morning, the same emotions I tried to scrub off in the shower, began bubbling back up to the surface. I knew I did not yet know Mashama well enough to lose my shit or cry, so I did my best to remain stoic.

"Okay," I said, "I'm going to leave you two ladies to deal with these birthday preparations. I'll just head home and we can talk next week when it's all over."

"We can meet now," Mashama said in protest of my leaving. "Zuwena and I have plenty of time this afternoon to get everything done that we need to."

"No, it's all good," I shot back, doing a bad job of lying through my teeth. "You guys do your thing. I will just go do some work. No biggie."

I don't remember him saying even this much before he stormed out.

I walked out of the apartment without giving either of them more time to seriously protest my departure. I guess everything would wait another few days.

Menu development wasn't going to happen on that day. Our agenda was too long to flesh out a menu, and Johno knew we were not very close in that department. I did have my own agenda items to talk about, though, such as finding suppliers and reliable food sources.

Walking home slowly, I wanted to scream. Again. I tried to control my impulses, or at least the worst of my impulses. But I couldn't. I made a big mistake in that moment and pulled my cell phone out of my back pocket. I began dialing Mashama's number. Unfortunately, she answered halfway through the first ring, "Hi. Listen," I said, trying to mask my frustration, "we had a ten o'clock meeting."

"I know. I was ready to do it," was her answer, which, frankly, felt almost canned to me, like she knew I would be calling and had already formulated a response.

Of course I knew he was going to call me after leaving so quickly. When he left, he was *frustrated*.

"It was a business meeting," I responded. "It may not have felt like business because it wasn't in an office but, trust me . . . it was business," I said, my impatience building.

"I know it was business."

"Then why was your sister at our business meeting?" I asked.

"Because we have stuff to do later in the day," she said, her defensiveness building.

I was really confused that he was so surprised.

"But it's Tuesday. It's a workday. Why do you have plans with your sister on a Tuesday? Why didn't we meet someplace your sister wasn't? My house? The site?"

"I didn't know we had a full day of things to do," she now snapped back at me. "I told you that I needed to clean my apartment."

"We always have a full day of things to do. We still don't have a menu for our opening. We haven't tested more than a couple of dishes. We still have a million things to do. There's always something to do and you're drawing a salary to be here. I need you to take this as seriously as I do." My second bout of anger of the day was bubbling up to the surface the more I spoke.

In the beginning, I often felt like I was being lectured or coached by Johno. As we began to understand our business, it was just the two of us and I was often a sounding board for his theories about restaurant service and culture. I felt like we were casual with one another but rarely did he hold anything in and was often trying to convince me of one way of doing things or another. The approach I have developed with him over time is to hear him out, let it register, and then give him my feedback. In this instance, still new to the dynamics of the partnership and our communication, our arguing back and forth just elevated matters.

"Johno, I take this seriously," she said, pausing to draw a breath. "As seriously as you do? I'm not sure. I'm not even sure what that means. Do we really want two of us taking this as seriously as you do? I don't think it'd be smart to have two of us acting like you. And don't throw the fact that I need money to live in my face. That's not fair. What should I do? Get a job at the Pink House till we open?"

I paused a second too long, considering her offer.

Then, "That's stupid," I blurted out reactively, "but we need a menu. We really do."

"I know we do, and I could have met this morning, done what we needed to do, and then had the afternoon with my sister to get ready for this weekend. This damned project is still going to move along at the same snail's pace it's been moving at since I got here. It even feels like it's beginning to slow down some."

It felt that way to me too—especially after my experience at the site earlier that day, but I said nothing and let the silence hang for a bit.

She took another breath and composed herself, finishing with, "Do you want to meet?"

"No, I don't. I don't like you springing this shit on me. We had a plan. It's a workday and you just have your sister show up. It's kind of bullshit. It's not professional," I said, making it personal.

He did make it personal. We have had dozens of meetings at his house when his personal life spilled into our time.

"Fine. We won't meet today. Probably for the best," Mashama said, her voice cracking with emotion.

"Okay," I said.

She added, "I am professional and I do take this seriously. I moved here. I picked up my life and I brought it here. That's how seriously I take it. Don't you get that?"

I did get that. I knew from witnessing it that Mashama had put herself in a new situation, one that yanked her completely out of her comfort zone.

"But that doesn't mean that I gave up my whole life for you or a restaurant," she continued. "I'm a grown woman and I know what we have to do and I'm doing it.

If you think, though, that because I'm turning forty and that means something to me, or that I have other things in my life besides you and a restaurant, that makes me unprofessional, I can't help that. You are who you are and I am who I am. *And we're different."*

It was clear with this weekend that I was pulling away from our normal routine. I was wearing a lot of hats at the time. Moving into this next phase, I needed to start menu development. I was looking for suppliers and farmers at the health food store or in the local yellow pages, trying to find someone who could help me, or even show me how wholesalers and purveyors worked in Savannah. This was taking longer than I thought. It was impossible to do any networking with local chefs because, before I moved to Savannah, we had decided to only reveal my occupation on a need-to-know basis. Which was silly when you think about it because the restaurant business is built on a network. Our train of thought was that keeping the nature of our relationship a secret gave us control of the situation. In reality, it gave Johno control over everything, including me and how I was trying to source ingredients. Sure, we would be able to manage people's expectations of who would be doing the cooking, what the space would be like, and when we would actually open, and this allowed us to not have to deal with those pressures. But Johno having control over everything else did not need to happen. He should have focused on his part and I should have focused on my parts of the restaurant, but because of the secrecy, everything funneled through him. This frustrated him even more and he knew about stuff he didn't need to know about, including my personal life. He had too much information surrounding my birthday weekend.

"Yes," I agreed, "we are very different. Bye," I said, hanging up the phone.

I got back to my house and went to my desk. I just sat in my chair for a few minutes and took stock. It had all happened so quickly. Somehow, almost without even noticing, I was now living in Savannah, Georgia, a city I barely knew. I was building a very expensive restaurant and exploring an industry I knew nothing about with a brand-new partner with whom I was maybe not as similar to or familiar with as I had first thought. I was, effectively, relying on a bunch of people who were complete unknowns to me.

Was I overreaching? I couldn't build a building or lay out a commercial kitchen by myself. I certainly could not develop a menu. I needed someone to do it with me, someone who wanted to do it with me. And then a thought flashed through my brain. I pretended I hadn't noticed it. I told myself I hadn't. But I had.

We were two months into our partnership, two months of learning to operate as a team and my teammate said she needed a break. She needed a moment to recharge. She needed time away from me, the project, some of it, all of it, to regroup. This worried me on every level. Our undertaking was to be for years and I figured they were going to be hard, grueling years. And here we were, still in the starting blocks and we were maybe confronting a significant difference in how we worked. I was full steam ahead, have a breakdown, lose your shit, dust yourself off, and keep going forward. But Mashama was different than that, we had just established that in our phone call. She needed space and perspective. But was it more than that?

It flashed again. . . .

Is it a Black thing?

A family thing?

A culture thing?

A Black, family, culture thing?

Or, was *this* the Black Power that Mashama had talked about? Was this just an exercise in power dynamics?

Black Power is not about exercising power over White people. It is not about stereotypes of Black culture or validating those things. It is about understanding that we *are* in a subjugated position, shining a light on that fact and helping each other by creating and sharing opportunities for self-determination.

And then, deliberately, I steadied myself and let the thoughts in the recesses of my brain reveal themselves.

These thoughts and questions in my head began to shape themselves into the one question that I feared the most.

Was I questioning Mashama's work ethic *because* she is Black?

Was this a part of my racism, my legacy, that remained hidden away in my unconscious?

Had I not vanquished such an abhorrent thought from the inside out?

Of course I had.

Maybe not?

Yes! I had.

Maybe not?

My mind continued to spin frantically.

Where was this coming from?

Why was I even thinking about skin color? Race? Racism? My racism.

Why do Black people remain stuck in a collectively subjugated position in America? Is it the Black community's fault? Society's fault? White people's fault? Everyone's fault?

Johno's question makes me think of Dr. King. Our subjugated position in America is designed by the very system that stigmatizes our skin color. Black people are the only ethnic group that have been enslaved on American soil. People who remained enslaved until the Emancipation Proclamation was signed and we were set free with an empty promise of 40 acres and a mule. The people who helped build the economic base for America were repaid with no land, no property, no business, and no path to prosperity. We were set free to starve. The concept of reparations for Black folks in this country seems to be dismissed, but we are owed that.

I considered all of the books about race, class, and culture in America that I had read in my thirties. What had I learned? Anything? Nothing?

Why am I even fucking around with this restaurant and all of this societal bull-shit that is so far out of my comfort zone?

If Mashama was just not cut out to work at the necessary intensity level, did the reasons for that—whatever they were—even matter?

With all that I was risking, was it possible that Mashama was not the right partner?

As I sat in my desk chair, grappling with all of these questions, it also occurred to me that it might be that I am a racist asshole—the type of person I had all but exiled from my life. Was I that guy who was talking a good game about progress, diversity, women's empowerment, and opportunity when it was easy for me to do so because there was nothing at stake? Did I then quickly fold when my own interactions with my new Black business partner didn't go exactly according to plan, to *my* plan?

This was a crossroads in the very fundamentals of what Mashama and I had agreed to try and build. We were taking a shot at something new for each of us. A new relationship, a new way of thinking by passing our thoughts through a joint lens rather than just mine or hers. Being in business with anyone new was going to be hard, but by purposely going into business because there was real difference and distinction between each of us, that would be more difficult. Right?

I began second-guessing my second-guessing. I sat there, thinking. How long? I can't say. I made myself confront the thoughts that I knew were the imprinting of my childhood, my upbringing, that very environment in which I was raised that I passionately loved and, sometimes, loathed simultaneously. I sat there until emotional exhaustion was the only thing I felt. Then I reminded myself of the woman I had gotten to know over the previous nine months. She was humble, human, kind, and, like all of us, flawed. She upended her life to do something bold, crazy even.

I sank further into my chair and my head began to clear. The cacophony that had begun with the sound of my own voice screaming at the subcontractors plastering the soffit earlier that morning began to quiet. I grew calmer and more reasoned. I began to focus my thoughts on Mashama and wondered what she was thinking at that very moment.

I usually don't like talking about every little thing. That shit was starting to drive me crazy. I damn sure don't like being managed, and working with Johno this closely was overwhelming. But, I was acting like I didn't have any stake in this and I was too insecure to reveal my hand. To show him how little I knew about building a restaurant was not an option for me. He knew that I was green and that was his to own. That I needed help—and I didn't know how or who to ask for it—was mine to own. He trusted me enough to invite me down here to build something and I felt like I was failing, which made me feel disappointed in myself. I was kind of pissed that he was piling shit on. He seemed to have no room for me to push any of my pressures back in his direction, so I didn't. That didn't feel like an option.

I remember on my first visit to Savannah, Johno and I were walking through Forsyth Park on our way to a restaurant and he asked me if I could be creative in a city so different from New York. Then we talked about traveling for inspiration and eating food together. In this conversation, he let me know that he understood creative people and that they needed inspiration in order to create. I liked that he understood that was important to me and that was a big part of why I moved down to Savannah, yet I was still treating him like he didn't get it, like he didn't understand what I needed to thrive. I was so out of my element that I resorted to calling old purveyors in New York, for goodness sakes. Johno checked on me daily and I never had much more to say than, "Yes, I'm working on it," or, "I have this product I want to use," which was all bullshit. The truth is that I had no idea how to open a restaurant, not even a little bit, and we had no resources. How could he not fucking figure that out? He knew who I was when I came to Savannah. I thought that he would understand that I needed time to adjust, but how would he know that if I didn't tell him? I never told him. What was I hiding? Can I command a kitchen staff? Will people want to eat my food? Can I do this? Should I do this? I couldn't keep stalling. I needed to figure something out. Being this close to everything—Johno, the building, the heat, the tension—had my vision cloudy. The fear of telling him exacerbated the fears that I already had. Pushing Johno away was not the answer and from that phone call I felt like we could've both been in a bad place. This was not a festive way to go into my birthday weekend.

Did she hate me? Was she ready to leave?

The frustration that I felt in her apartment earlier in the day was real and had definitely been building for me since she arrived in Savannah. Mashama was complicated. The vulnerability she showed during that first meeting in my office in NYC was part of who she was, but there was also a guardedness to her that I also noticed, which seemed to be, in many ways, increasing. I felt often that we were in a sparring match over being straight with each other. I wanted her to tell me the truth, the whole truth, and nothing but the truth. But I also knew that I was so jacked up from the pressure that I was not sure I would be receptive to real truth, her truth. Did she regret moving to Savannah? Was she in over her head? Did she want to kick me in the shins every morning when she saw me?

These were questions I wanted answers to, but I didn't know how to ask them and she was certainly not giving up any more information than she felt was necessary.

So, I did what I knew how to do . . . I just kept the pressure on with a constant stream of meetings, to-do lists, and reasons to be rushing toward a lot of different things simultaneously. I think I was running us both through a gauntlet, or running myself through a gauntlet and trying to drag Mashama by the hand through it with me, to gauge her commitment to this project and, I guess, to me. Her response to that seemed to be what was taking place between us over her birthday and the break she required from all of it. She didn't want me in her apartment this morning. She didn't want to work today. At least that is what it seemed to me. So why wouldn't she just tell me that?

I felt like what little trust we had established since we met was quickly eroding. My response to that was to push harder. And the more I pushed, the less she trusted me. The less I felt she trusted me, the more I pushed. We were entering a cycle that has been ending relationships of all sorts since the beginning of time.

When I envisioned our partnership, I never considered the downsides of it. I never considered that all of the differences between us—race, gender, upbringing, all those differences that I found so important—were also complicating factors and I hadn't allowed for that. I only considered what good would come out of those things. It is what I have always done. It is this very naivete that allows me to be an entrepreneur. It is the possibilities of things that get my attention; and when those things start going wrong, then I go through my cycle of "adjustment." It is how I live my life. I am not proud of this or ashamed of it. I am just reconciled to it. It is why, when I wake in the morning, I am usually in that fetal position, because I often spend the night thinking about what adjustments will be necessary that next day and how I am going to manage them. At this moment, in this relationship, there were adjustments to made.

Mashama and I had to fix this relationship, or it wouldn't last. We had to start building trust instead of eroding what little we had or we would fail. We needed to be straight with each other. We needed to be straight about our lack of trust— whether our lack of trust for each other was based on race or fear of vulnerability.

In spite of all of my self-reflection and the exhaustion I felt from having to unpack my subterranean bias about race, I was also just still pissed off at Mashama and I needed to get that cleared up too.

This partnership was too new for me to hand over everything, all of my inner thoughts. That's ridiculous, I know, but we were building something out of thin air and we didn't know if it was going to work. And I was afraid of not having any creative rights to what we had done so far in the process. I had

not known this man longer than six months. He's White and, in business, there are too many horror stories of White people taking advantage of Black people, especially creatively. That's not everything, but that was enough for me to be cautious, and my definition of cautious may be different from someone else's, like Johno's, but that's how it was for me. I had never been in a position of power since I'd arrived in this town and what little control I had, I wanted to keep, at least some of it, and not be completely vulnerable.

MY GRANDMOTHER'S SUNDAY GRAVY

Serves 12 to 16

TOMATO GRAVY

½ cup olive oil, plus more as needed

4 links sweet Italian sausage

4 links hot Italian sausage

1½ pounds oxtails

2 lamb shanks

3 or 4 pigs' feet

2 pounds beef eye round, tied

1 to 2 pounds pork or beef ribs

1½ pounds bone-in lamb stew meat, cut into chunks

2½ (6-ounce) cans tomato paste

Kosher salt

Freshly ground black pepper

4 (28.5-ounce) cans crushed San Marzano tomatoes

Sunday Gravy is the thing that has always comforted me more than any other meal. My grandmother made a two-gallon stockpot of gravy every Sunday morning, getting it on the stove by 8 a.m. so that it would be ready for supper at 2 p.m. sharp. You could scale this down to serve a small crowd, but Sunday Gravy is meant for a *real* crowd. The day of the soffit and my fight with Mashama was one of the worst days for me in the history of The Grey. I needed Sunday Gravy—and I needed it bad—to soothe all that ailed me.—JOM

For the gravy: Place an extra-large (25- to 30-quart) stockpot over medium heat. Pour the ½ cup olive oil into the pot. When the oil is shimmering, add all the meats and start browning in batches. You want as much surface area of your meat as possible to come into contact with the hot oil. Using tongs, turn the meat pieces until they are crispy and brown on all sides, then transfer them to a platter and continue cooking in batches, adding oil as needed, until all the meat has been cooked. Set aside.

Add the tomato paste to the pot in which you cooked the meat and stir to deglaze the bottom of the pot, melding with the oil and brown bits, for 3 to 5 minutes. Season with salt and pepper as you stir. Add the crushed tomatoes and stir to incorporate well. Add salt and pepper to taste. Return all of your browned meats to the pot over medium heat. Let the mixture come to a boil. Decrease the heat to low, cover (leaving a small gap between lid and pot), and simmer for 4 to 5 hours.

For the meatballs: While the gravy is simmering, peel off and discard the crust from the waterlogged bread, leaving just the white interior. Chunk up the bread and press it into a fine strainer until you have expressed as much of the liquid as possible.

In a large mixing bowl, combine the strained bread, ground pork, ground beef, garlic, parsley, eggs, Parmigiano-Reggiano, salt, and pepper and mix well with your hands until fully combined. You want a firm consistency that holds its shape but is not stiff. If your mixture is too soft, add some of the bread crumbs to bind.

Using your palms, roll the mixture into 16 (1- to 1½-inch) balls, placing them on a sheet pan as you work. Next, do what my grandmother did: Roll the remainder of the meat mixture into about 20 (½-inch) mini meatballs.

Line a platter with paper towels.

Place a large cast-iron skillet over medium-high heat and fill it halfway with olive oil (about ½-inch deep). In batches, add the large meatballs and fry, turning them while they cook until they have a nice, dark brown crust on all sides but are not cooked through. Transfer the meatballs to the paper towels to drain. Continue until all the meatballs have been cooked, replenishing the oil as needed. Turn off the heat under the skillet.

Add the meatballs to the gravy pot, tucking them in here and there. Let your gravy do its magic, continuing to slowly cook over low heat for the next 4 hours or so, until the meat cuts are falling apart and the flavor of the sauce has deepened.

Return the skillet with the residual oil to medium heat. Add the mini meatballs and fry until crispy, brown, and cooked through, transferring them to the paper towels to drain. Leave on the stove for

MEATBALLS

2 loaves stale Italian or French bread, soaked in lukewarm water for 2 hours

1 pound ground pork

2 pounds ground beef

4 cloves garlic, finely chopped

1 handful chopped Italian parsley

2 eggs

2 handfuls freshly grated Parmigiano-Reggiano cheese

½ teaspoon kosher salt

½ teaspoon freshly ground black pepper

½ to ¾ cup dry bread crumbs (optional)

1 quart olive oil for frying

CONTINUED →

MY GRANDMOTHER'S SUNDAY GRAVY
(CONT.)

Kosher salt

Olive oil for drizzling

4 pounds dried pasta
of your choice
(I prefer penne rigate
or rigatoni)

Freshly grated
Parmigiano-Reggiano
cheese for garnishing

2 handfuls chopped
Italian parsley

4 loaves crusty bread

4 bottles nice table
wine from Chianti
or Montepulciano
d'Abruzzo

1 pound ricotta cheese

Crushed red pepper
flakes for serving

people to nosh on as they come into and out of your kitchen while your gravy is cooking.

In a stockpot large enough to hold the water needed to comfortably boil the pasta, add a generous amount of salt, bring the water to a boil, and add a drizzle of olive oil. (The salt gives the pasta flavor, but I think the oil is just tradition.) Then dump in the pasta and let it boil for the requisite amount of time, stirring occasionally so it doesn't stick together. I usually set my timer for 2 minutes less than the cooking time on the box and taste it at that point, as I like an al dente pasta that is just north of crunchy.

While your pasta is cooking, skim the grease off the surface of the gravy. Transfer the meat to various serving platters. I like to put the meatballs and sausage on one platter (I usually cut the sausage into chunks); the shanks, ribs, pigs' feet, etc. onto another platter; and then I thinly slice the eye round and lay that on another platter, drizzling a little of the gravy over the top of the eye round.

At this point, your pasta should be ready to get off the stove. Pour it into a colander to drain and then quickly transfer the pasta to a jumbo bowl and pour enough gravy over it to coat all of the pasta as you mix it. Divide the remaining gravy among gravy boats or small bowls. Drizzle olive oil over the pasta and then garnish with a handful each of Parmiggiano-Reggiano and the parsley.

Place the loaves of bread and bottles of wine here and there on the table. Put everything else on the table all at once, passing bowls of the ricotta, crushed red pepper flakes, and extra Reggiano and the gravy so your guests can garnish their pasta just the way they like it. Enjoy your food, family, friends, and life.

CHAPTER 14

In April, just before Mashama relocated to Savannah, we decided to go on our first eating trip and to do it in Italy. And by "we" I probably mean me. As the guy who came up with the bright idea of opening a restaurant in the Southern United States and convincing Mashama to move down there and do it with me, I thought it was important to share the food of my grandparents and my childhood with Mashama—the food that made me love food. I became obsessed with the idea of us traveling together through Italy for a couple of weeks and exploring some of the areas that produced the things that were staples in my life—Parmigiano-Reggiano, mozzarella di bufala, prosciutto di Parma, bacalao, polenta, ragù di cinghiale, torta di ricotta, Chianti, Valpolicella, grappa, and limoncello . . . the list was endless.

It really isn't fair for Johno to think that we went to Italy only because of him. I love Italian food and was really excited to learn more about a cuisine that I was so interested in.

Mashama and I flew into Milan together and Carol met us there early that first evening, as she was already in Europe for business. We spent our first two days in that city, acclimating to the jet lag and exploring before we hopped into a car to drive around the smaller towns and cities throughout the top half of the boot. Our goal was to eat or drink something special or particular to each place in which we stopped for at least an overnight.

It was just after our arrival in Milan, and Mashama and I were looking for something to eat, cutting across the Piazza del Duomo, famous not only for the church, the duomo from which it took its name, but also for the West African and Indian street vendors selling tchotchkes to tourists. It was crowded in the square, and it was difficult for Mashama and me to keep track of each other. I moved quickly and was mostly uninterested in the knickknacks, but Mashama was stopping at the trinket-filled blankets that were laid out on the ground. On top of each, there was a variety of wares, such as small jewelry pieces, cheap paperweight statues of the Duomo, and flying things that the salesmen would launch into the air hoping to attract the eye of a child who would compel a parent to buy one.

I had never been to Milan and wanted to see everything.

I turned to look again for Mashama and saw that she was being followed and talked to by one of the African guys, so I made my way through the crowd and back toward her to intervene. From traveling for work and pleasure, I had learned that the best way to deal with an aggressive street vendor in any city was to be aggressive back.

"No, grazie," I said in a loud and emphatic voice as I approached him.

In near perfect English, he said back to me, "I don't want anything, mister." And then he turned back to Mashama and, as he tried to tie a thin, multicolored woven bracelet onto her wrist said, "Here, you take this. This is a gift from me."

Speaking loudly to him, I said, "She doesn't want it," trying to brush him off.

He ignored me, and so I took another step toward him.

"Johno," Mashama snapped, "it's fine."

She held out her wrist and allowed him to tie it on. "Is this your friend?" he said, looking at me.

He slipped that thin piece of string on my wrist so fast! This man was giving me this gift whether I wanted it or not.

Mashama nodded.

"One for you, too," he said, "because you're friends."

"No, I'm okay. I don't want one. But thank you."

He looked hurt, as did Mashama.

"We'll take it for my wife," I said, acquiescing. He smiled at us and this seemed to make Mashama feel better as he handed a second bracelet to her.

I dug into my pocket and pulled out a two-Euro coin and offered it to him.

"No, thank you, mister," he said. "It was a gift for friends."

"We appreciate it. Thank you. But here, take this," I responded.

"No, it is a gift," he insisted and then he did something I never expected. He just started walking in the other direction after having declined the money for the two bracelets he gave us, his "friends."

I turned to Mashama. "Why's the African guy giving you free stuff?" I asked.

"Really, Johno? Look around this square," Mashama directed. "How many Black people do you see who aren't selling something?"

I must admit, when the African salesman first approached me, I thought, *Oh, no, now I have to buy something and I was really just looking, taking it all in.* **Then I quickly realized he was just offering me a peaceful token. It was sweet.**

I looked around, taking a real look. There was a grand total of one Black person—Mashama. I looked back at her with nothing to add to her observation.

"He was just happy to see someone who looked like him here to buy things instead of having to sell them," she responded.

I'm not even sure if that was true. I'd bet money that I wasn't the first Black woman visiting that square. Maybe he just thought I was cute.

She was happy, really happy. The small connection she made with the guy made her feel something.

I was probably thinking about how street vendors have such an uncertain and difficult lifestyle. That would drive me nuts. I was happy that he was happy.

This interaction struck me because White people never come up to me and just give me shit for no good reason. Was this part of being Black, like being a Marine, where you are part of a group that always looks out for you? This stranger appreciated Mashama, even though he did not know her, because, it seemed to me, they shared a skin color. It was more puzzling because Mashama's Black experience was an American one and her admirer's experience was probably primarily an African one. It made me wonder if there was a universality to the Black experience, or at least being Black in the Caucasian world. No matter how hard I tried to relate to Mashama, there's a part of her experience that I would always be outside of and looking in. That's the way it has to be, I guess. But it was eye-opening for me to witness this interaction and not really understand it.

That evening we ate fresh seafood at a place in the heart of Milan. We entered into a busy market that would have been at home on the Jersey Shore. At a long counter, beautiful fish, squid, oysters, clams, and crustaceans were displayed on beds of ice. Young, hip Italians chaotically surrounded the counter to buy food to take home or to eat there at small, casual tables, washing down their meals with ice-cold bottles of Moretti beer or small juice glasses filled with red or white wine.

While we were tempted to just join in, we continued through the bustle to a back stairwell that led to a second floor and a more traditional restaurant setting upstairs. We had a reservation in that space, where the same beautiful seafood we saw in the market was served in a quieter environment. As we entered the room, affable waiters buzzed around, serving the freshest food to a full house. The mood of the room matched our mood perfectly. Mashama and I were still riding high since arriving in Italy, Carol had gotten to Milan from London without a hitch, and we were all just happy to be somewhere else and about to have a two-week-long eating adventure.

We ate fresh fish by the plateful and drank cheap Italian whites by the gallon. We laughed and critiqued all of the different things that hit our table. None of it was remarkable, with the exception of some stuffed baby squid that Mashama and I couldn't get enough of, but the night, overall, was an excellent one.

Suddenly, Mashama cried, "Oh, Carol, I forgot something," as she reached into her purse.

She pulled out the brightly colored bracelet the guy in the square had given to her. "This is for you. It's a friendship bracelet," she offered proudly.

Earlier that day I was given a gift by a stranger. This gift was significant to me because it was Johno's and my first trip traveling and eating together. I also loved the fact that Carol was meeting us. It gave us an opportunity to really get to know each other. I viewed the trip as the mark for our new start. I took pleasure in putting the bracelet on Carol's wrist just as the vendor had placed one on mine. This was a symbol of the friendship we were creating.

Carol's only reaction was to squeal and stick her arm straight out so Mashama could tie it on. "Yay. I love it," she said as Mashama began to secure it to her wrist and tell her how the bracelet was acquired earlier in the day.

When Mashama was finished tying it on and sharing her story of the West African vendor/soothsayer, we seemed to be well on our way to fulfilling his prediction—friends.

WHOLE GRILLED FISH
Serves 4

My father was obsessed with fishing and took particular joy in eating the *whole* fish—even a cat wouldn't bother with what he left uneaten. When Mashama put a whole grilled fish on our first menu, it immediately conjured up memories of my childhood.—JOM

Prepare a medium-hot charcoal fire or preheat a gas grill.

Season the inside and outside of the fish with salt. Stuff the fish with the bay leaves and orange rounds. Tie with butcher's twine below the gills and at the tail end of the pocket to secure the bay and orange rounds.

Grill the fish for 8 minutes per side, until the fish flakes. Don't grill longer or it will overcook.

Remove and discard the butcher's twine. Transfer the fish to a large serving plate. Remove the bay leaves and orange rounds and use them to pretty up your serving plate.

Use a knife to remove the dorsal, pectoral, and pelvic fins. Make a cut in the flesh below the gills from the spine to the cavity opening and the same cut at the tail end. Cut along the spine of the fish from the top cut to bottom cut. You should then be able to slide the tines of a serving fork under the flesh and lift the fillet right off the bone. (It takes practice, and you will know when you have it down.) Turn the fish and repeat for the other side. Arrange the cooked fish on a serving plate. Squeeze the remaining orange half over the fish and serve.

1 (2-pound) white-fleshed fish, gutted and scaled (we prefer snapper or sea bass)

Kosher salt

3 bay leaves

1 orange; half cut into two ¼-inch-thick rounds, and half left whole

CHAPTER 15

Mashama's fortieth birthday weekend came and went. We didn't speak much after that morning at her apartment and my ensuing phone call. She was wrapped up with friends arriving over the course of the next several days. The coordination of it all was difficult and, as these things often go, Mashama, as the host, had her fair share of stresses related to the planning and execution of her own party.

The night before they all left for Tybee Island, Mashama was driving and shuttling girls from the airport to her apartment. She was stocking up on provisions for the weekend, making trips to grocery and liquor stores. She called me occasionally for a piece of advice on where to get a certain thing or borrow a cooler or some similar request. We did our best to forget, or more to the point, to ignore, what had transpired between us, and all of our conversations were brief and polite.

I continued to try to reconcile the multitude of uneasy feelings this situation forced me to confront and what that meant to this relationship that we were building. My anger was also slowly subsiding.

Coincidentally, we had locked down the design for The Grey's initial swag T-shirts just before Mashama's birthday weekend. As a peace offering (or to self-soothe?), I had a bunch of shirts run off and dropped them with Mashama as a birthday gift to her so that she could give them to her friends as a memento from the weekend. It helped ease my conscience. I knew that sharing them with her friends would make her proud, and it was important that neither one of us lose sight of that—that we were doing something that, one day, I hoped we would be proud of.

I was uncomfortable too. We had just gotten into our first fight, and even with my friends there it took me a few hours to get into a festive mood. We were all excited about the delivery of The Grey swag, but I remember a few friends noticing that I was a little jumpy. Some thought he was hovering—and I thought so too—but I brushed it off. I knew that he was trying to make amends.

After the big weekend, we got back to our normal routine. I would spend much of the day at the site poring over the details. Mashama would join me for part of it and use the rest of the day to research recipes, meet farmers or other purveyors, and drive around the Low Country to see what was available to her in terms of ingredients that would help her conceive and build a menu. While there still wasn't much in the way of recipe testing, it did seem that Mashama was making progress.

Things were starting to come together.

And while I remained nervous about the menu, the backward step our relationship had taken that morning in Mashama's apartment was much more troubling to me. Even the throw-away banter we had gotten good at had dried up a bit.

As the relationship strained, Mashama grew more distant, and I genuinely began to worry that maybe she had soured on the entire thing. I continued to deal with my own doubts about her commitment, but she was in control of her next move. I wondered if she was considering pulling the plug and moving back to New York. Maybe our inherited discomfort would be too much to overcome. Maybe all of the common ground we found over food, family, and values wouldn't be enough. It was possible that she thought and would always think that I was controlling and only saw her as an employee. It was equally possible that all of the conflicted feelings I had that morning in her apartment were not to be so quickly reconciled.

Space was what I needed. Even though time was passing, things still felt uncomfortable. We needed to talk and I was waiting for the right time to bring it up.

As I often do, I felt like I had to fix things. I felt responsible for throwing us off course that morning and that it was on me to right this ship. I had to figure out a way to do it, I had to. We both put ourselves on the line. We were now in Savannah together and we would always be tied together through this common undertaking—this crazy scheme to open this restaurant that we hoped would be successful. We were not going to be able to do that unless we got back to building trust, not undermining it.

And then it hit me. Food! Food was the answer. It was the thing that had, in fact, brought us together. It was the thing that shined a light on our similarities. I would cook for Mashama.

About midway through that week, I invited Mashama over for Sunday dinner. It occurred to me that in all of the dinners, travel, auditions, menu development, and other food-related stuff we had been doing, I had eaten Mashama's food a handful of times, but I never cooked a meal for her. And while I was no chef, I was a slightly-better-than-adequate home cook—especially when I was cooking some of the Italian classics I had grown up with. Mashama accepted the invite, and we were on.

Carol had a business commitment that weekend and would not be able to get to Savannah, so it would just be the two of us, and it would give us the opportunity to relax, drink some wine, and spend a few hours together over homemade food. My food. I would make pasta carbonara—one of my favorites.

The morning of the dinner, I shopped—eggs, pecorino, De Cecco linguini (as if there's another brand of dry pasta), fresh Italian parsley, a nice fat onion, watered-down domestic pancetta (the real stuff is not available in Savannah), a head of garlic, and chicken stock. I know, I know—what the hell is chicken stock doing in pasta carbonara? Plus, Savannah's version of Italian bread, a simple green salad, and some nice red wine from Piedmont. My plan was complete.

Was I nervous? Yes.

I chopped the onion and garlic, not being one to believe in the bandied-about rule of not mixing the two. I chopped parsley and put it to the side to be thrown in at the last minute. I separated the yolks of three eggs from their whites.

I rendered diced pancetta. I sautéed the onion, then threw in the garlic. Added back the pancetta. Then I added chicken stock. Not a lot. Just a little. (I'm sorry, but I like a pasta that you can dip your bread into.) I threw the pasta into my boiling, salted water.

Mashama knocked on the door.

"Hey," she said.

"Hey," I responded, heading right back to the kitchen. "Sorry, pasta's in the water. We're almost ready to eat."

"Okay, cool," she answered. "I'm starving."

"Good. Me too."

She poured herself a glass of wine from the open bottle of Nebbiolo I had already been nipping at.

The pasta went into the colander and then into the serving bowl. I tossed in the soupy, onion-garlic-pancetta mixture. Then the egg yolks and a giant fistful of pecorino. I cracked white pepper over the top and mixed.

We sat down to our meal at a table on my side porch. It was all very civilized. There was little talking at first and much eating. While the comment we both made about being starving was done to help ward off the awkwardness we felt about purely socializing for the first time in a while, it was certainly true.

The pasta was not my best ever, but it was okay. And, more importantly, Mashama went in for seconds. I was happy to see she was enjoying it.

It was good. I love when people cook for me. Doesn't need to be anything special. I love the thoughtfulness and effort behind it. Plus, I *was* starving.

A second bottle of wine was opened as we wound down the eating.

We were full by then and transitioned into slowly sipping wine and enjoying the peace of a late Sunday afternoon, listening to the sounds of birds and people in the square and soaking in the lush greenery from our perch on the second-story side porch.

"Well, not the best pasta I've ever made, but not the worst," I offered after a bit of silence, fishing for a compliment.

"Oh, good," was all she said.

What does that mean? I thought.

Then I said it out loud, "Huh. So. . . ?"

"So? What?"

"So? So?" I said feigning bravado. "So, did you like it? Remember, you're supposedly this awesome chef," I said playfully, "and I just put my entire ego on the line to make a home-cooked meal for you. The least you could do is tell me that you liked it. Or not."

"Oh, okay. Let's talk about your ego," Mashama said, her enormous and disarming smile fully aglow. "Um, yes, it was good, Johno. It was good pasta carbonara."

"Good? That's it. Good."

"Yeah. Fine. It was very good," she reassured me.

"Good is not good," I snapped jokingly. "'Good' is 'Wow, your pasta really sucks.' That's what 'good' is."

"It did not suck. If it sucked, I would have said it was just 'okay.'"

The room was still pretty tense, but it was nice to see him being playful. I was even beginning to follow his lead as we started to volley back and forth with one another. There were a lot of thoughts swirling around in my head that night. We had some things to clear up—that was the motivation behind this dinner. I just hoped that I would say everything that I needed to say.

"So, what's wrong with it? What don't you like about it? I thought it was pretty good."

Fishing was over. I was now defending. Contesting.

"Fine. Pasta carbonara shouldn't be all wet and sloppy like that. That's all. The sauce should flavor the noodles. It shouldn't be all running around the bottom of the bowl. But it was tasty. Except the garlic. You don't put garlic in carbonara."

I was flabbergasted. "It wasn't sloppy. I like to dip my bread. I need some sauce to dip."

"I get it, and it's okay that you like to dip your bread. But what we just ate was not carbonara. It's fine, but it's just different than carbonara. It's like *your* take on carbonara. Which is cool. I guess."

"I can't even believe this is going on."

"What's going on? That a Black girl from Queens is telling an Italian kid from Staten Island what pasta carbonara is?"

"Um, yeah. Exactly that. What do you know about pasta carbonara?"

She laughed and drank some wine. "Clearly a helluva a lot more than you do. I made that shit every weekend for, like, three hundred covers for four years straight at Prune. That was one of our most popular brunch dishes. If I would've put up that soupy-assed dish, GH would have thrown it in the garbage."

I laughed, too, and raised my glass to touch hers. "It wasn't that good, was it?"

"No, it really wasn't. But at least we're both full now and kind of drunk."

"True."

We went quiet again, back to enjoying the Savannah evening and the idyllic setting as the sun sank lower in the sky, the cicadas increased the volume of their buzzing, and soon the birds and the people surrendered to them. The heat of the day softened, adding to the ease and comfortable laziness the red wine brought on.

The awkwardness between us had faded somewhere during the carbonara critique. Food!

Then, out of nowhere, Mashama whispered in my direction, "You know, you can't treat me like that."

"I do."

"Good."

As we continued sipping our wine, I added, "You know we have to trust each other. It's about family and trust for me. Trust has got to go both ways."

Another moment passed. I said quietly, "This restaurant means everything to me. It's so much of my money, my now, my future, my identity."

"I know," Mashama said reassuringly.

Another clink of our glasses.

"Trust just takes a long time for me, I'm working on it," she added, her voice even more quiet.

That was about all I could say without bringing myself to tears. Maybe it was my age or the situation that Johno and I found ourselves in, but I think that when you put your trust in someone else, these moments that test that trust are hard. I wasn't convinced yet if Johno felt any differently about me that day than he felt a week prior. I guess we would both have to wait and see if trusting each other would work out for the both of us.

"Me too, sister. Me too."

COUNTRY PASTA
Serves 6 to 8

This is Mashama's version of a pasta carbonara. When you look at the ingredients and see pork belly, you know it is going to be better than any version I have ever cooked. Our guests at The Grey wait with bated breath for this dish; and when it appears on the menu, I am always at the front of the line.—JOM

Preheat the oven to 325°F.

Season the pork belly with 1 tablespoon salt, 2 tablespoons of the black pepper, and 1 tablespoon of the red pepper flakes. Place the pork belly in a baking dish and cover with the lard. Cover the baking dish with foil. Bake for 4 to 6 hours, until fork-tender. Let the pork cool in the fat in the refrigerator overnight.

Remove the pork belly from the lard and, with a paring knife, separate the meat from the fat layer. Cube the meat into a ¼-inch dice. Reserve the pork fat.

Fill a large stockpot with water. Season generously with salt and bring to a boil over high heat.

Put 2 tablespoons of the pork fat in a sauté pan over medium-high heat. Add the diced pork belly meat and crisp so that it has a bit of a crust, 7 to 8 minutes.

Throw the pasta into the boiling water and cook till al dente. We always taste it 2 minutes before the instructions on the box tell you it'll be done, so we don't overcook it. (Nothing worse than mushy pasta.)

In a large serving bowl, combine the egg yolks, crisped pork belly, 1 tablespoon salt, the remaining 2 tablespoons black pepper, and 1 tablespoon red pepper flakes. Before you strain your pasta, take 2 tablespoons of the pasta water and whisk it into the egg mixture, tempering your egg yolks. Strain your pasta and dump it into the bowl. Add the 1 cup cheese and mix well. Serve it immediately, passing extra cheese and red pepper flakes at the table (never a bad idea).

2 pounds pork belly

Kosher salt

¼ cup cracked black pepper

2 tablespoons crushed red pepper flakes, plus more for serving

2 cups lard

2 pounds dry spaghetti (De Cecco, if you can get it)

8 egg yolks

1 cup shredded Parmigiano-Reggiano cheese, plus more for serving

CHAPTER 16

It was lunchtime and the three of us—Carol, Mashama, and I—were in Comacchio, Italy, at a restaurant called Al Cantinon. We had pulled into town an hour earlier, having left Milan that morning, dropped our bags at the bed-and-breakfast, and walked the short distance to our first stop in the eighteen hours we would spend in this out-of-the-way village just off the northern end of the Adriatic Sea.

We had made a special detour to get to this particular place for one reason and one reason only—to eat eel. Mashama and I had discovered in all of our dining out together in New York City that we both had a penchant for the long, slimy fish, and that's just a very random food to have in common. Comacchio, I learned prior to our trip from this Italian guy I knew, is the eel capital of Europe. The town has an eel museum, an eel festival, and is famous for a marinated eel that you buy in sardine-like tins that range in weight from a couple of ounces to industrial-size drums. Pretty much the entire population of the town subsists on the catching, processing, and eating of eel. It is, in fact, eel heaven.

This was a great idea because I had only eaten eel in Japanese restaurants. It was so interesting to think of it differently and to look at it from a new perspective. In a lot of ways, this little town would have a huge impact on our first menu.

At Al Cantinon, a traditional northern Italian trattoria with cream walls, exposed brick, simple wooden chairs, and white tablecloths, we found exactly what we were seeking. We arrived at the tail end of their lunch service, but the place was still packed with happy diners eating, laughing, and drinking. The mood was fun and energetic, and we were excited to be there. There was one open table, and we were quickly seated.

We started with some fried eel and eel carpaccio. Mashama and I were delighted. For Carol, our non-eel-eating lunchmate, we ordered a plate of citrus shrimp baked in pink Himalayan salt.

Well, thank goodness for Carol's dislike of eel. That shrimp turned out to be the first rock-star dish of our trip and also inspired one of the first menu items at The Grey. It exceeded mere deliciousness. The shrimp were enormous, cooked perfectly, and, by the time they reached the table, had taken on a hue similar to the bed of pink sea salt on which they rested. The shrimp shells allowed just the right amount of salt to seep through to the bodies and perfectly season the firm meat. They were unctuous, exploding in our mouths with a concentrated flavor of the briny sea, lemons, and butter—and that salt, oh, that salt.

Agreed. Hands down, one of the best ways to eat shrimp!

As Mashama finished the last of the shrimp on her plate, she looked at me. "Johno, we have to find out how these guys cook this shrimp. This dish is smart."

"Yeah, these need to go on the menu," Carol agreed.

"I'm not sure how to do that," I said, adding, "In case you didn't notice, we're in Italy and none of us speak Italian."

Carol said, "You speak Italian. You studied it for, like, a hundred years in school. Your grandparents spoke it. We've been listening to you for two days trying to speak it."

"Exactly. *Trying* to speak it. I don't remember it. It's hard."

"Come on, Johno," Mashama pleaded. "Carol might be right. If I can figure out how to do this, this could go on the menu."

"It's shrimp and salt. How hard can it be?" I asked.

This dish seemed simple enough, but the dishes that seem the simplest are the hardest to master. They are usually based on the ingredients and equipment and how well they go together to come up with something amazing. I still needed more details. How fresh were the shrimp—one day, two days old? Which worked best? What kind of salt? The crystals were unusually large. Did they heat the pan first? Did they heat the salt? Did they oil the pan? Was the salt wet? I didn't think the chef would reveal all of the secrets, but I thought I'd ask anyway.

"Please," they both said in unison.

A man I took to be the owner, a tall, distinguished-looking gentleman in a sport jacket and tie, was working the room with an obvious pride that I knew would make him only too happy to engage with us, so I signaled to get his attention. As he approached our table, I sweated as I translated in my head what I wanted to say into something resembling Italian. *"Scusi, signore,"* I said, taking a nervous breath. *"Questo piatto di gambaretti . . . Come si fa?"*

He laughed at me. Not smiled. Laughed!

It was hard to tell if it was my crummy Italian that he found funny or the question I was attempting to pose. Asking an Italian cook to give up a recipe that was likely centuries old was futile. I may as well have asked him to introduce me to his sister.

It was not going to happen, but after he was done chuckling, he leaned down close to my right ear. *"Signore,"* he said conspiratorially, *"si, è gamberi, è sale. Si?"*

I understood so far. *"Si, si."*

"Allora," he continued, *"quindi, cuocere i gamberetti nel sale."*

Then he stood up from his bent position and looked at me smiling.

I waited for him to come back down to my ear, but he was finished talking.

"Si, si. Questo è tutto?"

"Si, si, questo è tutto," he finished.

"Grazie mille, signore," I said, thanking him.

As he walked away, Mashama asked, "What'd he say?"

Now I laughed. "He said, 'It's shrimp and salt. Then you cook it.'"

"That's it?"

"That's it."

That was not IT! At least not for me.

But Mashama was not satisfied. She would not be thwarted. She decided that she was going to have her own run at the dashing owner. She turned on a 1,000-watt smile and blasted it in the direction of the man. He immediately smiled back. I noticed that Mashama was the only Black person in the restaurant as she adjusted herself in her seat to open up her body posture to more of the room and the gentleman from whom she sought family secrets. I wondered if being unique in this situation struck Mashama as an advantage or not.

I didn't think about anything else in that moment other than (dare I say it) speaking Italian. My goal was to get myself back in that kitchen and see how they used that shrimp and salt.

"How do I say 'This was good'?" she asked me, pointing to the shrimp shells. "In Italian," she added.

"I'm not good with the past tense. Just say '*Questo è molto buono*,'" I answered.

She immediately turned to the owner, who was standing a few feet away, and said enthusiastically, "*Molto buono, signore. Molto buono.*"

Huh. She threw in the "*signore*" and doubled up the "*molto buono*." *Well done*, I thought.

His face brightened a little. He came back to the table. "*Parli Italiano?*" he asked her.

"No, no." She blushed, adding, "Do you speak English?"

"A little," he answered sheepishly. She had him.

The conversation continued, and Mashama went on to explain that she was a cook in America and had never had such delicious shrimp before. Over the course of the next hour, some wine, and a sambuca alongside an espresso, she got enough out of the gentleman that she had an idea not only of the ingredients, but how to cook the shrimp dish when we returned to Savannah.

It was then and there that The Grey's first menu item was born—with those salt-baked, citrus shrimp.

There are only a few places in America that you can find fresh shrimp. Georgia shrimp has a proud following. People from the area can tell you everything about the crustacean—from the best way to cook them to how long they have been out of the water. Savannahians love their shrimp, and I knew a dish like this would be a hit there. After we opened, we put it on the menu but it proved to be more temperamental than I thought. We struggled with it for a while and then, really, it never truly worked out. We also realized people didn't love peeling their own shrimp in a restaurant like ours.

We stayed in Comacchio that night and had three more eel dishes, some other fishes, and a pasta for Carol at another eel-centric restaurant. A cabbage dish, similar to a *chou farci*, of course stuffed with eel, was another standout dish. That evening, Mashama and I sucked down just about everything on the table, other than Carol's pasta, which she protected with her life from the two of us. Comacchio was a hit.

Fried whiting and coleslaw is what I think that eel and cabbage dish would translate into in the South. My wheels were turning!

Our travels around Italy went on for another eight or nine days with stops that included Modena, where we had an encounter with world-famous chef Massimo Bottura; Orvieto, where we were introduced to the concept of fava beans and Reggiano cheese; and Rome, where Carol and Mashama nearly mutinied against me for leading them out for a "short walk" that turned into six miles in ninety-degree heat, both of them wearing the "wrong shoes." Luckily, a quick stop at a small café where we sipped ice-cold Aperol spritzes took some of the sting out of their swollen feet and disdain for yours truly.

Massimo Bottura was so charming and humble and he also sent us home with the most delicious balsamic vinegar. Orvieto was a beautiful mountain town with cobblestone streets and taxidermy boar heads hanging in every trattoria. Johno marched through the streets of Italy's capital like a member of the Roman auxiliary. My feet took a long time to recover. I swore off heels for the next two years.

By the end of our nearly two weeks together, we had accomplished what we had set out to do—eat, drink, and see the best and, occasionally, the worst of each other. The worst mostly being Carol and me arguing over something in the front-seat, like whether I should turn the car down the first impossibly narrow street or the second to get to the restaurant we were looking for, while Mashama pretended to be sleeping in the backseat and not listening to any of our bickering.

I really didn't know these people then and, at first, I was uncomfortable being in such close proximity to them. In the end, it was like watching your parents fight, and these episodes came and went quickly and I began to understand the dynamic between the two of them.

The fact that Mashama was positively influenced by our experiences in Italy meant to me that there was a chance that we might open a restaurant serving

Italian food. This, in my view, would have been a very good thing. It was, I thought, what Savannah needed, but rather than share this overtly, I was less direct. From the time Mashama had made the crab soup and rosemary-skewered chicken livers, she had always talked about wanting her cooking in Savannah to be Southern—the exciting part for her was to rediscover her roots.

I wanted to move down South and cook when I returned from France. Chefs in Charleston, like Sean Brock and Mike Lata, had the right idea, and there was room for more of that.

Black chefs in the South were not being recognized or celebrated, not like their counterparts. I wanted to be a part of this Southern food movement. I wanted to reimagine the Southern Black experience through food—cooking the same traditional foods, but with different techniques. This restaurant was a partnership and we needed to figure out what that meant. When it came to the food, I needed him to trust me.

While it was true that picking Italy as the first destination for a food trip for us was largely about my roots, it was also about me steering Mashama not only away from her ancestral cooking but toward mine. I was hoping to bring her to my side, thinking maybe she would reconsider her commitment to Southern food while in Italy—you know, weight her French and Italian technical skills that she had developed in New York City more heavily. In retrospect, this was a con-fusing—and wrong-headed—thing to do to her (and us). The menu process was going to be difficult enough without me mucking up the works, but that didn't stop me from throwing all of the pasta, polenta, and prosciutto at her that I could. This concept of trust that I was so hell-bent on establishing between the two of us was unconsciously pushed around a bit from the very beginning because of my own opinions on the type of food we should serve.

So sneaky! He really had no idea how this would need to work. In the end, it just elongated the process.

Did I have the good of our future business at heart? Of course. I wanted it and us to be successful, but I had become extremely self-reliant over the course of my career, and so my inclination was often to think that I knew best. Hence, going to Italy and my desire for Mashama to embrace her classical cooking skills. I do believe the trip helped with the overall process of finding a common language and developing a menu, because it did focus us completely on food. And Mashama's love for classical Italian cooking was genuine—it was easy to see that as we ate our way across the countryside. But there were costs associated with that trip, and those mostly manifested themselves in what became our slightly confused opening menu—it was caught somewhere between Southern and Italian. It would take another two and a half years after we opened The Grey for Mashama to find a clear voice and to create a menu and a format that was truly reflective of her as a chef and not some amalgamation of outside influences and opinions.

Fact is, those blended voices didn't work for us. As the restaurant has grown and come into its own, now we focus more on the seasons and continue to figure out ways to amplify the ingredients' flavors and expand on our region's traditions. We use the African diaspora as a guide and our local farmers as our resources to help us unlock what Southern food means and to guide how we cook it. Those are the classical skills needed to amplify Southern cooking.

BRAISED CABBAGE WITH TOMATOES AND FISH SAUCE
Serves 4

½ cup extra-virgin olive oil

1 large yellow onion, thinly sliced

6 cloves garlic, sliced

1 head Savoy cabbage, shredded

1 (28-ounce) can San Marzano tomatoes

Kosher salt

Freshly cracked black pepper

1 teaspoon smoked paprika

¼ cup Colatura di Alici fish sauce (you can buy it online)

We often talk about the braised eel and cabbage we ate in Comacchio, Italy, and wanted to include that recipe in this book. But we wondered, *Where in the hell are people going to get eel?* Mashama is like the MacGyver of cooks, so she decided that we'd give you a recipe that mimics the flavors of that dish with ingredients that are a lot easier to find.—JOM

In a large sauté pan, heat the olive oil over medium heat and then add the onion and garlic. Cook for 4 minutes.

Add the cabbage and tomatoes to the pan, crushing each tomato with your hand. Dump the tomato liquid from the can into the pan as well, season with salt and pepper, cover, and braise for 30 minutes.

Stir the paprika into the cabbage mixture. Remove from the heat and stir in the fish sauce. Transfer to a serving bowl and have at it.

CHAPTER 17

The road trip in Italy was informative. Aside from witnessing the inner dynamics of Johno and Carol's relationship, driving from one city to another allowed me to soak up that country's culture. The changes in weather and terroir really affect everything from how you dress to what you eat. That trip gave me a glimpse into how local Italians live. Shortly after we all returned from our trip, I realized I wanted to get reacquainted with the South in that same way.

Coming back from Italy, there was a lot to do. I had to continue to focus on the preservation of the building and construction of the restaurant, and Mashama had to pack up all of her shit, put it in her car, and make the move from her grandmother's house in Queens to an apartment on Montgomery Street in downtown Savannah. Once she got to town, her focus was, in theory, going to be on concepting and setting up that opening menu. But it was not a clean break between our two areas of responsibility. I wanted and needed Mashama's input on the restaurant design, layout, kitchen, bathrooms, all of it. I pushed for this for two reasons: first, she knew far more about the inner workings of a restaurant than I did and, second, because it was also important that she be invested in every aspect of what we were building. I felt certain that sharing these decisions would be a key to our long-term partnership and success.

Even though I had lived in Savannah as a child and visited my mother's family many summers, once we moved back to New York, our drives to and from the South were purely direct—there was no touring. Outside of this, Atlanta was really the only other Southern city I knew, and seeing the South through the eyes of a chef was something I had not considered before.

I packed up my car and drove from New York to Charlotte, across North Carolina, through Asheville, Knoxville, and Nashville, Tennessee. I visited smokehouses and dairy farms. I made my way to Jackson, Mississippi, and ate at the Mayflower. I stayed with friends from New Orleans to Atlanta. I covered a lot of culinary ground while trying to consume as much of what the South had to offer as I could.

I felt that my love of food and wine, combined with the years I had spent traveling professionally and personally, dining out regularly in a variety of cities and restaurants, gave me the foundation to have a role in the development of our first menu. I was certainly encouraged by the success of our Italian trip and all of the things we ate and how we had found lots of common ground. I believed that in order for us to maximize the value of the relationship we were building, both of our points of view needed to be reflected in the food we were serving to our guests and the space in which they were enjoying it.

Once we returned from Italy, I tried to be a reliable taster and sounding board for Mashama in her process of developing that first menu. We both knew that this would prove to be her most difficult challenge. Every experienced chef and person with whom we spoke nearly promised us that for a chef to find their voice in creating their very first menu from scratch was no small undertaking. It would be a process rife with setbacks and frustrations.

In spite of the excess of choices or ideas that the Italy trip may have provided, I did sincerely want Mashama to find her voice. I did not want to be the guy who was forcing an Italian concept—I wanted us both to believe in the menu we ended up with. Mashama was in Savannah because she could cook. I knew that. I worked harder at trusting her instincts on letting the region and the ingredients speak to her—the ingredients of the Southern United States.

As I became more educated about the region, I also realized that I didn't understand what Southern food was—at least not in the way Mashama considered it, the way she wanted to cook it. When I was initially envisioning the restaurant that would become The Grey, this type of food was never really on my radar. Edna Lewis, the queen of seasonal Southern cooking, was a name I had not known before I met Mashama. So when I heard the term "Southern food," I naively believed it to be solely what I watched Paula Deen, the only chef I'd ever associated with Savannah, cooking on television. That food was often fried, high in fat and sugar, and drowned in cheese or butter or sauce. I didn't want to eat that. Back then, television didn't offer a real alternative to Ms. Deen's brand of Southern cooking, such as Elizabeth Terry of Elizabeth on 37th (Street) who was executing a different version of Southern fare. Ms. Terry, who received Savannah's first James Beard Award in 1995 for Best Chef Southeast, was, out of the media's eyeshot, cooking food that used fresh local vegetables like Vidalia onions, Georgia shrimp, and other ingredients from the area, and, per all reports, she was preparing them simply and cleanly. That food, I could get down with, but I was swayed by what I saw on television, the "idiot-box" as my old man would have said.

So, each time Mashama brought up cooking the food of her grandmothers, one of whom had always lived in Waynesboro, Georgia, about two hours northwest of Savannah, I had visions of Ms. Deen's food, along with a small twinge of nerves in my stomach, a sharp pain in my aorta, and a spike in my blood sugar.

It's a big assumption that Southern food is unhealthy. I blame cheap, processed food and the fast-food revolution for increased health risks in lower-income communities, not Southern food. Beginning with slavery, the Black community in America has been forced to live on a diet that is low on the hog. We have kept some of those traditional foods in our diets. We have also embraced those traditions and renamed it as soul food, but many of those foods don't benefit our health as a community, instead inviting increased health risks that plague us for generations.

The more we got into it, though, the more Mashama explored the region's food-ways, I realized that it was not a binary equation. It was not Southern versus Italian. It was more nuanced than that. My earlier premise that this should be simple—come up with a dish and cook it until tastes good—was rudimentary. It was my accountant's brain, applying structure to a process that was going to define Mashama as a chef. A Black chef. A Black female chef. A Black female chef cooking food in the Deep South.

Cooking in the South was going to be a tall order to fill. The landscape is beautiful and local farms are everywhere. Cooks in the South want to cook Southern food, and I can't blame them. It seemed to me that every Southern chef was raised on some Southern farm, cooking with their grandmothers, and it was only natural that this would bring a real awareness to the region. I'm a city girl. I grew up surrounded by concrete, not grass and livestock.

During the menu-writing process, I had no choice but to pull from my own personal experiences surrounding food. I knew that if I was going to run a kitchen, I needed to be motivated. I needed to draw on all of the things that made me curious about food and cooking in the South. What about my upbringing and my family? What did they have to do with me arriving at this point, if anything? Both my grandmothers were very special. They gave a wonderful gift to their families and it was based on food. Whether I was in Waynesboro shelling peas on the front porch or driving to a dock in Long Island to buy fish just out of the local waters, they talked about the importance of family and food. After I decided that these two women would be the source of my inspiration, I could let all of the other influences in without changing who I was and what I wanted to cook.

All of these machinations around the menu did serve to highlight a fairly stark difference between Mashama and me. My background was in business. I had experience in the corporate world, start-ups, finance, media, and even some not-for-profits. The thing they all had in common? Lots of men doing almost all the decision making. It has been my experience that where you have a lot of men, more often than not White men, a lot of alpha dogs, running things, you have complex power dynamics, politics, and struggles. You learn how to survive and thrive in that environment, and, in my case, you learn how to embrace it, contribute to it, and perpetuate it. You become political. If you are really good at it, you become a politician who doesn't look like someone politicking. You get people "invested" in ideas. You sell things "upstream" and "downstream." You "huddle."

Once you learn this, it is a very hard thing to unlearn. Our trip to Italy was partially about this—me selling Mashama, getting her invested in a certain concept, the concept of an Italian menu. But the world in which Mashama had operated professionally didn't involve politics or gamesmanship. Restaurants are cultural dictatorships. The chef runs things and everyone else follows suit. Our dynamic as business partners and collaborators was going to require us both to learn, unlearn, change, and adjust almost everything we did and how we did it. At least we would have to do that if we wanted to be successful.

Well, it's not as cut-and-dry as that. The very old way of looking at the kitchen brigade system could read as a dictatorship, but if you look closer you see that it isn't true. The executive chef runs things and she does have the last word. If you look deeper than that, there are chefs de cuisine, pastry chefs, sous-chefs, and chefs de partie working creatively in collaboration with the chef. It takes the entire team, with different skills, to help bring the chef's vision into focus.

As we learned how to be around one another, how to collaborate, and how to give each other some space, maybe the most difficult thing for me to learn was that Mashama was in the process of working through layers and layers of not only ingredients but also history. We were beginning to taste things more frequently and this was exciting. But, we also knew it was time to start trying out these dishes on people besides the two of us. We decided to plan a last-minute dinner party and host a group at my house on a Friday evening, plying them with potential menu items. We would keep it casual and make sure the drinks were flowing to facilitate honest feedback.

This was about the third tasting and by far the most memorable one. It was late summer in Savannah, and the markets were bombarded with muscadine grapes, eggplant, tomatoes, and peppers, allowing me to work on preserves, relishes, and jellies for our opening. At our previous tastings, we tried out dishes like green tomato aspic with za'atar spice, double-crust egg pie with salted sour cream, chicken country captain, and a country-style pasta carbonara, but we didn't have a menu yet. I was relying heavily on the Farmers' Market for produce and wasn't sure if all of what I was getting there would

be available when we opened. The tasting we were planning then was about predicting the dishes that would make sense a few months later.

On short notice, I called some friends and the first people to accept were some downtown neighbors, Chris and Staci. They lived a couple of blocks from Carol and me, and we had become friendly after Carol and I met Staci when she was on the other side of the real estate transaction for our first home in Savannah. Staci said they had some friends visiting from California and asked if it would be all right to bring them. She assured me that they were into food and would eat anything, so we didn't have to worry about dietary restrictions. We had two-thirds of the six available seats at the table filled. We were cooking with gas.

Mashama insisted we not limit the attendees to strictly White, well-to-do folks who lived in the Historic District—where we both lived. At first, when Mashama would say things like this, I got my feelings hurt. The same way that middle-aged men never feel like the old guys in the room even when they're graying and in their fifties. I had never really seen myself as anything but the fireman's son from a lower-middle-class neighborhood in Staten Island— certainly not a well-to-do White guy—and I always tried very hard to stay true to the values I learned from growing up that way.

Johno *is* a well-to-do White guy. But even during our first meeting at the Arts Club, he stuck out to me. He wasn't like other rich men I've seen up close. He has a way of not getting too big for his britches. It is important to him to stay humble. He seems committed to investing in the people and community around him.

Early on in our relationship, such requests felt like segregators. Mashama put me and my White friends in one box and defined herself and all African Americans as different, in another box. Was this separatism or pragmatism? Did Black folks receive food differently than White folks? I just did not know.

White and Black people usually don't attend the same schools or churches or live in the same neighborhoods. Some of this is city planning, due to economics or race politics, and some of it is by choice. Let's face it, we are all different, and appreciating those differences makes for a better human experience. I don't know if we African Americans will ever fully heal from the way we have been treated throughout American history. I think having dinners, recognizing those differences—for example, what we eat or what our political views are based on and the needs within our communities—helps create the dialogue that is necessary to begin to effect widespread changes that could help balance the scales of equity.

I guess that when I thought about reaching "all of the Savannah community," as I had phrased it when I talked about finding a business partner different from me, I had not really considered what that meant in terms of cooking food for that larger community. I assumed some sort of homogeny in how Southern people ate. In other words, I thought people in the South ate Southern food regardless of the color of their skin. Whereas, when Mashama and I started to get to know one another, I was surprised that a Black girl from Queens and an Italian kid from Staten Island had so much in common around food. My surprise came from the ethnic and cultural diversity that I expected from a city like New York. But in coming to the South, I didn't allow for that. I just assumed that food was food there.

Southern food is regional, sub-regional, and even micro-regional, varying from town to town. Looking at the South from a distance, you would think that all Southerners use the same ingredients and cook them the same way, but differences between Blacks and Whites, rich and poor, certain neighborhoods and towns is, in part, what creates the diversity of eating in the South.

With my feathers slightly ruffled, I didn't invite anyone else that I knew, but rather put it to Mashama. "Not sure if I mentioned this, but I don't really have a lot of Black friends here or anywhere for that matter, "I retorted." So, if you want someone at the table who is African American, you're going to have to help me figure it out." Then I added, passive-aggressively, "The downtown White folks are my bailiwick."

Mashama, still new to Savannah, was stumped for a second. I may not have had many Black friends, but Mashama just didn't know very many people here at all. She thought about it for another minute or two and then said, "What about Cynthia Hayes?"

Cynthia, who has sadly since passed away, was the co-founder and executive director of an organization called Southeastern African American Farmers Organic Network (SAAFON). She had recently won a James Beard Foundation Leadership Award for her life's work, specifically her work for SAAFON. She and Mashama were beginning to get to know each other, which, obviously, was a good thing as Savannah did not have many residents whose reach into the culinary and foodways universe went beyond the county borders. Cynthia's did.

The time or two when I had been with Cynthia, I got the feeling that she didn't like me much or the fact that I was opening a restaurant with Mashama. And I thought that this was because I was White and an outsider.

The two other tastings we'd done for The Grey had been very casual. In attendance was usually a group of people who were involved with the restaurant for some reason or another—a photographer whose pictures hang in the restaurant, our advisor on the initial wine list who owns a small wine shop (called Le Chai) off Forsyth Park, and the woman who came down to Savannah to cook with me from New York City. This was the first tasting that would be soliciting the opinions of people with a fresh perspective. I am usually nervous before I cook for people, even when I know them well, but I was just acquaintances with these people. Staci, Chris, Cynthia, and Terry—I only knew them professionally. I remember some hesitation about inviting Cynthia and Terry, but from what I could see, I thought they were people who pushed the narrative around food as it related to race and class, particularly in Georgia but also the South, and I wanted them to come. They were well-traveled folks and I liked that. They reminded me of my parents, conscious and outspoken about the state of African Americans in America. If we were going to build something in this city, we needed the opinion of more than just the people who had something directly invested in what we were building. We needed to hear from the community we intended to serve.

"Sure," I said, "Cynthia Hayes. Why not?"

"No good?" Mashama asked, sensing my trepidation.

"She's fine. I just don't think she cares for me, so it might be a little weird."

Smiling at me, she said, "Johno, Black people are going to be a little funny about this thing. This entire thing. Just like the White people. You may as well just start getting used to it. We both should."

"What's funny?" I asked. "The fact that you're doing this with a White guy or the fact that you are doing it at all?"

"Both, probably."

I was confused by this. "Why wouldn't the Black community view this as a good thing?"

"Why doesn't the White community?"

"I don't think most of them care what I am doing or with whom," I answered.

"That's not true. Some of them care and some of them don't like it."

"I can't worry about racists or rednecks. I'm not trying to change the world, just build a restaurant." And then I asked, "Are you implying that Cynthia doesn't like it?"

"I'm not implying anything," Mashama continued. "What I'm saying is that your idea that you and me being together is going to draw attention means it's going to draw attention from *everyone* in Savannah. Your people, my people, people we don't even know yet. You want to think that the Black community should be grateful or something right out of the gate." She paused for a second, adding, "Well, that's just not realistic. Black people aren't any different from everyone else. In fact, they'll be suspicious. At least some of them."

"Suspicious of what?"

"Of this," she said, pointing at me and then her. "Suspicious of you. Suspicious of the bus terminal. Suspicious of everything. Maybe that's where Cynthia's head is at. So, let's have her over and find out."

"It's going to be weird," I said, agreeing with a nod.

"Sure is."

There's always a question of intent when Black folks and White folks do business together. That's what a history of being fucked over does to you. It makes you cautious. It makes you consider factors that wouldn't matter if you were the same race. Those factors could be one person's family or their social status. The playing field wasn't even, but at least we were starting to communicate about it in conversations like this. This was progress. It was during moments like these that we were bringing our different perspectives about race out into the light instead of letting them fester, as we had done early on.

Mashama spent the day cooking in my kitchen—it being more set up than the one in her rental unit—something that was happening with more regularity as we got into the fall of that year. She somehow sourced eel (not an easy product to get in Savannah) to make a knockoff of the eel-stuffed braised cabbage dish that we had eaten in Comacchio. She pan-roasted whole snapper with salsa verde, beef liver over polenta, and made the same chicken schnitzel she had cooked at the audition she did in my New York City apartment. She smoked collard greens and served a few other things. It was a spread.

I played prep cook and host. I took full advantage of Mashama's need for assistance to raise my standing in the kitchen with her after my first crack at impressing her with my soupy pasta carbonara had gone wrong. I did basic kitchen grunt work—chopping things (unevenly), peeling stuff (trying not to cut myself), and washing dishes (which I was good at). I was awkward and nervous working next to her, but I did it. Mashama, on the other hand, was patient and calm but never stopped moving. She also can get very quiet when she cooks and I was not sure if that was normal or some commentary on my capabilities.

That evening's menu had a lot of moving parts. I was outside smoking things in the garden, making sauces, and breading and frying things. As prep time began to spill over into setting-the-table and getting-the-house-ready time, stage fright started to surface in the form of the same old question: Will they like the food?

We worked away the afternoon preparing, but unlike the afternoon of Mashama's audition in New York City, when the air was more festive and hopeful, this particular afternoon it all felt a little ominous. I got the sense from Mashama, through her facial expressions and some barely audible grunts, groans, and mutterings, that, while we were making progress, she was not too happy with the direction in which the final product was heading.

At seven sharp that evening, Cynthia and Terry Hayes arrived in Terry's weathered and well-worn red pickup truck, the truck of a man who works hard for a living. I greeted them at the door while Mashama continued plugging away in the kitchen. Cynthia, a woman who was quick to smile, struck a strong presence in the entrance to my house with her loose, long curls sitting high on her head in a shock of black and silver hair. Terry, a thin and wiry gentleman, whose hair and beard were both cut close, followed her into the house.

The Hayeses called that red truck "the watermelon truck." They had searched for a secondhand vehicle in that color and used it to pick up watermelons from the local farmers within the SAAFON network. They used them to make the watermelon juice they would sell at their stand in the local farmers' market in Forsyth Park. Everyone would go to that stand on hot Saturday mornings.

I did what I always do when a guest comes into my house, asking, "What can I get you to drink? I have white, red, beer, and booze. You name it."

"Water," said Cynthia, pleasantly.

Oy! Nondrinkers in Savannah? This was a rarity. There's an old joke: In Atlanta, people ask you, "What do you do for a living?" In Charleston, people ask you, "What's your mother's maiden name?" In Macon, they ask you, "What church you belong to?" And, in Savannah, they ask, "Hey, what do you want to drink?"

"Same," said Terry.

"You got it. Hey, Mashama, Cynthia and Terry are here."

Greetings were exchanged in the kitchen while Mashama put the finishing touches on a number of the dishes in front of her.

Just then, another knock on the door. Staci, Chris, and their friends from California had arrived. As I opened it, they were a bit more animated than the Hayeses. They all had half-full to-go cups in their hands.

"Heyyyy," was the greeting from Staci, a thin, athletic blonde, as she hugged me hello, practiced at not spilling her drink.

Chris, tall and clean-cut, followed her in, and we exchanged a handshake and a bro hug.

He introduced their friends. "Johno, this is Scott and Yvonne."

"Hey, guys, welcome," I said, as I shook hands with Scott and got a nice-to-meet-you hug from Yvonne. "I see you guys brought some drinks, but can I get you something else? White, red, beer, booze?"

The orders came in quick succession.

"White."

"White."

"Red."

"Beer, please."

"We've been out for a little while. Scott and Yvonne just got to town, so you know, when in Savannah, have a few drinks," Staci explained as they giggled their way into my home.

"Oh, I know," I agreed as I walked them into the dining room and introduced them to Cynthia and Terry.

Greetings were cordially exchanged between the tipsy, downtown partyers and the more subdued Cynthia and Terry. It was awkward in the way things can be awkward when you put together people who don't know each other and seem on the surface to be quite different, with some a bit lubricated and the others completely sober.

I did not need to introduce any of the Staci group to Mashama because Staci was in the kitchen in a flash, making intros and saying hi to Mashama and surveying the evening's menu. Instead I managed, as best I could, to facilitate conversation between the disparate groups sitting at the dining room table.

"So, you know," I started, "thanks for coming. The restaurant should open in a few weeks, and Mashama and I were just trying to get some feedback from folks who live here in town. Mashama is making some of the dishes she has planned for our menu, and we just want to see what you think."

"Okay," someone responded.

Cynthia asked, "So what's my girl cooking? I hope it's the food from here. That's important."

It was, mostly, from near Savannah, but I had not yet been introduced to the farmers I would come to work with. Ultimately Cynthia would be the connection to that regional network of farmers and a great resource for me.

"Uh huh," I answered, "I think it's the food is from here, but you can be the judge of that."

Cynthia nodded. "It's important that if you do this you be respectful of this part of the world. Don't just make it a New York restaurant gracing Savannah."

I nodded back at her, and an awkward silence fell over the room.

I excused myself and went into the kitchen to help Mashama, leaving our six guests to themselves.

"How's it going in there?" Mashama asked.

"As I predicted. Weird."

"It'll get better."

"I hope so. Anything I can help with?" I inquired, hoping there was a job for me to keep me out of the dining room.

"Nope," Mashama said. "Just entertain our guests."

"Yes, dear," and I made my way back to the dining room.

When I returned, Staci had taken over. She was a real estate broker downtown and had the type of unapologetic energy that you ultimately gave in to—it was just a question of how long surrender took. Over the next little while, everyone succumbed to it and the awkwardness that defined the early part of the evening subsided as people settled into their seats and conversation assumed a more normal cadence. Ultimately, all Savannah residents at least have Savannah in common and it wasn't long before Staci, Chris, Cynthia, and Terry recognized one another from the Saturday Farmers' Market. They then touched upon this person or that person that they knew in common. The drinkers, as drinkers usually do, drove the conversation, but Cynthia and Terry were active participants, and they seemed to be very comfortable in the conversation. They offered thoughtful perspective on the more raucous exchanges that were taking place—particularly Cynthia, who was whip smart and unafraid to share her thoughts. She had no problem taking a position different from that of the majority, not something I was always comfortable with myself, and she did so charmingly and with grace.

After a few more minutes, Mashama declared that dinner was ready and she and I began setting it on the table. When everything was in place, Terry led us in prayer, which is not something that normally takes place in our house and always makes me wonder if a bolt of lightning is going to strike me as I sat there recalling the days when being actively Catholic was a bigger part of my life.

As we ate, the voices quieted. People were hungry, and not much was said other than the requisite "This is very good, Mashama."

Cynthia was inquisitive about some of the ingredients and their preparation. "Mashama, where'd you get these collard greens?"

"Kroger's," Mashama said quietly, almost ashamed.

"Mmm hmm, I figured as much. No collards in season 'round here right now."

I wanted to test a vegan collard greens recipe I had been playing with using this Jamaican pimento wood. In Jamaica, they use this wood to cook jerk over, and I thought cooking vegetables on it could be cool. I recall the collards being a hit. I had a spicy vinegar sauce on the table and people couldn't get enough.

Mashama flashed an embarrassed smile.

"You need to come with me and meet some more of the farmers who are growing the food down here. We're going to do that next week."

Mashama nodded respectfully. "Yes, ma'am, that sounds great. I would really love to do that."

"How about this snapper—where's that from?"

"Russo's."

Russo's is our local retail fish market in town and we all shop there. But that was another thing I found difficult to find in Savannah—a seafood wholesaler—and that seemed so odd to me with Savannah being a coastal city.

"Mmm hmmm."

"You know, we have this entire network of farmers down here." Cynthia said as she looked at me. "Been growing 'organic' food since the beginning. Wasn't called organic back then. They just called it 'growing.' I'm going to introduce y'all to them. Be good for you and the restaurant. The food that we grow in the Low Country and all through the South is important. Down here, an introduction is the key thing, though. People don't like strangers just showing up, no matter if you have a brand-new restaurant or not."

"Thanks, Cynthia. That's exciting," I said, not completely sure if it was help she was offering or an admonishment.

As we continued to chat, Mashama, Staci, Chris, Scott, Yvonne, and I shared a couple of bottles of red wine. We passed plates around the table and helped spoon this or that onto someone's dish. We all talked more about Savannah life, plans for the weekend, and food in general.

As I looked around the table, seeing Mashama do the same, I took notice of what people were eating and what was being passed over. The roasted fish sat mostly uneaten. Undercooked? Maybe. The beef liver was devoured. The eel was kind of picked over by everyone, but nobody went at it hard. A 50 percent hit ratio on the dishes on the table seemed to hold true. It wasn't awesome.

I took a stab to see if I could get more from people than just a long view of the food that was eaten and the food that was not. "Delicious, Mashama," I said to the table. "Love that beef liver."

Everyone nodded and agreed that they loved the beef liver too.

"I thought the fish was a little hard to eat though," I continued.

"It was good," Cynthia said, "but it was hard to eat. And those collards, it's just not their season."

"Yup," Mashama agreed.

"I liked the eel," I offered.

Everyone nodded politely.

Nobody else offered much in the way of praise or critique.

As a final course, Mashama served a chocolate pudding with spicy peanuts and whipped cream. Everyone there loved this finale, but I was skeptical because chocolate pudding just was not my thing. This, however, would become the very first dessert on the menu and rightfully so—even I thought it was great.

After a little more chitchat, the night started to come to a close. The Hayeses got up first. Terry had an early morning at the Farmers' Market, and it was already pushing eleven. I walked them to the door and thanked them for helping us figure out the strengths and weaknesses in our menu. Terry shook my hand warmly and Cynthia gave me a big hug.

Progress? Maybe.

A few days after that dinner, Cynthia called up and offered to drive me down the Georgia Coast. She stayed true to her word and introduced me to people within her network. During the hour or so drive, she asked me what I was

looking for. She wanted to reassure me that she was there to support me. She wanted to know what I had to say with my food and what I wanted to cook. She asked what it was that I wanted that I could not get, and she told me that she could help.

That trip was just the therapy session I needed. First, I told her about myself, my family, and why I had come back to Savannah. Then I told her that I was looking for a good distributor (other than Sysco) for our basic needs, like paper towels, salt, and cooking oil. I told her that we were going to have an oyster program and we wanted local oysters for it. I told her about wanting to serve seafood. I wanted to tell my story, the story of how I got here and the influences that had steered me in this direction my whole life. How I had been learning about this food through cookbooks. I wanted the oral histories and to listen to the elders about the traditions that gave us this food. She listened closely. When I was done, she paused for a minute, picked up her phone, and made two phone calls. We then drove to the coastal town of Brunswick and met people. First, we had lunch with a farmer who was connected in the local foodways; after that, it was to the home of Geechee-Gullah historian Wilson Moran; and then, finally, we caught up with oysterman Ernest McIntosh. These were exactly the right people and Cynthia knew it all along. With my head spinning, we slowly made our way back to Savannah early that evening. I remember ending that day with so much more than when I started. I had the name and contact information for a rep who could stock the restaurant's pantry, I had a local fisherman's contact, I had a place that sold local seafood, and Wilson and his family told me all about Savannah, its coast, and what people ate. I left that car ride with direction and resources. I will forever be indebted to Mrs. Cynthia Hayes.

The rest of us had a nightcap, and after I walked Staci and friends out—they were going to head to the next stop along the way to keep up the revelry—Mashama and I began cleaning up.

"What did you think?" I asked Mashama.

"I think some things were okay. I think most of it needs work. I don't think the Hayeses really got it at all. I think Staci, Chris, and her friends liked it. Some of it, anyway."

"I think it was tough to eat a lot of it family style," which is how we served it. "Especially with no one knowing each other. That was a little awkward, and I think people may have eaten more if we plated it."

"Yeah," Mashama acquiesced nearly to herself. "I don't know. I want the restaurant to be about sharing food. I think the menu just needs some work. It's got to make more sense. The things that are on it have to make more sense."

I was disappointed. I still wanted to impress Johno at the time and this was an example of how I let him control our narrative early on. I didn't think that this dinner would be so hard. We were reacting to the people in the room and not looking at the food—at least, I wasn't. I lacked clarity. In the end, a lot of those dishes anchored the first menu. And I learned a lot that night: the need for restraint when working creatively, the importance of staying flexible and reading the room, and the power that outside influences can have on personal expression. Looking back, it took time for those lessons to take hold.

"It's a little all over the place."

"Yeah. All over the place," Mashama agreed.

"Mmm hmm. Tell a story, maybe. It needs a beginning, middle, and an end."

"Maybe. That might make sense. Three parts? Small plates, middle size, and large?"

"Yeah. Something like that. That sounds Italian to me," I popped in, hitting my old refrain. "Like antipasto, primo, and secondo. That's how we were eating in Italy."

"Yeah, except I'm not cooking Italian."

"I know. But that's it. It doesn't have to be. Just steal that construct. Antipasto can be pickled shrimp. Local grains, the second course. Maybe a pasta carbonara," I slipped in with a smile. "Then the proteins are the secondo."

"Maybe. I'll work on it. Something will be ready by the time we open."

One of the first things I registered about Savannah was that it was rice country. One of my fondest food memories from my summers in Waynesboro was the fish and grits my grandmother would serve us for dinner, with the fish my granddaddy caught earlier that day. Highlighting grains in the South works, focusing on proteins as a main course works, oysters and smaller dishes—it all just works. I liked the idea of looking at Southern food this way. A menu structured like this could work.

SPICY PEANUT-CHOCOLATE PARFAIT

Serves 6

Mashama is definitely a savory cook by trade, but her skills run far and wide, and this dessert is representative of her approach to cooking: A twist on this, a play on that, add a little spice... Have some fun with this one—she sure did.—JOM

For the peanuts: Preheat the oven to 250°F. Line a baking sheet with parchment paper or a silicone mat.

In a bowl, whip the egg white until frothy. Whisk in the granulated sugar, water, salt, cayenne, and chile powder. Stir in the peanuts until evenly coated.

Lay the peanuts in a single layer on the prepared baking sheet. Bake for 45 minutes, stirring once so they toast evenly. Let cool. When cool enough to handle, break apart and set aside.

For the pudding: Place both chocolates in a large bowl and set aside. In a saucepan, whisk together the milk, cream, and granulated sugar and cook over medium heat just until it comes to a boil. Remove from the heat and set aside.

In another bowl, whisk the egg yolks. Drizzle half of the cream mixture into the eggs while whisking, gently tempering the eggs. Pour the yolk mixture back into the saucepan with the cream mixture and whisk together. Stir the mixture with a silicone spatula over medium-low heat just until the custard thickens slightly, approximately 20 minutes.

Fill a bowl with ice water and nest another bowl in it.

Pour the custard over the chocolate and let stand for 1 minute. Gently whisk to combine and melt the chocolate. Pour the mixture into a blender and pulse briefly to blend until smooth. Transfer the chocolate

SPICY PEANUTS

1½ teaspoons egg white

2 tablespoons granulated sugar

1½ teaspoons water

¾ teaspoon kosher salt

½ teaspoon cayenne pepper

¼ teaspoon dark chile powder

1 cup roasted, unsalted peanuts

CHOCOLATE PUDDING

12 ounces 53% cacao chocolate, finely chopped

6 ounces 60% cacao chocolate, finely chopped

3 cups whole milk

3 cups heavy cream

¾ cup granulated sugar

6 egg yolks

PEANUT BUTTER WHIPPED CREAM

1 cup heavy cream

2 tablespoons powdered sugar

¾ cup peanut butter powder

¾ teaspoon vanilla paste

CONTINUED →

SPICY PEANUT-CHOCOLATE PARFAIT
(CONT.)

mixture to the bowl in the ice bath. Refrigerate overnight.

For the whipped cream: Place the cream, powdered sugar, peanut butter powder, and vanilla paste in a bowl and mix with a handheld electric mixer until it holds soft peaks.

Divide the pudding among six small parfait glasses or small jars. Using half of the peanuts and three-fourths of the whipped cream, top each pudding with some peanuts and then a dollop of whipped cream. Divide ¼ cup of the peanuts among the glasses and then top with the remainder of the whipped cream. Finish with the remaining ¼ cup peanuts. Impress the hell out of your friends. A Malmsey Madeira sounds like a good idea with this one.

CHAPTER 18

"We should re-create the entire sign just as it was," I said to Mashama. "People need to know what went on here—in this building and in the South."

Mashama at first said, "Yeah, maybe."

"What's your hesitation?" I asked.

"I'm just thinking that if I'm sitting here eating, do I really want to be looking at a sign that says 'Colored Waiting Room'? Do I need to be told that right here in this building, Black folks used to be forced to segregate while I'm in the middle of enjoying my meal, a meal I'm paying a lot of money for?" she asked, as we were having a conversation about the historical signage that was on my beloved, now-perfectly-smooth-as-a-baby's-bottom soffit. While menu testing was nearing its final phases, we also had a lot of other shit to deal with. Shit like this. The things that often seemed like minutiae but were the kind of details that would take our restaurant from pleasing to thoughtful to, maybe even, architecturally and historically relevant.

The layout and the preservation of the building were a huge draw for me. It was a relic and yet it could still function as it did so many years prior to Johno purchasing it. There was no denying the history of the American South and the impact it has had on the country. I was sure we could find another way to illustrate the racial divide at that time in history; I wasn't sure that showing it through the original signage was necessary. If you know the history and looked for traces of it throughout Savannah, you would spot those traces in this building.

It was really becoming crunch time and in addition to that stuff, detailed wood, glass and stainless-steel finish work on the bars, exterior doors, and server stations were also going on at a painfully slow pace. Our furniture, due to a continuously extended construction schedule, was completed and delivered long before the interior of the restaurant was actually ready for occupancy. So, for the last couple of months of the project, the essentials of our dining room, banquettes, tables, chairs, and shelving all sat in the middle of a mostly completed space under sheets of plastic to keep sawdust, plaster dust, metal dust, and plain ol' dust from soiling and or damaging everything. We navigated around the shrouded pile of expensive furniture whenever we were working on site, having late-stage conversations like this one.

"Are you thinking about a Black guest or a White guest who is not going to want to read that sign?" I asked Mashama.

"Does it matter?" she said, volleying the question back to me.

"Yeah, it matters, the history matters. Part of this whole process is that it's an exercise in the preservation of history, the good and the bad. We need to identify that space somehow. So, do you think everyone will be offended by it?"

"I don't know if it's offensive, but it's damned sure going to be uncomfortable. You know, I don't think being so blatant with it is the way to do it. If this were a museum, then yes. I would be the first person to insist that it says 'Colored Fucking Waiting Room.' But people are coming here to have fun, a night out. They want to enjoy themselves. If they want to look deeper into the history, they can, but I think we don't need to do that by hanging a sign. That sign."

"Yeah. Okay. All fair, but I'm not sure I'm there," I said, pushing back.

She thought for a moment and looked toward Gretchen Callejas, one of the preservation architects, who was with us as we were all trying to finalize the decision for Leigh Nelson, our branding person from the firm LMNOP in Brooklyn, who was listening in on the phone as we all talked it through. "Okay, I get that you're not there. But on this one, I think, we're going to *have* to get you there, Johno," Mashama shot back. "This one's a big deal, I think."

I nodded as Mashama, Gretchen, and I stared at the blank soffit over the back end of the dining room, over what was formerly the segregated waiting room and bathrooms.

I started to say something, but Mashama beat me to it, "What if we just put a sign up that says 'Waiting Room' and we let people ask the question if they want to ask it?"

We all processed the suggestion for a short period. Leigh spoke first, "Yeah, I like that. I think that works."

I looked at Gretchen, she smiled at us and nodded her agreement, "Yup, me too."

I looked at Mashama who shrugged her shoulders and said to me, "You going to be the holdout on this one Mr. I-gotta-preserve-the-history guy?"

I thought about it. I took my time. I didn't want to give in on this point because I had always imagined that the signage would be re-created. I was emotionally attached to that idea. I was emotionally attached to everything about that soffit and none of it was going according to plan. I procrastinated a little more. Mashama's logic was sound. I had no choice, "Nope, I'm down with that idea. It's good. I think that's the right thing to do."

Calling the colored waiting room just "Waiting Room" brings us into the future. It doesn't hold us to the segregated history of the past.

To augment the sign, we also purchased work from another of Savannah's artists, Jerry Harris, a photographer who spent much of his career in New York City but returned to Savannah in his retirement. He had taken a series of black-and-white photos of famed gospel singer and preacher James Cleveland's visit to First African Baptist (FAB) Church, which is only a couple of streets away from The Grey, and he still had the original gelatin silver prints when he and I met. He took these photos in the late 1970s while working at a local newspaper, and they are an extraordinary mix of Mr. Cleveland and the congregation in spiritual and musical bliss. We hung them throughout the old colored waiting room and outside of the colored bathrooms as a soft acknowledgment of the rich Black history of Savannah. And while I was still struggling with the nuances of race and my views, Mashama and I were making these decisions together. We hung Marcus Kenney's *Collected Stories*, Jerry's photos, and the soffit signage together. These decisions were reflective of both of our points of view—at least our points of view at a moment in time in our own personal evolutions. Had Mashama not been my new business partner, I would have, more likely than not, made the soffit sign "Colored Waiting Room" and just as likely would have had to change it right after opening because she was probably right—people would have been uncomfortable with that. But taking chances with the artwork, Jerry's photos and Marcus' painting, while not without some criticism from our guests, stimulated the cultural conversation in a direction that has always seemed, at least to us, to be constructive and a positive.

As we worked through these decisions together, we were learning that becoming true partners was going to happen little by little. I wanted the connection to be instantaneous, but partnerships were built over time and not invented or willed into being. Mashama was just getting to the point in her own professional development to take on the title of executive chef, so the idea of being a partner in the underlying business had to be completely foreign to her. The result of all of this was that we didn't really know how to communicate the true nature of what we were trying to do together—be partners. So the media, our vendors, suppliers, distributors, and guests, projected their views of our relationship upon us. Our portrayals in press accounts would position me as the "multimillionaire investor" or other similar descriptor, who had *hired* this Black woman to come down and work at my restaurant. In the beginning, we would read about ourselves only in ways that sounded anachronistic—exactly what we were trying not to build—and that made us feel defeated before we were even fully out of the gates. Mashama came to Savannah to own real equity in the business we were building—equity that she would control and grow as our business(es) grew. I brought ideas and capital while Mashama brought her skills and creativity as a chef, leader, and human. We thought coming together might effect change. It was troubling, given the intricacies of our circumstances, for me to be reduced to an "investor" and Mashama described simply as "my" or "The Grey's" executive chef.

It *was* troubling because it all felt so fake to me—equity didn't feel like real money. My talent was my equity and back then I didn't think it was worth very much. I didn't begin to feel ownership in the restaurant for a year or two because understanding the equity in something doesn't make any sense until you start to figure out its value. Thinking of myself as *the* chef was the first obstacle that I needed to hurdle. The superficial media coverage helped perpetuate that. Focusing on my role as chef required fewer explanations from either of us when we were still figuring it out, and the writers could use just that "executive chef" part to anchor their stories' predetermined point of view. That message was simple and clear.

As far as ownership, there were a few things I had to learn throughout this process, which, through gut instinct, I got right:

1. Negotiate to preserve your voice. Even if you don't know what exactly your voice is yet or how powerful it can become. You need to establish trust in a partnership and if you don't think you can talk to your business partner without consequences, then it is not going to work.

2. Constantly stay engaged with your business partner. Things change and if you are not in constant communication, then you drift apart. Your first thoughts about the business are often just that. As the business develops and you grow into your roles, you must ensure that your needs are being met and the only way to do that is to stay close to each other.

3. Lastly, balance. Understand where the balance lies that keeps you happy in your partnership, and the value that balance holds for you. Johno and

I have revisited and adjusted our original agreement three times in order to find balance.

After we finished our discussion about the soffit signage that day, we headed back to my house to finish choosing glassware, a project of why-do-now-what-you-can-put-off-till-another-time. Filling an empty glass for each of us, we spent the remainder of the afternoon discussing tableware and wine goblets. As we were getting into it, Mashama hit me with another question: "You know the kind of people we need to hire?"

"Good ones?" I asked only half-jokingly.

"Don't be a jerk. But think about this," she said. She stopped opening the boxes of samples to make sure I was listening to her. "We want to work with people we like, right?"

"I guess that's the ideal. I would take competence over likability. Sometimes you just have to do that, I think, when you are building from the ground up."

"Not in this business, you don't! Johno, come on, this business is all about chemistry. If the people who work with us don't have chemistry, our guests are going to know it, and they're not going to like it."

"Okay, I agree with that. I think," I said, handicapped by a lack of any practical knowledge of restaurant staffing and guest care.

"What do you do with people you like?"

I took a second to think about it. "You spend time with them," I surmised.

"Yeah. But be more specific."

I was stumped.

"Holidays!"

"Holidays? Aren't holidays family time?"

The holidays in my life were just as much about friends as about family. Many of my closest friends I consider to be family.

"Yes, of course they are. But you're Italian," Mashama continued. "Didn't you have a bunch of 'cousins' who were around you and your whole family throughout your life? The people who weren't actually related to you but you considered family?"

"Sure we did, and that's exactly because we're Italian. That's what I've been trying to say about being family. We do things for each other. We have each other's backs. That's what makes someone your family. It might not be as thick as blood, but it's pretty damn close. We had tons of 'Italian cousins' growing up. Still do."

"Me too. Those are the people we need to work with. The people we would have Thanksgiving dinner with," she said before thinking another second longer. "Think about your own holidays. My holidays. The standard family is there: the person who eats too much, drinks too much, talks too much, undoes the top button on their pants, and sits in front of the television watching football while everyone else socializes."

"In my parents' house, we always had the 'orphans' over too," I said. "Someone we knew who was from someplace else and had no family of their own to go to on a holiday."

"Mmm hmm, that's what I mean," Mashama answered excitedly. "We're going to have all kinds of people trying to come work with us. Some of them will be good but may not fit with what we're about. Our test for new hires should be that we would be happy to sit around the holiday dinner table with them, and . . . ," Mashama paused, searching for the end of her thought, "and enjoy their company."

"I love it," I said, considering that we were coming up on the holiday season with Thanksgiving being only a few weeks away. "Let's go even further—the way we did at my parents' house. Let's host Thanksgiving dinner each year at the restaurant for the staff. And anyone else and their families who want to join us as well. That'd be cool."

We touched glasses, an agreement between us finalized.

This was the beginning of establishing our company culture. Having a meal with people, discovering you like them, and starting to build a community. Some of the best work environments focus on the health and well-being of their staff, but when staff support each other it makes the job better. Knowing that your co-workers wouldn't let you burn the toast in the

salamander or that they would clear one of your tables when the guests' desserts are in the pickup window and you're in the weeds. Solidarity and mutual respect among the staff—and management—is how every restaurant should be. It's what the overall culture of this business is built on.

The Thanksgiving Day event immediately took hold. In fact, the first meal we ever cooked at The Grey, prior to actually serving a single guest, was Thanksgiving dinner that first year after the restaurant was built and we were in the process of training our new team for opening, which finally occurred on December 18.

That dinner has grown from twenty-five or thirty of us that first year to sometimes close to a hundred. Some of our "Italian cousins" from Savannah attend—meaning folks who don't actually work at The Grey but are our friends, special guests, or just people in need of some companionship for a holiday. And our team, everyone in attendance, goes out of their way to welcome those folks. It is our nature and our raison d'etre.

The big pitfalls in restaurant culture, from what I was learning, reading about, and discussing with people in the industry, centered around divisions and factions: Front-of-house and back-of-house staff at many restaurants felt as if they were members of two different teams. Cooks vied to move up the ranks to get a coveted sous-chef slot. Servers vied for the lucrative tables that would tip well. Being crafty about making the most money for the least amount of work is sometimes an applauded trait in hospitality.

Thanksgiving and all that we were trying to create culturally was always about being a team and maintaining a familial environment, which came with its own set of challenges that any family unit confronts.

When we posted our first job ad, we felt strongly that it should be unconventional and reflect the culture we wanted to create. We wanted to communicate our values to potential candidates so that they could consider whether they shared those values and if they would be excited to work with people who insisted on them.

. . .

THE GREY IS SEEKING APPLICANTS FOR ALL POSITIONS

Who We Are

The Grey is a new restaurant in Savannah, Georgia, slated to open this October. It is the culmination of a near two-year project around the restoration and conversion of an abandoned Greyhound bus terminal built in 1938. It was the building's streamlined design that first made us fall in love with it and next convinced us that this was a spot that should house something special within this lovely and historic city. So, we decided to go for it and we have been designing, building, and sweating over it every day since. We hope that what results from this passion of ours is not only a restored bit of history, but an exciting new eating and gathering place for locals and travelers alike. With interior and exterior spaces that are simultaneously elegant and relaxed, The Grey should provide a venue for high-energy, eclectic, and memorable times for our guests and staff.

Our Chef

The Grey is headed up by Chef Mashama Bailey who returns to her Southern roots after spending over ten years cooking in New York City, the last four of which were at James Beard Award–winning Prune on Manhattan's Lower East Side. Mashama draws inspiration from her culinary experiences in New York, her travels abroad, and her childhood, part of which was spent in Savannah, to develop dishes that represent her interpretation of classic Southern cuisine.

Our Staffing Philosophy

The Grey is committed to success by providing the restaurant's team with the tools required to achieve that success. Our long-term goal at The Grey is to not just build a competent staff but to create a family of like-minded professionals to whom self-reliance and teamwork go hand in hand. We hope this manifests itself in a great working environment of which we are all proud, and reassures our guests that, in a town of great dining choices, they have made an excellent decision by visiting The Grey.

Our Ideal Candidates

We are seeking applicants at all levels for both front and back of the house. This includes managers, cooks, porters, servers, and wine and beverage staff. Before you consider applying to The Grey, please be sure you can answer yes to the following questions:

Am I of the highest integrity?

Am I passionate about food, wine, and service?

Do I believe that teamwork is the key to my success?

Do I desire to treat guests as if they are guests in my own home?

Do I have a dynamic sense of humor?

Do I rise up to meet challenges, have an excellent work ethic, finish what I start, get motivated by fast-paced environments, bring a positive attitude to my work, and give maximum effort at all times?

At The Grey we seek leadership, passion, and commitment to excellence above all else. Should you personify these qualities and those attributes necessary in a service environment, you should send us a résumé. While there is no substitute for experience, the quality of the individual is the most important thing to us, so if you do have limited experience or are even considering moving into the hospitality industry from something else, you should send us a résumé. You might be surprised by our willingness to be a bit unconventional.

The Positions

Managers—Evangelizing our culture and tone begins with you. You must be committed to excellence and be a natural leader and teacher. If your background is in general or service management, floor, wine, beverage, or operations management, etc., please send your résumé and cover letter to managers@thegreyrestaurant.com.

Cooks, porters, and other BOH—This is the lifeblood of what we do. Creative, hardworking, and disciplined are the traits we are focused upon. If you are seeking a position cooking, baking, or other BOH, please send your résumé and cover letter to BOH@thegreyrestaurant.com.

Servers, bartenders, and other FOH—Service is your drug of choice. You want to make people happy and you like creating memorable moments. You are hospitable, self-assured, and genuinely curious about food and wine. If you are seeking a position as a server, bartender, or other FOH, please send your résumé and cover letter to FOH@thegreyrestaurant.com.

We will be accepting résumés until August 18 and hiring will be completed by September 1. We look forward to talking to you in the near future.

PLEASE BE SURE TO INCLUDE A COVER LETTER OR INTRODUCTORY EMAIL THAT INDICATES WHICH POSITION YOU ARE APPLYING FOR AND WHAT YOUR PERSONAL CAREER GOALS ARE.

The Grey is an Equal Opportunity Employer.

That ad was good, right? I would want to work at The Grey. The ad attracted many young people working in restaurants. Some were experienced and looking to challenge themselves. For others, working at The Grey could have been a good way to skip over the old-guard servers at some of the more established restaurants in town. They could hone their skills at a new place and help set the standards.

From that ad, we ended up with quite a cast of characters—the Island of Misfit Toys. It went strangely according to plan in that we were short on experience and long on character, characters, senses of humor, and a willingness to buy into our ideals.

This ad, however, didn't bring the African American community to the restaurant looking for jobs. I'm not sure why. If I had to guess, I'd wager it was the location, the old-world wine list, my nouveau port city Southern cooking, or because all our talk about family and culture had Black folks suspicious. I bet some candidates thought, *My own family is enough and I don't even know y'all, thank you very much!* Or it could have been that people already had good jobs and didn't want to take a chance on a new restaurant. Lastly, in the beginning, I don't think anyone knew that the chef is Black. I took this part of the hiring very personally. I can't help but reflect on it.

In the beginning, there wasn't a lot of color in the building. I wanted to walk into The Grey and see people like me. I wanted to feed them and I wanted to work with them.

In order for me to be truly represented in this restaurant, we needed Black cooks, servers, and managers. We wanted all of our guests to feel comfortable. It's not enough to see a Black chef, when most of the Black staff is unseen in the kitchen and just a few Black staff are sprinkled around the dining room floor. All the roles within our restaurant should be diverse and representative. Through our reputation and exposure, in time, we finally have a more diverse staff. We now have an ability to reach the Black community and beyond.

Opening The Grey was quite an achievement when you consider that one of our leaders was me—a middle-aged White guy with no restaurant experience who worked the floor every night for the first year and a half, making every mistake possible—and the other was Mashama—a first-time executive chef and business owner. And even though we got it opened, there was still plenty of work to do between us. I can promise you that Mashama still didn't fully trust me that opening night and I still was, from time to time, suspicious of her motives and what was driving them. This is normal between new business partners, I think, but skin color aggravated some of these mutual misgivings. We put in the work to get better as professionals and colleagues, in the days, weeks, and months that followed, but it was definitely a long, hard road to build common ground and give ourselves something firm to stand on.

Is it just me, but isn't not fully trusting and being suspicious of one's motives the same thing? It didn't feel this way at the time but being suspicious of each other was normal. We had met a little over a year before, neither of us had opened a restaurant before, we were not from Savannah, and we had a very young and inexperienced staff. That we were able to get the restaurant open is pretty phenomenal if you really think about it. Thank goodness we never stepped back to view it from 10,000 feet away because, if we had, we might have realized we'd set a seemingly impossible goal for ourselves. It was madness and yet, somehow, we managed to open and not kill each other.

That is the messaging we used to start The Grey and how we built our opening team.

Our first service director, Brian Chan, was a young Chinese American guy who established the foundational service model for The Grey, much of which we still use today. He moved from New York City, where he was entrenched in the service culture, and settled into life in sleepy Savannah. He was loved and, at times, feared by the team for his unwavering approach to elevated service and his tendency to get into it with people, myself and Mashama included. But I can safely say that without Brian, that first year would have been much, much more difficult.

Brian was *tough*. We bumped heads often, but he helped cement our standards and practices even though we didn't agree with him all the time.

Our first sous-chef was a gentleman named Theo Smith who had previously owned his own restaurant in town that people loved. He tirelessly worked the line each night while struggling through some issues around his eyesight and his knees, often painstakingly getting within an inch of a dish in order to be able to garnish it properly. By month three, his bum knee could take it no more and he let us know one night that it would be his last. Those first few months were hard and it took Theo a couple of years to return to The Grey as a guest. He was key to getting us opened and he did it with grace, grit, and sheer will.

Theo has a gorgeous spirit and more confidence than most movie stars. He worked hard for us and remained by my side for the first six months. I had no

idea how to manage a sous chef and didn't trust him with most things because I didn't yet trust myself. Luckily, we survived those early days and have built a mutual respect and friendship with each another.

Our first bar manager was a young man named Cody Henson. When we met, he was thinking about going to back to school to get his PhD in biology. Instead, he decided to take what he learned while bartending his way through college and transform himself into a food and beverage professional. The Grey would be the first stop on his new career path and his first gig running a bar program. He delivered something that Mashama and I were not capable of doing and his influence remains on our backbar's shelves to this day.

A star in the making. Best bartender ever, not to mention that the man is well-read and a great dancer.

Our first lead line cook, Paola Mesadieu, a young Haitian American woman who followed Mashama down from New York City, had a degree and background in economic development but had decided to go into cooking. In the run-up to opening, Paola helped Mashama recipe test and she helped me with the administration and trafficking of goods and furniture for the start-up phase of the business. One of my favorite memories of the pre-opening days of The Grey is when Paola ordered our branded paper bags, the ones we would use for folks who wanted to take their leftovers home. They arrived at the restaurant one morning, much to our collective surprise, on two enormous pallets, having to be fork-lifted off the delivery truck. We had to rent a storage facility to house them, and it took us three years to run through all of them. She remains one of our closest friends and most ardent supporters.

Paola saved my life. She trusted me and made many sacrifices for me and The Grey. I am thankful for her loyalty and will always treasure her support.

Our lead bartender was a theater major from North Carolina who was also a leader in the local LGBTQ community by the time he was twenty-seven. He left a high-paying job at one of Savannah's corporate restaurants to try his hand at working with us—this group of people who were going to fly by the seat of their pants and see if they could pull off a small miracle. His name was Scott Waldrup, and if recollection serves me, Scott was the person who dubbed The Grey as the Island of Misfit Toys. That was because, with Scott as our spiritual leader and filled out by a staff of servers, porters, cooks, and hosts, we came together in a way that no one expected. In the early days of running the restaurant, we quickly fell in love with each other and made sure that we always had each other's backs.

Max Connor, Julia Kois, Bri Daniels, Colleen Ferris, Daniel Dameron, Kaleb Craft, and Kenny Menken, among many others, were all instrumental in our survival that first year or two and in learning how to become an effective team and, more importantly, a family.

All of these people played such an important role. Their dedication and support during that crazy time will keep us all connected for life.

It seems that when you, as an organization, appeal to the qualitative attributes in people, they respond to you in a different way than they would have had we just posted a standard job ad that read: "The Grey seeks servers, cooks, hosts, dishwashers, and porters."

Culture, a healthy internal culture, has always been the most important aspect of building The Grey. I have been involved in start-ups most of my career and learned over those years that when you're building a business, quite literally from the ground up, as we were doing at The Grey, every element of our work and messaging that can be seen, touched, or heard by any stakeholder—the team, the guest, or the community—must be reflective of that culture and articulated as such, in substance and in form.

An unexpected benefit of teaming up with Mashama Bailey to build this business was how incredibly impactful our partnership has been on shaping our internal culture. It seems as plain as the sizable nose on my face now, but I was so focused on the community and the tarnished history of the bus terminal prior to desegregation that I underestimated the benefits of what plain ol' diversity in leadership would do for the trust of our team. Our culture starts with the fact that Mashama and I are different—Black and White, female and male, a creative type and a business guy, Queens and Staten Island, Beyoncé and Bruce Springsteen. It creates balance and boundless opportunity for ingenuity, integrity, and collaboration.

This was good. I think back to the day we sat at the bar in Local11Ten. These same thoughts had brought on fear and uncertainty, but now, seeing our partnership up close through the eyes of the staff, our differences had a positive effect. Also, I'm more like Janet, Nina, or Erykah. No disrespect, Queen B!

Yet, we have gotten so much wrong since we started this, but we try to face those things too. If one of us fucks up, we own it. And the mistakes we have made over the years, unfortunately, almost always have had to do with the team. Everything we have done as leaders within this organization has an impact on the team. And when you are making personnel decisions, it is never as clear as you'd hope. For the first few years, yelling was a part of our culture and I bear a lot of the responsibility for that. Much like the day I lost it when they plastered over our soffit or when we had no oysters for our New Year's Day oyster roast, I have reproduced that type of outburst three or four other times inside the walls of The Grey since we opened. After the last time I did it, over bar drains that were not being properly cleaned and had become a nest for fruit flies, I committed to not doing it again. There is no place for it. It is disrespectful and sends the absolutely wrong message.

I was a tyrant in those early years. Many of the things that go along with operating and running The Grey were new to me, and I often took out my frustration on those who worked closest to me. I handled menu changes, purchasing, linens, deliveries, meetings, prepping, and expediting. When I couldn't meet my expectations, I often blamed the cooks for not meeting my expectations of them. I would yell when tickets dragged. I was upset when we weren't set up for service on time or confused by why a dish was too complicated for others to plate properly. Our cooks constantly pushed themselves and I still wanted more from them. What I didn't understand was that I hadn't provided support systems for the staff at any of the different experience. How could they be set up on time when they didn't have the prep support or the proper recipes for the dishes? We never had enough line cooks for service, so of course tickets dragged! When the kitchen couldn't keep up with the dining room, I would pace back and forth full of anxiety and disappointment. I would often find myself filled with regret after a rough service—regret for the harsh things I had said to "motivate" them.

Back in those days there were many nights when I was yelling and banging the counter, when it was too late to change the fact that we were not prepared for the night. The environment became stressful and somewhat toxic. It wasn't until my sous chef, who had been cooking on the line for almost two years, who was also exhausted, started acting a lot like me when I knew I wasn't leading by the right example. I had to make adjustments because, on those nights, I no longer liked myself. The boys' club kitchen culture that I was reared in wasn't going to work for me as a leader. (And, frankly, I hadn't had the privilege of enjoying many of the boys' club benefits, so why perpetuate it?) I could motivate people, but I didn't understand how to provide support. I sought advice and talked to the other managers. I talked to the staff and listened to why they thought working at The Grey was so frustrating. We developed a proper training program in the Back of the House to establish accountability. We also needed different staffing, so we dissolved existing positions in order to develop a smaller core team. We figured out how to support them. Those small steps helped change the course of our program and powered the energy in the kitchen.

There are hazards in every aspect of hiring and firing. You get desperate and hire someone because you need the body, but they may not fit the culture. Yeah, we've done that. You stick with someone too long because you like them well after they have demonstrably given up on your organization. Yeah, we have done that too. You invest in someone who has interpersonal issues because you feel it is better to positively influence their behavior, rather than kicking that can down the road, but you don't explain to the key members of your team why you have made that decision. We are guilty of that one.

Yeah, mistakes galore. Honestly, we've made too many to count. Working through them and learning from them is the best we can hope for. And that is what we try to do—keep each other in check and try to listen to the people around us.

For the first couple of years we were open, we could not keep our porters from walking out on us. Being a porter is a hard gig. It's entry level. It's long, physical hours. It's high pressure because these folks are integral to keeping the restaurant operating during busy services. If they cannot keep clean glassware, plates, silverware, pots, and pans coming out of the dishpit as quickly as they go in, the entire restaurant breaks down. Completely.

In Savannah, most of the guys applying for these jobs tend to be African American men from the end of town that has been ignored or long forgotten by most people and businesses in the Historic District. A lot of them have had kids at a young age, have or had legal problems, and come to this position out of need.

Every time we thought we had someone in that position who seemed to like it and who seemed to understand how integral they were to our success, something would happen and they would soon be out the door, often just picking up and leaving in the middle of a busy service. Like any other position, some of them were just not meant for The Grey. But most of them just seemed to not like the job, the environment, Mashama, and/or me.

Mashama, in particular, had her share of challenges in dealing with these employees. Many of these guys didn't seem interested in taking direction from or reporting to a woman. Because Mashama knew that they questioned her authority, there was a period of time when she was especially hard on those working in that position. It became almost a battle between her and them. She would ride them and, when they were at their breaking point, they would come to me. They would weave together euphemisms to explain to me why they couldn't work for Mashama, saying things along the lines of, "She's being disrespectful talking to me like that."

I would answer by saying, "Like what? Like your boss?"

From the front of the building and the Diner Bar you can see the dishpit and polishing station in the kitchen. Walking from the entryway to your table in the main dining room, you can see the entire cooking line—front and back. Everything we do in the kitchen area is on display to our guests. This was by design, but it means that the dishwashers have more responsibility than washing the dishes or taking out the trash. We need the windows cleaned and the floors swept all the time during service. The pit can't be backed up because people can see that too. We need people to be self-starters, hardworking, and committed to their jobs.

Whenever one of those conversations occurred, I knew that the person would not be with us for much longer. And, if I intervened beyond that, all I would have accomplished would have been to usurp Mashama's authority. Because so many entry-level positions in the South are filled by African Americans, at first I thought our difficulty keeping porters was a race-related challenge, at least to some degree. But it turned out that it was also due to a contest of gender and power, which was an immense blind spot for us. Mashama and I were fairly tone deaf to those factors and we could not figure out how to fix it.

The original people who came to The Grey to work in the dishpit were the most transient people in the restaurant. Their sensitivities and tolerances were different because of that transience. It seemed impossible to get them to understand our ethos and that it was different from the other places they had worked. They could all leave on a moment's notice and get a job paying the same rate at another restaurant that maybe didn't hold them to the same set of standards we had: no smoking, no cell phone use on the job, and total focus on the job (which meant no talking). This made the dishwashers the toughest to manage. They didn't work as if they were part of the team, no matter what shift it was. I've come from some fined-tuned kitchens, where most all of the dishwashers seemed comfortable and some even happy. I wanted happy and productive dishwashers and didn't know how to make that happen. I didn't know how to motivate them or get them invested in what we were doing any other way than by simply paying them. I tried befriending them, but that just read as me being soft and indirect. I tried ignoring them, effectively excusing their lateness or absences, when I thought they were a little high or a little drunk. All of these things began to build up. Pushing them to clean the space correctly would turn into me bargaining with them. My management style had become too personal, geared toward the individual, and I was giving out too many hall passes. This wasn't working for them and it wasn't working for the restaurant. Between the cooks and the dishwashers, this was a shitty time in my professional development. I needed to take stock of myself and bridge this gap. Not only did I have to alter my management style, but we also had to make some changes to the kind of people we were hiring. After that, we looked for people who were a bit more mature, those who maybe had realized that they too needed a change in their lives. We looked for just a hint that would-be new hires believed that being part of a thoughtful business had value beyond the paycheck and making ends meet. This was hard shit.

So, we tried to address these challenges by reacting and making constant changes to our management style and techniques. There was no consistency in our communication or our expectations. For a year or so, we tinkered with everyone's schedules. We tried different hierarchical structures and reporting lines. We tried putting different people in place as supervisors. We promoted within the ranks. We gave people titles. We cut people who were not a cultural fit. We started holding separate porters-only meetings so that they could voice their ideas as well as their concerns.

The very first one almost turned into a riot. But those meetings really helped us improve things. The best thing we could have done was to start holding open forums during which everyone could air their grievances. That helped us improve our porters' work environment.

With all of that, we could not solve the problem. And then one day, we hit rock bottom. Every porter who worked for us left over the course of a few days, and we had none. Not a one. We were going to have to limit dinner service just so we could get through the evening.

Actually, we had one porter. Just one: Chris Punti.

Desperation forced a short-term solution. We asked every person in the restaurant to work a dishpit shift and a building-cleaning shift to not only help us get through service, but to help us figure out what Mashama and I were doing to make the porter job unbearable. Unwittingly, we co-opted everyone into solving the problem. Within a couple of hours of asking for volunteers, we had every shift covered.

I took the first shift. People who had never worked the dishpit got a chance to see what life was like when co-workers were hurling dirty dishes at you in a high-pressure environment. We learned that when people are not respectful in their approach to the dish area, it feels like the person back there may never survive what seems like a never-ending parade of people dumping plates of half-eaten food, along with countless 300-degree pots and pans, plus hundreds of pieces of glassware and silver that must spotlessly exit an area that is dirty by definition. All this comes at you while you steam yourself stupid from the hot sink and dish machine in a kitchen that is usually about a hundred degrees.

The support and feedback from the team was instrumental in sorting out the issues our porters rightfully had with how the rest of us worked with them. What we heard was that we needed to give weight to the voices of the porters, be respectful when dropping plates, post schedules sooner, provide consistent feedback, create our team-building events in a way that attracted all of our staff so that everyone could create personal bonds, and the list went on and on.

But the biggest thing we learned was to stop trying to create one management style for porters and another for everyone else. We stopped treating them like special cases or hard cases or broken cases. We treated them like any other team member—same standards, applied consistently. We held them and their work areas to the same standards as the rest of the staff, and we supported them in the same meaningful ways that we did our cooks and front-of-house staff. We had their backs and they began to have ours. The word was always out there that the kitchen at The Grey, no matter your position, was a difficult place to work—that you had to be quiet during service and you couldn't use your cell phone or take smoke breaks. But then, slowly, the word also spread that we were a fair and respectful place and that we placed value on *every* position—that we *were* a team.

As we started to form an inclusive group and the porters felt heard and respected, they were better able to perform. We were finally working together, as a team, to make their work more organized and efficient, and this resulted in fewer stressful distractions and less conflict. The overall communication improved between everyone in the workspace. At last, the culture we had been practicing throughout the rest of the restaurant was true for the dishpit too.

We now have long-standing employees in our dishpit and the porter ranks. We have committed to the people doing those jobs and changed the pay and promotion structure, so that this position, which has historically paid only minimum wage to ten or eleven bucks an hour, pays a living wage increasing to fifteen dollars an hour, mitigating the need to work multiple jobs to make ends meet.

It was a hard-learned lesson and one that I wish we had figured out sooner so that so many of the early folks who worked those positions would have been set up for success from the start.

SALTED HONEY CHESS PIE
Serves 6 to 8

Chess pie is a simple Southern dessert. And it is delicious. Our pastry chef Natasha Gaskill is a whiz at them and has elevated the standard chess pie to something a bit more elegant. When she made this salted honey version for us, we both freaked out for it.—JOM

For the crust: In a small bowl, stir together the water and vinegar. In a food processor, combine the flour, sugar, and salt. Add half the butter to the processor and pulse five or six times. Add the other half of the butter and pulse another five or six times. Dump into a large mixing bowl. Remove the large pieces of butter and return to the food processor with 1 cup of the flour mixture. Pulse until the butter pieces are pea size. Return the mixture in the food processor to the mixing bowl. Give the vinegar-water a stir and then sprinkle ¼ cup of it, 1 tablespoon at a time, over the flour mixture, scraping the bowl and folding in the flour while shaking the bowl between additions. Pinch the dough; when it holds together, it's ready. If it's too dry, add another 1 to 2 tablespoons of the vinegar-water, scraping and folding after each addition.

Lightly flour a work surface. Turn the dough out onto the surface. Split the dough into two even balls. Flatten each ball into a disk, wrap tightly in plastic wrap, and refrigerate for at least 1 hour for up to 2 days. (You will use one disk for this pie and can freeze the other disk for up to 2 months. Thaw in the refrigerator overnight.)

Remove the dough disk from the refrigerator and roll out into an 11-inch circle, about ¼ inch thick.

Fit the dough into a 9-inch pie tin so that you have 100 percent surface contact between the dough and

PIE CRUST

1 cup ice water

1 tablespoon apple cider vinegar

2¼ cups all-purpose flour

1 tablespoon sugar

1 teaspoon kosher salt

1 cup cold unsalted butter, cut into 8 pieces

1 egg

2 teaspoons water, at room temperature

PIE FILLING

½ cup unsalted butter, melted

½ cup cream

⅓ cup honey

3 eggs

¾ cup sugar

2 tablespoons cornmeal

½ teaspoon kosher salt

2 teaspoons apple cider vinegar

1 teaspoon vanilla extract

Maldon sea salt

CONTINUED →

SALTED HONEY CHESS PIE
(CONT.)

pan. Trim the excess pie dough, leaving a uniform
½-inch overhang. Then tuck this overhang under the
rim of the pie tin and crimp the edges for a decora-
tive appearance. (YouTube this if you need a visual.)
Take a dinner fork and prick the pie dough everywhere. Freeze the pie tin for 1 hour.

Preheat the oven to 400°F. Whisk together the egg
and room temperature water to make an egg wash.

Remove the pie tin from the freezer. Place a piece of
parchment in the pie dough and weight it down with
dry beans or pie weights. Bake for 20 minutes. Lift
out the parchment, removing the weights. Brush the
pie dough with the egg wash and return to the oven
to bake for an additional 10 minutes, until golden
brown. (If this all sounds incredibly time-consuming
and difficult, call us at The Grey Market and we'll
ship you a couple of frozen pie shells.) Decrease the
oven temperature to 325°F.

For the filling: Combine the butter, cream, and
honey in a small saucepan over medium heat and stir
until the butter has melted. In a bowl, beat the eggs
and then stir in the sugar, cornmeal, and kosher salt.
Slowly stream in the butter-honey mixture, whisking
constantly. Stir in the vinegar and vanilla.

Take that pain-in-the-ass-to-make pie crust and fill
it. Bake for 35 to 40 minutes, until the filling is a little
jiggly in the center and the crust is golden brown. If
your crust starts to get too brown on the edges, protect it with an aluminum foil wrap. Let cool on a wire
rack. Top with sea salt, cut, and serve. Store leftovers, covered, in the refrigerator for up to 2 days.

CHAPTER 19

The call that I received from Mashama just after midnight because our general manager, Scott Waldrup, had been struck by a car while the two of them crossed Bay Street, was a turning point for The Grey, Mashama, and me on so many levels—some obvious and some not.

That night ultimately got as chaotic and confused as it could have. It turns out that Scott and Mashama were most certainly caught up in the violence that seemed to take place all too often in Savannah and on this evening had spilled into the city's primary tourist area. The streets continued to feel tumultuous as Carol and I were finally able to lead Mashama to our car after the police had finished interviewing her. Groups of teens and young adults were still wandering around; and because of the mention of gangs by the policeman I had spoken with earlier, many seemed menacing, at least they did to me. I instinctively began to size up all of the people walking past me and took note of the Black teens and young adults, because it was this group that I associated with gang crime in Savannah. My nerves were rattled and I felt unsure of everything and everyone. The kids wearing the gear and colors that I viewed as potentially gang affiliated got a third glance from me. I noted anyone who seemed agitated or intoxicated, if they eyeballed me, or if there was any discernible bulge in their waistbands or pockets. I felt unsafe in those moments, just as I would have if I were walking a late-night street in an unfamiliar New York City neighborhood. I was afraid of the people who created this night. Were they here on these streets with me, my wife, Mashama? I felt like I needed to protect the three of us from any other danger, from harm. My right hand took comfort being concealed in my briefcase.

I was numb. My eyes blurred with my tears and I had a slight chill that seemed to be setting into my bones. I couldn't shake that feeling. I held myself tightly. I wanted to hide until it was all over. The minor pokes from the police questioning and all the noise from the sidewalk crowd had left me feeling nothing. It was loud and I couldn't discern one sound from another. People were lurking just out of my blurred range of sight as the three of us walked the four long blocks to get back to Johno's car. I could feel people watching us as we walked by. As we got closer to the vehicle that was going to take me anywhere else but there, the air seemed lighter. The people in the streets seemed removed from the violence. They continued their holiday antics, stepping to the side when we passed, like a flash mob dispersing. I think they knew instinctively to move away because the three of us looked scared. When I got to the car, I felt safe, the safest I had felt all night.

Having left the scene without any confirmation of what had happened to Scott, my mood was hollow, unsettled. I wanted to do something, I needed to act. In my family, that is what we did in an emergency—we acted. My brain was going a million miles an hour on the short walk to the car. Mashama was becoming a bit more communicative, but only in fits and starts. As she recalled some aspect of the event, she'd ask a question or make a statement and then would return to silence. The shock, which is what I thought she was going through, appeared to be deepening.

Once we were safe inside the car, we headed back to our home, Mashama softly crying in the backseat. I dialed Colleen's number, one of our managers and our human resources person. Colleen had been with us from the very beginning, having started as a back server who then worked her way up to manager. She was as close to Scott (and all of us) as anyone. It was somewhere around one in the morning on July 5 when I rang her and she answered her phone groggily. "Hey, what's up?" she asked, likely thinking the same thing as I had when my phone rang about an hour earlier: *this cannot be good.*

"Hey. There's been a really bad accident," I said calmly. Without emotion or outward expression of compassion for how this would affect her, I delivered the news: "Scott was hit by a car a little while ago. I don't know how he is, but it was very, very serious."

I know the late-night phone call all too well. I am from New York Fucking City. My cousin Julian Jones and his half-brother, Leslie, fell eleven stories down an elevator shaft in 2007. They were both killed on impact. Julian's sister called me and told me the news. Our family was crushed. The call I had made to Johno took me right back to that night.

I waited a moment as what I said to her sank in and began blasting the cobwebs of sleep from her head.

Poor Colleen. The shock and burden of receiving a phone call like that is something she will never forget, is all I remember thinking. I wanted to talk to her—she was close friends with Scott too—but I just couldn't.

"What?" she asked. "Scott? Is he okay?"

"I don't know, but I'm trying to find out. Right now, though, I have to figure out how to get in touch with Tart," I said, referring to Scott's partner, who was away visiting his family in New Orleans, "and I need to get a number for

Scott's mother. I think she lives in North Carolina. Where can I find that info at The Grey?"

Silence on the other end, so I spoke with more force: "Colleen! I need you to listen to me right now so we can get some answers. Okay?"

"Yeah, okay. Yes, she lives in Raleigh or something. There should be an emergency contact sheet in his employee folder. It's in the top drawer of the file cabinet. If you want, I can come down there and get it for you."

"No, stay in your house. Don't leave and do not come down here. Downtown's still kind of a mess. It's dangerous. Just stay in your house. I'll call you when I get there if I can't find it."

"Okay. I'll see if I can find Tart's number while you're doing that."

Sitting in the backseat, I could hear Colleen's voice on the line. *I have Tart's number* I remember thinking. I called him right after *it* happened but I couldn't say anything. I just stared out the car window as the voices in the frontseat faded into the background.

"Yeah, do that please, thanks. But don't call any of the other managers or any of the staff until I know something. No point in freaking everyone out. I'll call you in a little while, as soon as I have some more info."

By the time I hung up, we had covered the distance to my house and I pulled into the garage. Carol and I walked Mashama upstairs to our living room. It was the first time I had seen her in the light. Her face was even more swollen than I'd thought and the life in her eyes was masked red by blood vessels. The emotion of the evening had overtaken her. Even her tears had subsided, leaving a zigzag of salty tracks on her cheeks, as she walked to the sofa, practically falling into it. I could see the relief in her as her body relaxed and allowed itself to be swallowed up by the cushions.

As I Googled "Savannah trauma center," Carol asked, "What are you going to do?"

"Go to The Grey and see if I can find Scott's mother's number in his file. I need to call her and let her know what's going on. And then to Memorial Hospital," I added.

"What should I do?"

"Stay here and I'll call you as soon as I find something out. See if Mashama can get some sleep, this is going to be a long haul."

Carol nodded and kissed me good-bye as I grabbed a bottle of water out of our fridge and headed back down the stairs to our garage.

The ride to The Grey did not match up with what was going on that evening on Bay Street. I drove through Monterey and Chatham Squares, two of the city's most beautiful. In the dark of a warm, sultry July night, the ambient glow from the sky, the large windows of the nineteenth-century homes, and streetlamps put the live oaks and the Spanish moss in their most hauntingly beautiful light. The trees were both steady and animated, with gigantic and motionless tree trunks serving as a base for the ballet that took place between the limbs and the light, resulting in the infinite shadows that contributed to Savannah's reputation for being haunted. That night it felt like the city was abuzz with all that took place in those shadows.

As I turned right onto Martin Luther King Jr. Boulevard, I left the squares, the peace, the quiet, and the shadows behind. It was bright now, the way that a main thoroughfare in a city is at any time of day. Headlights, streetlights, stoplights, and flashing lights illuminated the road all around me. The highway overpass of I-16 was in front of me, a Parker's gas station to my left, and fast-food restaurants in either direction. A few pedestrians shuffled, stumbled, or meandered along.

I drove slowly north, toward the river and The Grey, taking it all in. I was thinking about Mashama and wondering about Scott and whether or not he was alive.

When I pulled into the driveway on the north side of The Grey's facade, my surroundings had gone from bright back to dark again—but it was not peaceful. Our stretch of MLK was desolate and dimly lit at that time of night. I could see through the expanse of our yard, the yard that once staged passenger buses, into the back alley that bordered Yamacraw Village, the public housing project. There was enough pedestrian traffic back there to make me nervous. I couldn't help it; Yamacraw made me nervous that night.

The three downtown housing projects in Savannah are behind the two major streets that border the Historic District to the east and west. These communities are tucked away in the shadows, separated from the highly trafficked tourist area. Many people who live in these neighborhoods can walk to their jobs downtown. The newer, updated Greyhound Station, in conjunction with

the city's bus depot, is just a block or two behind The Grey. People who work downtown and live too far away to walk home, use our alley as a shortcut to the working bus station. There are always people walking back and forth through the alley, and, as with any alley, the later it gets, the sketchier it gets.

Yamacraw has a reputation in Savannah and it's a rough one. Good people live there but a few bad apples—mostly kids—have been known to start fighting, steal a car for a joy ride, or, worse, fire gunshots. That behavior has never spilled over into the alley behind The Grey, but we all know that it's a possibility and we keep our guards up.

Before I exited my car, I removed the keys to The Grey from my briefcase and selected the key to the front door so it was at the ready. I wanted to be off that sidewalk as quickly as possible and back behind a locked door. Then I pulled the small 9mm that I kept a firm grip on out of my briefcase. The sight of the angular black metal and the red wood handle comforted me. I flicked the thumb safety downward, cocked it once, sliding a round into the chamber, and flipped the safety upward again. I had practiced this movement so many times, since deciding to buy a gun a couple of years prior, that it was as natural to me as tying my shoes. This was, however, the first time I had ever done it with the thought, albeit a distant one, that I might actually fire a nonpractice round. I put the cocked gun in the front pocket of the cargo shorts I was wearing and I kept my right hand wrapped around the wood grip with my index finger extended down the length of the cold slide.

I looked over my shoulder as I exited the car and headed to the front door. I quickly let myself in, locked the door behind me, and turned off the alarm. I turned on some lights—I felt as if I were a child in a dark room, afraid that danger lurked in every recess. I opened the back door of the restaurant and peeked out into the alley to make sure there was no sign of trouble out there. I checked the bathrooms and the kitchens to ensure, irrationally, that I was alone.

The bus station can feel a little haunted late at the night. I always hurry inside, scurrying along like a palmetto bug to the fast tempo of the beeping alarm. I know this makes me appear vulnerable, but I quickly lock the door behind me just in case anyone is watching.

For the most part, after midnight that stretch of MLK is uneventful. You'll have your partygoers making their way home or a homeless person asking for change. It's mostly quiet, but that night I can understand why Johno was totally freaked out.

I headed down the stairs to our dark basement that housed the small office and I began rifling through our employee files. In the dim light, I located Scott's folder and found that his emergency contact listed his partner, Tart, and not his mom. I was disappointed to not get a number for her, but I now knew that I would have to call Tart.

The day prior to this mess, Carol and I hosted an annual pool party at our house for the entire The Grey team. It was an epic affair with the life of the party, of course, being none other than Scott Waldrup. He was dressed in red, white, and blue and my memory from that day is of him fifteen feet in the air, standing on the balcony off our kitchen overlooking the pool, which was filled with and surrounded by the thirty or forty of our employees, their girlfriends and boyfriends, and the various people who had become part of our extended family. He was up there because he and Nicole Elliott, our lead front-of-house manager for years and great friend to all of us, had bought a bunch of gag gifts earlier that day for some of the team members who had distinguished themselves in some unusual way, such as "The Most Difficult Person to Understand When They Are Cooking on the Hotline." It was moments like this that Scott lived for. He loved to be joyous and to bring joy to other people. He was absolutely beaming up there, his smile as bright as the sunshine that day. I remember thinking he was like a king surveying his people, his big, red beard bouncing in time with his movements, wearing his signature summertime tank top, and drinking his drink. It was the highlight of that day for me, and, I think, for many of us. The only thing missing from that picture was Tart, the love of Scott's life and his near constant companion.

As I sat down at the desk, I looked at my watch. It was coming up on two in the morning—one o'clock New Orleans time. I steadied myself for a minute and sketched out a quick plan in my head as to how I would tell Tart what was going on. Then I dialed his cell.

No answer!

Shit!

"Tart, it's Johno. Scott's been in an accident. Please call me as soon as you get this. Thanks."

I employed the same jumpy procedures in reverse as I left the building.

I drove to the hospital and then roamed the emergency room, asking various nurses if the injured from the accident downtown were there. They were. Was

Scott there? They couldn't tell me—I was not next of kin. Well, who was there? They couldn't tell me.

The waiting room was becoming more crowded by the minute as the friends and family members of the various victims from that evening's violence received their own phone calls and were arriving in an attempt to locate the people important to them or assess how badly someone might be hurt. Most of the people around me were African American. I felt awkward and angry. I can't remember if I was the only White guy in the room, but if not I was in a very small minority. I was angry for being caught up in a world—the gang world—that wasn't mine. There was one young kid, maybe seventeen, whose baggy jeans were smeared with blood. I wondered, *Was he at the shooting or part of the car chase that had me there?* Moms and aunts, cousins, dads and uncles were arriving seeking their own answers. They were as disoriented as me. I felt for them.

The anger from that night has yet to set in for me. Mostly, I feel so sad for Scott and those boys who caused the accident. Violence is born of poverty and attracts children from the same communities that need mentorship, programs, and support. This is a cycle that has to stop. Positive role models, financial support, healthcare investment, and educational mentors all working within our communities can change this.

Including Scott, the casualty count was eleven, I learned from a nurse. He didn't say how many were dead or alive. I pressed the same nurse as he seemed to be the only person willing to give me any information, "I'm looking for a guy who works with us. He's our general manager. Big red beard, and his name is Scott Waldrup."

The nurse went bug-eyed. "I know Scott. You're one of the owners of The Grey—right?"

I had hope for a second that he would share something with me. "Yeah, I am."

"I love Scott. We love your restaurant."

"Thanks. I really appreciate that," I said, trying to be polite. "But listen, Scott was apparently caught up in this shit tonight. He was down at the river with some of the people we work with and when he was walking home he was hit by the getaway car."

The young nurse's eyes sunk to the desk, absorbing the news of his friend.

I leaned in a little. "Listen, because I'm not related to Scott I can't get any information. But Tart, his boyfriend. . ."

He cut me off, "I know Tart too. We love both of them," he whispered.

"Me too," I responded. "But because I'm not related to Scott, and Tart is in New Orleans, and Scott's family lives in North Carolina, no one will tell me anything." As he nodded at me, muttering something about next of kin, I asked him, employing my best Staten Island affect, "Listen, can you do me a favor? Would you? Just go back there and have a look at who's here. See if any of the victims are Scott. You don't have to tell me anything more than that. I'll owe you one, I swear, if you can just tell me that."

He nodded and went into the netherworld of the hospital without saying another word. He was gone for what seemed like an hour but in reality was closer to ten minutes. When he returned, his face was red and looked as if he himself had been crying. I thought the worst. But he just shook his head. "He's not back there. Maybe they brought him to Candler Hospital," he offered with fleeting hope in his voice.

"Candler? Do you think?"

He just shrugged his shoulders. I shook his hand and I headed out the door.

Memorial is the trauma center, I remember thinking. *Was he crying?*

I decided to pass on Candler and drive home and check in on Carol and Mashama.

When I arrived, Mashama looked peaceful on the sofa, having surrendered to fitful sleep. Carol woke up when I came in and looked at me with worry wrinkling her forehead. "I don't think he's at the hospital," I said.

I don't remember sleeping at all. I just remember feeling sad and knowing that when morning came it would all be real.

"What does that mean?" she asked, wiping the grogginess from her eyes.

"Means the morgue and the police are my next stops."

I called Colleen back and explained that I had learned nothing.

I tried Tart's phone a second time. Still no answer. I did not leave another message.

When I was standing on the curb, right after the accident, I called Tart. Leaving a message for him was the most difficult, painful thing I have ever done. I couldn't imagine being him or Scott's family. It was all so surreal.

After calling Tart's cell, I then called the Raleigh, North Carolina, police department and told them that I was trying to track down Scott's family, that he had been involved in an accident. I said that I thought I remembered his mother's name was Terry Waldrup, having met her once when she visited Scott in Savannah. I gave them all of the information I had and my cell phone number. I asked them to have Scott's mom call me if they were able to reach her. They sounded earnest in their promises to do so.

I got back in my car and began to drive toward the main downtown police precinct. The night was now completely silent. Even the shadow lurkers and drunks had gone to bed. As I drove, I called the morgue and spoke to someone who told me that if I was not next of kin, they could not tell me anything.

As I was circling back around the block to park at the police station, my phone rang. It was a North Carolina number. "Hello?" I answered pulling over to the side of the road, anticipating that it was either the Raleigh PD or. . .

"Johno, this is Terry Waldrup, Scott's mother." Her voice surprised me. It was actually her.

I held my phone to my chest for a second and blew out a short, loud breath, like I was getting ready to lift something really heavy. I put the phone back to my ear and I launched into it. "Oh, thank God, Terry. I'm glad you called. This is hard but I'm just going to say it. Scott was in a terrible accident earlier tonight. He was with Mashama and he was hit by a car. I've been trying to find him, but I don't have any answers yet. Still checking the hospitals and police stations to get whatever information I can. But no one will tell me anything because I'm not next of kin. I'm at the local precinct right now and I'm about to go in. I know a captain here in town, so they might help me. I wish I knew more, but I don't. I've tried to track down Tart, but he's in New Orleans. I just don't know how bad it is, but Mashama thinks it was pretty bad. I wish I could tell you more. . ."

As I petered out, dumping everything I knew on her, she calmly said, "Johno, Scott was killed earlier tonight. You can stop looking."

My God, I thought. *He is dead.*

My world froze for another second. *Scott's mom just broke the news to me that her son is dead.*

"How did you find out?" was my only response.

"The police came to my house earlier and told us. The Savannah cops found his cell phone at the scene and tracked us down, I guess. He was killed instantly. They said he didn't suffer at all."

I hugged Scott's mom when she arrived at The Grey, and standing behind me were all the other people in Savannah who loved her son. She had a warm smile on her face. I told her that he hadn't suffered, and she seemed at peace with that. I remember thinking, *I'm glad he went quick—like a firework in the sky, fading into the darkness on his favorite holiday.*

"Oh my God, Terry. I'm so sorry. I don't know what to say."

"I know, Johno. I am sorry for you. Scott loved you."

"Did they tell you what the hell happened?" I asked.

"Yes, but very few details. They said there were three young men who were involved in a shooting a few blocks away. They shot some other people on the street. They jumped into their car and it looks like the police started chasing them. As they were fleeing the scene of the shooting, that's when they hit Scott and crashed into a light pole. Two of the boys in the car were killed as well. Only one of them lived."

"Oh my God," I gasped, drawing in a breath, and added, "Why would the police chase them in the middle of downtown? That makes no sense. Okay, I have to tell Mashama and Carol about Scott. I have to go home and tell them. Mashama was with him when it happened."

"Oh my Lord, I didn't know that. Is she okay?"

"Yes, she's fine. Very shaken, but somehow, not a scratch on her. I'm so sorry, Terry."

"I know you are. Now, go see those two gals," Terry said, with a calm and a caring for our well-being that came through the line as clearly as her voice. "My girls, Scott's sisters, are on their way. We're going to come to Savannah in the morning. You go talk to Mashama and Carol. We can talk in a little while."

What a wonderful woman, who raised a wonderful man. I could see where Scott got his compassion from. She turned out be strong enough for all of us as I hope we all were for her.

"Okay, I will call you as soon as I get home. We'll figure out how to get you to Savannah. I can come pick you up if you want. I think it's only a five- or six-hour drive. And, you stay with us when you get here tomorrow. We have the room. Don't screw around with hotels."

"Okay, that's really kind of you. My brother is figuring all of that out now," she said. "I'll know more about getting to Savannah then too. Go take care of your wife and Mashama."

Her calm was disarming and surprising. It was soothing. *How was this woman, this mother of a boy she just lost, able to comfort me?* I think I will always remember that call.

I went home and told Mashama and Carol. Mashama just collapsed back into the sofa; the anguish had created such a deep exhaustion in her that her legs would simply not support her, and she just sank back into its softness.

The news of Scott's death, I guessed, was really not news to her. She had witnessed the impact of the car, which, we would learn later, actually severed him in two. She knew what had happened. The only thing preventing her from completely accepting it up until that moment is the eternal optimism that defines Mashama Bailey.

As I stood there, I was not sure what to do next. Suddenly my mission for the night, finding Scott Waldrup, had ended. Carol came to me and hugged me tightly, and I let her. I could feel the tears come to my eyes as my own emotions prepared to release. But, just then, my phone rang. It was Tart.

I answered it, composing myself as I walked into the other room. He had just gotten home after a night out celebrating the holiday. It was approaching four in the morning our time. He knew nothing of the evening's events other than the message I had left, telling him that Scott had been in an accident. I explained to him, with the same directness I had employed when I called Colleen, that his partner of eight years was no longer.

He was somber, stoic. His only words were that he would see me in Savannah before the end of the day that we were already four hours into.

It took two years after that horrific night for Tart and me not to feel deeply sad for each other. I was Scott's friend, his friend at work and his friend outside of work. We shut The Grey that day to host an impromptu memorial for, unsurprisingly, hundreds of people who needed to be close to the people who were close to Scott, who needed refuge. When Tart walked in late that afternoon he was immediately surrounded by his core group of friends. Those people supported him during this time, they were his anchor in a town that he wasn't from but one where he had made a life with Scott for the last eight years. Upon seeing him, having never been particularly close to him, all I could feel was guilt that I had survived and Scott hadn't. I couldn't get past Scott's death and how painful this must be for Tart. I always thought that maybe Tart felt it wasn't fair that I, not someone Scott was closest to, was the last person with him before he died. It was hard because every time we saw each other after the memorial, I think we felt like we had to talk about Scott. We needed to find our own common ground beyond Scott and that was going to take time. And we did. We do. That freak accident, Scott's death, and the fact that I was right in the middle of it, will connect him and me for life.

My first reaction that night, after concern for Scott and Mashama, was fear. Fear of the perpetrators of these multiple acts of heinous violence committed that night. I feared them as my neighbors. I feared the housing projects where gang activity and violence take place, including Yamacraw, where the occasional sound of gunfire at night startled but never surprised those of us at work. I feared the people who walked on the street next to me and that fear was so hard for me to manage because I could not tell who people were. Was this person or that person there to victimize someone the way Scott was victimized the night of his death? You couldn't tell the gang kids from the *kid* kids, at least I couldn't. *The police and the city government couldn't even figure out how to identify the perpetrators and keep the rest of us safe, to keep Scott and Mashama safe,* I thought, so I feared their ineptitude as well. Some of these fears may be justified when you consider the results of that evening, and some of them are bred of ignorance and racism as we walk backward and pick up the inherent-bias baggage many of us carry around.

When violence erupts, I always hope it's not some young Black kid in search of power or pride. I hope that it isn't someone who suffers from an untreated mental illness or who is so desperate that they have no bearing in reality or faith in the living. Unfortunately, that was the case that night. Those kids set out with intentions to harm or even kill. We don't know why—and we don't know their circumstances—but we do know that they killed themselves as well as others. This is the by-product of hate. Hate for one's community, hate for one's neighborhood, and hate for someone's prosperity. Without any of the bystanders seeing it coming or knowing the hate these boys had internalized, they took Scott's life and changed the lives of all of the victims, their friends, and their family's lives. Forever.

The premise of The Grey was to be a place that welcomed the entire Savannah community—Black, straight, gay, White, everyone. But what I learned over the course of that evening and as a result of Scott's death is that many of us revert to our base emotions in times of trouble, or boredom, or complacency. I did. I was immediately brought back to my childhood, listening to firemen and cops talking about the people of color as being their enemies in the communities they served.

Was I, in the White enclave of Savannah's Historic District, sliding back into that? As I thought about the housing projects, the gang kids, the violent perpetrators of Scott's death, was I just segmenting people into groups in a way that allowed me to avoid saying that I was afraid of the Black community? Was I reverting back to the cops and firemen I knew in my youth, seeing the people of color in my own community as the enemy? I had thought for a very long time that I was well beyond my childhood community's thinking. Just as I thought that I didn't see skin color when Mashama and I hit the first bumps in our relationship. But I did. I do. God, this is all so very disheartening.

My thoughts turned to my childhood and my grandfather—the man at whose home I ate Sunday Gravy and where I found a few hours of solace from my own troubled household. The man who could magically fish a quarter out of a front pocket filled with coins so that I could buy a candy bar. The man who, when I was just seven years old, was murdered by a drug-addicted, African American guy who demanded my grandfather's possessions as he traveled home from his job as a tailor in Manhattan's Little Italy neighborhood aboard Staten Island Ferry boat, *John F. Kennedy*. The man who was bludgeoned and left to die in a urine-soaked bathroom stall perhaps because the man who attacked him had lost hope and any sense of remorse or empathy. The man whose death helped vilify a segment of the Black community in the eyes of my family and in my young eyes.

No matter how tolerant I believed myself to be, I had unconsciously absorbed the messaging that we should only trust our own. We should be separate and recede into our own tribes.

Using the thinly veiled and loaded term "nationalism" as cover, a movement of retreating to intolerance and hatred for difference was surging in our own country the summer of Scott's death. Seeing many of our most powerful leaders ignoring or even supporting the cultural division in our country was a constant source of pain for Scott in the months prior to his murder.

As we received people at The Grey over those next couple of days—the restaurant equivalent of sitting shiva—collectively trying to shake the fog of this epic tragedy, it became the community connector that Mashama and I had always hoped it could be. It had become the meeting point for all of Savannah. Everyone who loved Scott and Savannah came. They came by the hundreds. They rejected hate in the aftermath—a bright spot during an otherwise bleak time in Savannah and the swell of "nationalism" in our country.

Other restaurants brought us trays of food. Our distributors brought us cases of wine, beer, and all that we needed to serve a full house. Our whole team gathered. We hugged each other. Past employees returned, as well as our friends, neighbors, colleagues, competitors, and people we didn't even know came.

We were indeed one community for that brief and tragic period. It reminded me why I chose Savannah to start this chapter in my life. It assured me that my love for Savannah, albeit a complicated place, was well founded.

Living in separate communities is an implicit affirmation that we are too different to be one community, enabling institutions—whether governmental, business, or religious—to treat communities differently. In Black communities, you might have businesses owned by Blacks, Italians, Jewish, and White people, and many other ethnicities and backgrounds. But, it is unlikely that in any of those other communities you would have a Black-owned business.

Black people have lived and worked among different races throughout history in this country. Before the civil rights movement, there were places and neighborhoods where Blacks were able to keep their consumer dollars within the community. Most of these examples have been systematically eroded, infiltrated, burned down, broke down, or otherwise dispersed. Over the last sixty years, this breakdown had resulted in subconscious fear or hate. In these communities, where there is no reinvestment and less consumer

control by the folks who live there, there are fewer resources and jobs and the residents are forced to find that shining example of success in a different way. Sometimes it's found through education, sports, music, or religion, but it can also be found through the streets—via hustling, drugs, and crime. In some ways, our communities, Black communities, have never felt like our own safe places. It always seems as if someone else is in control, and that control breaks down hope when people are forced to look outside of themselves and their communities for support. The control that is exercised over our communities is rarely ever neutral and is more often subjugating and destructive.

I remained confused about where and at whom I should direct my fear and anger for what had happened to Scott. On the first full day after his death, I was walking to the restaurant early in the morning, down one of Savannah's beautiful tree-lined streets. I was in a daze. I ran into a man, a friend named Kevin, who, at the time, was working for one of the city agencies. He expressed his sincere condolences. And, well, I exploded in emotion. He did not deserve it. I yelled and swore in the middle of Bull Street about the incompetence of our government. About our failures as citizens and as a city. About how all of this shit that magazines, tourist bureaus, writers, authors, and politicians were espousing about the "New South" was all just straight-up bullshit. There was no "new" South in Savannah. It was the same old fucked-up South in the same old fucked-up America, and it appeared it would remain that way.

As I vented my anger, it became clear to me who it was directed at. It was for all of us. All of us who are complacent in allowing societal pain to fester. It was directed at myself, who had been silent on all of these issues prior to Scott's death, both in my hometown of New York City and my adopted town of Savannah. I had worked hard in my life, but I had worked within the borders of my comfort zone. Until Scott was killed, the systemic problems that our society faces, Savannah faces, were purely issues that existed outside of my purview and I felt, in a lot of ways, were not my problem. This complacency happens to individuals in government, within religious organizations, and across our entire system. It perpetuates division. And, beyond complacency, there are those leaders who leverage our fears to further divide us, trivializing the real consequences: there is nothing but loss—loss of hope, loss of future, loss of shared values, loss of life—at the end of the path of division.

And corruption! Not leveling the playing field must be fueled by something; something other than hate and fear. Is it money, power, control, wealth, privilege, all of that? The motivations are being exposed the more we talk about the differences between us in this country even though this has been going on for generations. Why would you fear us if you own everything? Why would you hate us if we have nothing that you want? The pain is deep and sometimes unspeakable. But we need to keep talking about it, we need to talk about it a lot more. We can't change our history, but we can change our future by openly talking about our past and getting closure in the form of reparations.

As the hours wore on after Scott's death, I realized that it had to be different for me this time around. When my grandfather was murdered, as a child I absorbed the fears, biases, and bigotry of my environment and the world. This time, I was not going to allow all that to permeate me.

When I looked around, in front of me at every turn, there was my partner and friend, Mashama Bailey. And when I looked at her now, I felt trust and support. This person, this capable woman who went from stranger to acquaintance to business partner to family member, definitely helped to alter my sight lines. And that's what was different this time around. I am committed to continuing to confront my fears, suspicions, and biases—unconscious and conscious. I must accept that I am a work in progress.

Suspicion versus racial biases? Did my prejudices manifest themselves as mistrust and fear? Something I needed to figure out was whether I distrusted Johno because he is White. And whether history had conditioned me to automatically distrust White people. The answer is, yes, my suspicion is an inherent bias. I also needed to ask myself if I distrusted Johno because he was a businessman and had, in my eyes, the majority of control of our start-up, knowing that, for me, control equals power.

My distrust subsided when I began to exercise my voice, my power. Once we began to use our combined voice to not only build a business but to create a self-sustaining business culture, my suspicion resolved. We had to have each other's backs first before I began to believe him and before our team would ever begin to trust us. The night of Scott's death, Johno was there for me, in the middle of the night, just like a member of my family would have been. That was the night I realized he was more than my business partner—he was a friend.

Yeah, big parts of the South are still fucked up. Just take a drive around Savannah—really ride all around it, not just through the idyllic squares. Ride around the projects in Yamacraw, River Point, or Simon Frazier. Ride around the far east and west sides of town. You'll see these stark differences, the inequity. But it doesn't have to remain that way because the Savannah and the South that

I have come to know and love is also so very beautiful and hopeful in its layers of history and complexity. So are the people. All the people. The relationship that Mashama and I share is, in a way, emblematic of this. It is strong and yet it is complicated by who we are, our histories, our experiences, our biases, and our ambitions. We seek the truth from each other and balance and equity between us, but outside forces sometimes play their role in this. Our community(ies), families, supporters, and detractors, perceived and real, add layers of complexity as we run our little business and consider the possibilities of what that business can be, what it can represent.

If you ask me, that's what people like about The Grey. It's the possibilities. The possibility that me, a middle-aged guy, with no shortage of failings and faults, who knew nothing about restaurants, could envision one that ain't half bad and heal himself just a little bit along the way.

The possibility that a Black woman can own a business in a building that, as it was originally run, she would have only been allowed to enter through the back door.

As time has passed, I have begun to process my fears, anger, and guilt. I feel the irrational, self-centered guilt for a member of our team who was killed while I was in a position of leadership—on my watch.

I feel anger for the local government that did not show up to protect Scott or to mourn him. In total, I met with two people from the city in the aftermath of Scott Waldrup's killing. Both meetings were off the record, and I believe that the people with whom I met only did so because I was prone to bouts of rage in the middle of Bull Street, shouting into the ears of anyone who would listen. Those meetings were unfulfilling at best.

The institution of the city of Savannah did not send a sympathy card, it did not send a bouquet of flowers, and it did not offer to help Scott's family in any meaningful way during this time of need. The mourner in me was angry because I felt it was disrespectful to Scott and his memory. The businessman in me was angry because during The Grey's time in business, we had generated millions and millions of dollars of publicity and exposure for the city, and yet its leadership did not even send condolences or formally acknowledge that Scott, our general manager, a key player in making The Grey noteworthy on a national level, had been killed in their downtown—on their watch.

When I challenged one city representative on this fact, the response was that they couldn't show up for Scott because they hadn't shown up for the previous twenty-three families who had lost loved ones to violence already that year, the majority of whom were Black victims.

And that's when I realized that the issues that Savannah faces, which resulted in twenty-seven homicides by the Fourth of July of that year, including Scott and two of the boys who were in the car that hit him, are not Black and White issues. No, Savannah's issues, the South's issues, America's issues, run so much deeper than that. Scott was not the only victim that night. Spencer Stuckey, seventeen, and Gabriel Magulias, twenty, were also killed when the car they were in tore through Scott and crashed into that light pole as they escaped the scene of the shooting. Jerry Chambers, who was driving the car that snuffed out those three lives was convicted of felony murder and was sentenced to life in prison with the possibility of parole. Four young men were victims that night. They are all victims of the fear and hopelessness that infiltrates so much of our society— fear and hopelessness that is stoked by a defective and, ultimately, destructive power dynamic.

Our issues in America, which show up as microcosms in businesses, board rooms, neighborhoods, and every place that people congregate, strike me as issues of power and control. The people with the power trying to keep the power, even if that means dividing us further; people who want the power trying to get the power; people who had the power trying to take the power back; and the people who have been powerless demanding the power.

"Black Power" is a political slogan, one I have heard within my family's household my entire life. It was the slogan of the movement in the late 1960s, founded by Huey P. Newton and Bobby Seale, that was based on the ideal of eradicating injustices in society toward Black people. It was a movement about civil rights and racial pride, achieved by establishing institutions to preserve and celebrate Black culture. It was a rallying cry to remind Black people that we are in a system that is against us. It was about standing up for ourselves, not about promoting division. Our history has been forever changed by others, and this movement was designed to encourage us to understand ourselves and our diverse African heritage.

Our very simple job at The Grey is to make food and serve it to our guests to the best of our ability, making them feel warm and welcome as we do it. But what I said at the beginning of this book remains true: it was always so much more important to me to build something that achieved more than the goals of good hospitality. I was lost when I purchased the abandoned bus terminal on MLK. My career had hit a wall, I was full of self-doubt, and I was questioning nearly everything about my professional life choices. In the layers of interrelated history and complexities inherent in this building and Savannah, I thought I might have seen a way to restore myself by taking a leap of faith on a new business and a new city. As the saying goes, what could possibly go wrong? And then I met Mashama Bailey who, it turns out, was as game as I was. Together, we set out on this journey to learn from each other and live a life that I could have never dreamed would be so fulfilling while simultaneously being so damned uncomfortable: uncomfortable running a business I knew nothing about; uncomfortable in my relationship to race, class, and culture; uncomfortable learning so much about myself and human decency from the most unsuspecting people and places; uncomfortable in our successes; uncomfortable with our failings, my failings.

And all this learning, challenging of our views, my views, all of this discomfort that we have gone through over the early life of this business has maybe allowed The Grey to become one example of what change to the status quo can look like. And, even if we have not accomplished that, at least we are having the conversation. Mashama and I have that conversation by virtue of who we are and who we are becoming. We have the conversation with each other, with our team, with our guests, with our friends, and with our families because it is now the life we are living.

The silenced voices of the disenfranchised are now being heard. The exposure of wrongdoings and injustices are coming more and more into the light. Our cell phones and our use of social media help educate people and the platform for these conversations is growing worldwide. I'm not sure what the future may hold, or if that will include healing, forgiveness, or redemption. But I do know that you cannot unsee what you have already seen. I have seen change and progress. It's slow and sometimes it looks motionless, but it's there, happening, for those who want to witness it and be part of the change.

Quite simply, The Grey is our work in progress.

THE REVOLVER
Serves 2

4 ounces Russell's Reserve 6-Year-Old Rye Whiskey (or similar)

1 ounce Borghetti Liqueur di Vero Caffè Espresso (you can use Galliano Ristretto)

½ ounce simple syrup

4 dashes orange bitters

2 orange twists, flamed with a match to release the oils in the peel

In my humble opinion, this is the best after-dinner cocktail ever created—the sweetness of the rye, the back note of the coffee liquer. YUM! We were introduced to it by our first bar manager, Cody Henson. The note about me and this drink in our reservation system, where we jot down guest details we want to remember, reads, "When it comes to Revolvers, two is one too many." Truer words have never been written.—JOM

Fill a mixing glass with ice. Add the whiskey, espresso liqueur, simple syrup, and bitters. Stir for 15 to 20 seconds.

Strain into two Nick & Nora glasses and garnish each with an orange twist. Clink glasses and say, "Cheers" to each other before you take your first sip.

EPILOGUE

BY JOHN O. MORISANO

Paris, COVID-19, and Bolognese

Each morning, in a two-bedroom flat in the 7th arrondissement of Paris, after we made a couple of espressos, I would begin reading aloud to Mashama all that we had written to date. We would write more, make changes, add and delete paragraphs, reread, rewrite, eat, argue, drink, hug, laugh, and cry, all in the furtherance of telling our story.

Monday through Friday were reserved exclusively for writing. Saturdays, we took the day off and walked the city, went to flea and food markets, got tattoos commemorating this and that, had lunch someplace on the outskirts of town or sat in a café alternating espressos with glasses of wine. On Sundays, we worked half a day, slept a little, did laundry, and always ate Asian or Indian food in the evening.

This took place during the first six weeks of 2020.

Somewhere in the middle of the third week, it started to feel, finally, like the book, this book, was morphing from two disparate voices into one. At least to us, it did. It was exiting the realm of forced presentation and the words and points of view began to comingle and contrast, accurately reflecting the dialogue that Mashama and I have been having since we met.

Several months prior to our time in Paris, we had sent a draft of the book out for something publishers refer to as "audience reads." We imposed upon about a dozen friends, family, other writers, and subject matter experts to read our book. Most of those readers were complimentary—they said they liked it, that it was good. But there were several who did not find the book, well, to be frank, very good at all. A couple were offended by layers of its content, inaccuracies in some of the fine details, different recollections of events, the conflicting points of view, and things, said and unsaid, by and between Mashama and me. We understood that the book required more context, explanation, self-exploration, debate, and/or resolution.

We were rattled by this feedback. Some of it felt harsh—an obvious cost of business that comes with writing a book. We knew that writing on topics about which we were not subject matter experts, and taking them on purely from our own points of view, would prompt reactions from people. Our goal, though, was to paint a picture of who we are—two middle-aged business partners in a relationship with each other—and what our business does, and how we personally confront the issues of gender, race, class, and culture that swirl around us. We did not espouse to know all of the questions that should be asked or have the right answers, whatever that means, but were interested in sharing our perspectives as a means of putting our internal dialogue, which has benefited us greatly, out there for people to access.

We didn't pick to do this in Paris because it's sexy—although it is. We picked that city because to do what we do for a living, we need to eat food. A lot of it. It benefits our product immeasurably to see what is going on in the world's great cities, kitchens, and culinary scenes and helps afford us the opportunity to contribute to the ongoing conversation around food. We actively seek to be challenged and inspired by other chefs, restaurateurs, service models, wine lists, techniques, and settings. While I am by no means claiming Paris was a hardship, Mashama and I decided to allocate just about all of our annual travel and food budget to rent that flat in Paris so that when we weren't writing, we were eating—effectively killing two birds with one big, expensive rock. So, for the month of January and part of February, we occupied the sparse sitting area of that Left Bank flat on the rue de Lille, a few blocks from the river. I sat at a simple wood table most days, in a spindly steel-tube chair, staring too often at the disparate artworks and photographs hanging on the plaster walls, as Mashama constantly adjusted her laptop and position on an overstuffed, off-white chaise lounge just a few feet away.

We ran the Nespresso maker ragged.

I have always felt more at home in Paris than almost anywhere else in the world since I lived there in my twenties. I am drawn to everything about it. The beauty, the language, and the lifestyle suit who I most want to be rather than who I am on a daily basis. Mashama, who often poked fun at me for what she must have viewed as my clichéd love for a city that millions upon millions of people hold dear, had, I think, during our time there, come to see why my affection for Paris is not at all clichéd, but, maybe, justified.

At the end of each day of writing, we would take some time to catch up with our team back in Savannah. We answered questions, provided guidance, helped solve problems, and kvetched about the ins, outs, ups, and downs of doing what we all do for a living. Nightly phone calls were followed by (or included) a glass of wine and then our nighttime gig—eating—began. Usually, it was a simple dinner like a croque madame and fries at Le Comptoir des Saint-Pères around the corner on the rue de l'Université; a plate of crudo, a tin of sardines, charcuterie, and crusty bread at a small bistro, down the street from us, called La Calèche; Korean food at Guibine in the 1st arrondissement; or Indian food at Ravi on rue de Verneuil. Other (more expensive) nights, we would venture to see what interesting chefs, young and old, were doing in their spaces—Le Bon Georges, yam'Tcha, La Vieille, La Bourse et La Vie, La Poule au Pot, Voltaire, Chez L'Ami Jean, Martin, Mokonuts, Juveniles, Septime, Clamato, Oui Mon Général, Piero, Le Baratin, and Maison were all on our list.

In the morning, we would wake up and do it all over again—the Parisian version of Groundhog Day. A morning run along the Seine, maybe to the Eiffel Tower, would help offset the sedentariness of writing and the bacchanal of the food and wine from the evening prior.

On our final morning, we finished packing in that frantic and chaotic way that seems inevitable after such a long trip—when you have crossed over from visitor to resident. We took a taxi to the airport in silence, the misty rain adding to the gloom of an overcast sky. It was bittersweet in that we were anxious to return home to Savannah, but leaving Paris and all that it now represented to us, was sad. We had gotten better there—better friends, better business partners, and, hopefully, better writers of a better book. We left satisfied and buoyed by our work—the daytime and nighttime efforts.

But in the Charles de Gaulle Airport that morning, as we were doing the things that would get us back home, something telling happened. In retrospect, it was ominous. We did not then have an inkling about how seriously we should have received the omen delivered to us by the gentleman asking the standard security questions about our upcoming trip:

"Did you pack your bags yourselves?" he asked.

"Yes," we responded in unison.

"Have they been in your possession the entire time since you packed them?"

"Yes," we answered again.

"Did anyone give you anything to carry for them?"

"No."

"Where else did you travel on this trip?"

"Nowhere, just Paris."

"Are you both sure?"

We looked at each other and then back at him. "Yes," we said, nodding.

"Have you been to China?"

China?

Mashama and I looked at each other again, "Um, no, we haven't been to China," she answered, laughing nervously.

"Anywhere in Asia?" he pressed.

"No!" we said emphatically.

News of COVID-19 had started to become serious in Europe just as we were leaving. There were known cases at a French ski resort in the Alps. Northern Italy was in the midst of an outbreak. China, the epicenter, was under lockdown. But Paris? Mashama and me? We were just fine. We were so buried in our own little Frenchified world of writing and eating that we had not yet grasped the magnitude of what we would soon face. No one in America had.

So, we flew home. We watched movies on the plane, drank cheap Bordeaux and white Burgundy out of those little airplane bottles, and ate oversalted airplane food. It was fun—a mini vacation at 38,000 feet as the final chapter of our writing sabbatical ended.

When we got back to Savannah, things were better than ever. The restaurants were as busy as they get. And, while we were gone, the team exceeded mere proficiency in operating without us. Instead, they had learned how to excel at it and they had become truly self-reliant. The high that we were on upon our return was only outdone by the mood of the team; they had performed so well and were elated. The year was shaping up to be a good one.

A few days after our return, the pace at which we had been working continued, and we left for Blackberry Farm in Tennessee where Mashama would cook dinner as part of a chef program they hosted for a small group of guests, and she and I would give a talk about this book to that same intimate group. We were on a roll.

However, the rumblings of COVID-19 began to get louder. Italy closed. France closed. Germany, Spain, and other European countries were shutting down and, yet, the States still seemed to be immune. Our federal government assured us, repeatedly, that all was fine and most of America pressed forward.

During the second week in March, Carol and I were in New York City for a grand opening and cocktail reception at the Metropolitan Museum of Art, honoring the daughter of friends from Savannah. The virus was starting to hit New York City hard that week. As I rode the subway, to various meetings around town, I was becoming mindful to keep my distance from people. The train cars' yellow and orange polyform seats, the stainless-steel interior, all purposely intended to look perpetually shiny and clean, instead took on a sinister sheen. I tried to touch nothing, rather than grab on to a handhold, preferring to balance myself in the center of the carriage on wide feet as the car ricocheted from side to side. I began opening doors with my elbows as I entered buildings en route to meetings. On that Tuesday night, March 10, we had dinner in Brooklyn with friends we hadn't seen in years. The restaurant was packed. I was uneasy, but conversation, food, and wine placated my nerves. We arrived back in Savannah the next morning and our restaurants continued to operate normally through the end of that weekend—Savannah seemed okay. On Monday morning, a day on which The Grey is always closed, Mashama and I still had no idea that the Sunday night before was the last time The Grey would be open for many months, as news of shutdowns across industries and the country came in fast and furiously as that day wore on. The Grey Market shut down a few days after that. Within thirty-five days of our return from Paris, both of our restaurants, like most restaurants throughout the world, were no longer operating.

All of our coming together that we managed in Paris, all of the book writing, all of the hard work of the seven years prior to build and open our dream, were instantly put in jeopardy by a virus. Just like that, everything we had been doing that felt so weighty to us was rendered insignificant as the virus overtook everything. Before the month of March had ended, Carol and I watched two of our dearest friends in Savannah, the couple whose daughter had been honored at the Met Gala, who were by far The Grey's most fervent cheerleading team, succumb to the virus, which they had contracted in New York City the week we were there together.

Nothing would be the same again. The fragility of everything was brought sharply into focus.

The weeks following the initial outbreak of COVID-19 were surreal. That period tested everyone and everything. Mashama and I lost track of each other immediately following the shutdown. We had been so used to seeing each other nearly every day since we opened The Grey that we didn't know there would be fallout from *not* seeing each other. We gave up our regular opportunities to share a thought, a concern, or a suggestion and retreated into our own little interior worlds. The few moments a week that we did see or talk to each other, we were being pulled in so many directions that we very rarely, if at all, had normal conversations or asked each other the basic question, "How are you doing?"

We fixated on the areas of the business that each of us had become comfortable with. I worked feverishly on PPP loans, sweated unemployment insurance, tried to write articles about saving restaurants, talked with other restaurateurs to outline strategies for comebacks, organized meetings with the team via Zoom to keep them abreast of developments, and spent time with Carol, whose schedule of professional travel, usually done at a breakneck pace, had been completely shut down. Mashama ordered ingredients for farm boxes that we distributed to the industry each Saturday, worked on new menus, fielded requests for media interviews, organized cleaning parties of our spaces, kept up with her direct reports, read cookbooks, and spent time paying attention to her home, which she had owned for a couple of years but had rarely done more in than sleep because of our pre-COVID-19 schedules. Gone were the evenings, after a busy night of service, when we would meet up in the Diner Bar and discuss the week behind or ahead of us. Gone were our impromptu dinners at the Crystal Beer Parlor on a Monday night, eating burgers and chicken wings. COVID-19 was everything.

The more I retreated into myself, the more I justified my solitude by telling myself that this was great for Mashama. I knew she relished her personal space. So, I continued to do my thing, at times actively avoiding Mashama because I didn't want to burden her with my problems—the things in our business that fell to me. She had her own set of responsibilities to deal with. I hunkered down and assumed that when this was all over, we would pick up right where we left off.

Well, I was wrong, and by the fifth week of being closed, any meaningful communication between us had all but ended. If personal space was your drug, you could easily overdose on it during the pandemic.

When we saw each other, it was awkward and quiet. I would fill in Mashama on the superficial goings-on of my life and ask her a couple of questions about what she had been up to the past few days. The conversation didn't really go much further than this and I took that as proof that I needed to continue to give Mashama her space while I tended to the things that were tugging at me—mostly our finances.

One afternoon, I was sitting in our shuttered restaurant by myself working on whatever I worked on at that time. We had just finished a virtual meeting with our management team and something about Mashama's demeanor during that call seemed off—she seemed withdrawn. I called her. As soon as she answered the phone, she said something like, "Hey, where are you?"

"I'm at The Grey."

"Okay, I am going to take a ride down there right now," she said, adding "we need to talk."

"Yeah, that's why I was calling. You okay?" I asked.

"I'm coming down now. Let's just talk when I get there."

Mashama got to our restaurant and, at an appropriate social distance, explained to me that she felt all alone. She felt that the way we had come to rely upon each other over the past years, the way we supported each other, just wasn't happening during this period of extreme crisis. She was emotional and, before long, I was emotional too.

"I was just trying to give you space," I said, explaining my thought process.

She seemed perplexed by my comment and said something along the lines of, "Well, aren't we most effective together?"

Yes, we were most effective together. But I still felt that Mashama needed space in spite of what she was saying to me. Her demeanor, as I saw it, and her words did not seem to add up to me.

Over the next week, we made a couple of attempts to restore the comfortable communication between us, but they went nearly nowhere. I kept doing my thing, and she kept doing hers.

Then, one early evening, Mashama and I were at The Grey Market strategizing about how to reopen it for curbside pickups. The meeting, which lasted a couple of hours, was planned, but the impromptu glass of wine after it was not and, slowly, we moved from our formal agenda to just talking. Within a half hour—and after that half glass of wine—talking was easier than it had been in a couple of months.

I took a risk and asked, "Hey, I made a big batch of Bolognese yesterday. I'm going to cook some pasta when I get home. You want to come over?"

"Sure," she answered. "I'm starving."

We locked up the Market and headed to my house. When we arrived, I set about pulling together a supper of penne Bolognese. Mashama talked Carol through the roasting of a couple of heads of broccoli in garlic, olive oil, and Parmigiano-Reggiano. We drank some wine while Parisian radio station TSF Jazz played in the background. The three of us talked easily as dinner cooked.

We talked about The Grey, the Market, what was next, how we could get better, where we could build upon things, and where we might need to change things, scale them back. Suddenly the planning of our future, a conversation we typically had often, seemed natural for the first time since the day we had closed our doors.

We sat down at the table when the pasta was ready and, other than the music, the kitchen fell silent as we ate. The food was good, my Bolognese far outshining the Carbonara I had cooked for Mashama all those years ago. The broccoli that Carol made, which Mashama had guided her through, was superb.

As we wound down the eating, we sipped wine and used bread to sop up the remnants of an excellent meal. We chatted, laughed, and just were.

Food is a very good thing, I thought. *It can cure a lot of ills.*

In that moment and the days that followed that dinner, I thought a lot about The Grey and The Grey Market, about Mashama and our business relationship. Until that point, I had been fixated on our dangerously broken finances and the fact that we went from having two growing businesses that were generating millions of dollars a year in revenue to ones that were now generating zero. I thought about why I could not reconcile what Mashama said to me in The Grey a couple of weeks prior and how I perceived her state of mind. And, that's when it kind of hit me.

I'm the money guy at The Grey. I funded it. That's what got me my ownership in it. Mashama cooks for hers. And no matter how much we are partners, the reality is that if the pandemic were too much for me to bear financially, I might be compelled to make the decision to shut down our restaurants—maybe for good.

If things during the pandemic got bad enough and I couldn't afford to float the restaurants through this unprecedented collapse in business, The Grey could just go away—like it never existed. Just like that, it could all be over and our lives would never be the same. We would both go from doing nothing else for the past seven years but living and breathing our restaurants to not having them. I would have to figure out how to get as much of my money out of the real estate as I could. Mashama would have to figure out what was next for her. A new business venture? A job? Write more books?

This is, far too often, the reality of the situation for Blacks and Whites in America. Even for Mashama and me to change it, two people working hard at that change, it is going to take a long, long time. Until Mashama has accumulated enough wealth of her own, through her ownership and the growth of our businesses, until she has the ability to contribute beyond her blood, sweat, and tears for her equity, the final decision making remains in the hands of the person with the money—in this case, me. This is one insidious outcome of a system that has been built from its very inception by White people and on the backs of the Black community. Simply put, Whites have amassed wealth and Blacks have not. That's not liberal bullshit. It's the truth.

Our business, pre-pandemic, was well on its way to creating that kind of value the Black community has been purposely excluded from since enslaved people were brought to America. Mashama and I had found an equitable balance along the way, one that we evolved as our circumstances evolved. Our partnership, which had always been values-balanced, was progressing into an economic equilibrium as we created more and more value through what we were building together. Yes, we have been knocked down by this virus, this global health and economic crisis, but we have not been knocked out. And we have come a ways personally since we started this venture. As I invest my assets, business experience, and time, and Mashama invests her time and rare skills as one of the country's great chefs, the anachronistic power-wealth dynamic changes between us. With us sharing not only points of view, but the equity in the underlying businesses, ours is not just another example of White people creating more value for themselves—in this case, myself—but of us creating value together, for ourselves, each other, and our team. It will continue to take time, but we will get there. We must keep at it if we hope to contribute to the fix of what truly ails American culture. The problem has to be fixed at the most fundamental economic levels and that cannot be left up to the government. We all must be willing to think differently and make real change in our communities, counties, cities, and states. What Mashama and I each bring and give to our businesses is exactly what levels the playing field between us and, as long as we are honest with each other, the outcome can be equitable.

Hey, it ain't a lot, but it is something.

ACKNOWLEDGMENTS

There have been so many people who have encouraged us in the building and running of The Grey and telling this story—too many to count, frankly. This is a short list of the people who have impacted us during the lifelong journeys that landed us here, together, at this moment in time and in this place. We thank you.

Larry Aber
Jim and Terry Alberts
Catherine and David Bailey
Danielle Bailey
Dawud Bailey
Margaret Bailey
Zuwena Bailey
Barnacle
Dianne Bernhard
David Black
David Bloomquist
Danny Bradley
Betsy Cain
Gretchen Callejas
John Caracappa
Brian Chan
Andrew Cohen
Dorothy Colling
Maxime Connor
Richard Coomer
Kaleb Craft
Daisy
Doug Dalmedo
Daniel Dameron
Brione Daniels
B.J. Dennis
Christian Depken
Nicole Elliott
Trevor Elliott
John T. Edge
Lolis Eric Elie
Osayi Endolyn
Amy Factor

Brian Felder
Colleen Ferris
Brian Fiasconaro
Flounder
Natasha Gaskill
David Gelb
Allison Glock
Jeff Gordinier
Gabrielle Hamilton
Jerry Harris
Cynthia and Terry Hayes
Cody Henson
Dee Herb
Eleanora and Nicola Infantino
Tart Johnson
Casey Kahn
Howie Kahn
Brian Kelly
Marcus Kenney
Julia Kois
Adam Kuehl
Andrew Thomas Lee
Jeremy Levitt
Edna Lewis
T.C. Lumbar
Jacqui Mason
Brian McGinn
Ernest McIntosh
Doug McManamy
Helen Medvedovsky
Kenny Menken
Paola Mesadieu
Danny Meyer

Wilson Moran	Chris Rowe
Allison Morisano	Ed Sabounghi
Anthony Morisano Jr.	Steven Satterfield
Frank Morisano	Carol Sawdye
Glen Morisano	Theo Smith
Glenda and Anthony Morisano	Cathy and Philip Solomons
Maria Morisano	Kelly Spivey
Audrey Morris	Libbie Summers
Tim Morris	Arnold and Lorlee Tenenbaum
Leigh Nelson	Scott Waldrup
David Paddison	Terry Waldrup
Becca Parrish	Tim Waters
Chris Poe and David Zyla	Mattie Mae West-Lodge
Anne Quatrano	Geneva West
Joe Randall	Walter "Sonny" Winfree

And in the category of there are just too many people who have added to our everything over the years, we would also like to say "hey" to the following folks:

The 8-Ball Crew

Those rock-solid Staten Islanders and the Farrell boys

The Manhattanites

**The Savannahians who have been with us from the get-go—
y'all know who you are.**

Our families, friends, and nemeses, who have supported and challenged us to do better along the way. (Pro-tip: Never underestimate the value of a good nemesis.)

The farmers, purveyors, and distributors who grow and bring all the wonderful things that allow this place to do what it does each day.

A special thanks to the people who have breathed life into The Grey—our guests. Finally, most importantly, a gigantic HEY to all of the people who have been a part of our team and The Grey family over these years. You have truly worked your asses off for this place, this idea, and have our eternal thanks and gratitude.

—MASHAMA AND JOHNO

INDEX

Published in the United States by Lorena Jones Books, an imprint of Random House, a division of Penguin Random House LLC, New York.

www.tenspeed.com

This is a work of nonfiction. Nonetheless, some of the names and personal characteristics of some of the individuals involved have been changed in order to disguise their identities. Any resulting resemblance to persons living or dead is entirely coincidental and unintentional.

Library of Congress Cataloging-in-Publication Data

Names: Bailey, Mashama, 1974- author. | Morisano, John O., author.

Title: Black, white, and The Grey: the story of an unexpected friendship and a beloved restaurant / John O. Morisano and Mashama Bailey.

Description: First edition. | [Emeryville, CA] : Lorena Jones Books, an imprint of Ten Speed Press, 2020.

Identifiers: LCCN 2019030187 | ISBN 978-1-9848-5620-3 (hardcover) | ISBN 978-1-9848-5621-0 (epub)

Subjects: LCSH: Grey (Restaurant: Savannah, Ga.) | Morisano, John O.—Friends and associates. | Bailey, Mashama—Friends and associates. | Restaurateurs—Professional relationships—United States. | Interracial friendship.

Classification: LCC TX945.5.G73 M65 2020 | DDC 647.95092/2—dc23 LC record available at https://lccn.loc.gov/2019030187

Hardcover ISBN: 978-1-9848-5620-3
eBook ISBN: 978-1-9848-5621-0

Editor: Lorena Jones
Designer: Annie Marino | Art director: Emma Campion
Production designer: Mari Gill
Co-production manager: Dan Myers | Co-production manager: Jane Chinn
Copyeditor: Janina Lawrence | Proofreader: Leda Scheintaub
Indexer: Ken DellaPenta
Publicist: Kristin Casemore | Marketer: Stephanie Davis

Printed in the United States of America

10 9 8 7 6 5 4 3 2 1

First Edition